Adventures in the Dream Trade

Neil Gaiman

Edited by Tony Lewis and Priscilla Olson

The NESFA Press
Post Office Box 809
Framingham, MA 01701
2002

Trade Paperback Edition, August 2002
International Standard Book Number:
1-886778-42-6

Adventures in the Dream Trade was first printed in an edition of 2000 numbered
hardcover books, of which the first 300 were signed by the author and artist,
bound with special endpapers, and slipcased. Of these 300 copies, the first 10
were lettered A through J and the remainder were numbered 1 through 290.
The trade copies were numbered 291 through 1990.

No other copies will be printed in hardcover.

Copyrights and First Appearances

"The Dark Knight Returns," *Foundation: The International Review of Science Fiction* 38, Winter 1986/1987.

"Curiosities: *Lud-in-the-Mist* by Hope Mirrlees," *The Magazine of Fantasy & Science Fiction,* July 1999.

"Banging the Drum for Harlan Ellison," *Readercon 11 Program Book,* Readercon, July 1999.

"Neil's Thankyou Pome," *The Magian Line,* v2.2, October 1994.

"The Old Warlock's Reverie: A Pantoum," *Once Upon a Midnight,* Unnameable Press, 1995.

In Re: Pansy Smith and Violet Jones," Liner notes for The Flash Girls: *The Return of Pansy Smith and Violet Jones,* Spin Art, 1993.

"Banshee", recorded by The Flash Girls on *Maurice and I,* Fabulous Records, 1995; *Warning: Contains Language,* DreamHaven Inc., 1995

"Post-Mortem on Our Love", *Angels & Visitations: A Miscellany,* DreamHaven Books, 1993; *The Magian Line* v1.2, 1993; recorded by The Flash Girls on *The Return of Pansy Smith and Violet Jones,* Spin Art, 1993.

"Personal Thing", recorded by The Flash Girls on *Play Each Morning Wild Queen,* Fabulous Records, 2001.

"All Purpose Folk Song (Child Ballad #1)," *The Magian Line* v1.4, 1994; recorded by The Flash Girls on *Play Each Morning Wild Queen,* Fabulous Records, 2001.

"A Girl Needs A Knife", recorded by The Flash Girls on *Maurice and I,* Fabulous Records, 1995.

"Hallowe'en," *Time Out* Magazine, Hallowe'en 1996.

"December 7, 1995," Tori Amos Dew Drop Inn Tour book, 1995.

"Good Boys Deserve Favours," *Overstreet's FAN,* volume 1, #5, October 1995.

"The Flints of Memory Lane," *Dancing with the Dark,* Vista, 1997.

"Essay for Patti," *The Faces of Fantasy,* Tor, 1996.

CONTENTS

Adventures
in the Dream Trade

THE INTRODUCTION

At the Request of Norton I, Emperor of the United States, the Imperial Historical Pantaloon and Jester-Without-Portfolio Enters the Following:

This is the moment when we, kerfuffle, introductions to books, rhubarb natter, material here presented will certainly, noises offstage, useful as training wheels on a surfboard, the paying customers are eyeing the exits, but of course the work speaks for itself.

Which is to say, I won't keep you long, but I am happy to be here.

I'm happily here because Neil asked me to be, which, considering the number and quality of people he could have asked, was deeply kind and generous of him (as it was kind and generous of him to introduce a book like this for me). But the book ain't about me, folks.

Or, as someone else might have put it:

In the hills of Transylvania, where they never will explain ya
Why you can't go to the castle with the drayman,
Very late they scotch the shandy for the purplish-amber brandy,
And they all soon will be talking of Neil Gaiman.

Where the action is frenetic, or the order is hermetic,
Under open skies or hidden from the layman,
True believer or zetetic, all shall soon be copacetic,
Drums and voices will be talking of Neil Gaiman.

Which is an in-joke, yes, but not a secret beyond decipherment, and if nothing else it illustrates the correct pronunciation of Neil's surname, a Q which is A'd surprisingly F.

People ask what Neil is like, but the Stage Manager is eyeing me and the first-act curtain rope with an intensely synergistic gleam, so I will limit my remarks.

First, he is not Terry Pratchett. I have conversed with both of them at once, and even Peter Sellers couldn't do that without technical assistance. His humorous delivery tends to the British-dry-gin variety, something like the late Peter Cook, but with more authentic merriment. (Cook always seemed to be sizing up his companion for sale by weight, as in the last line of a Lovecraft pastiche.)

Not that there isn't a silly-funny Neil as well, with the love of onomatopoeia that kids like better than meaning in words (his conversations with his younger daughter Maddy can be like opals spinning in sunlight), and grownups—well, the *Bullwinkle Show* writers could name a Wall Street fussbudget 'Fiduciary Blurt,' and people who don't laugh at that could probably lower their blood pressure by fifty points if they learned how.

As many rimshots as I'm hitting here, I really do mean this about words. A staggering number of people who want to be writers do not seem to like words very much. They want to produce a kind of pH-neutral prose, usually described as 'transparent,' that simply generates fully nuanced scenes in the reader's head without, well, the damp and wriggly bits, and are convinced that was how James Michener and Lev Tolstoi did it, adding two fingers of the best straight up for Hemingway.

(Apologies. This is the intrusion of a sometime manuscript reader, still carrying his memories of the dark place and the cold black river of coffee and the insistent drumming in the left temple near the eye. 'Mistah Strunk—he dead.')

But you gotta love the words, friends. You've got to love them for themselves, for the sounds they make and the figures they cut on the page and the light they give off when they facet together; love them even when they don't seem to be doing anything. Especially then.

Neil loves them, which brings us inevitably to *Sandman*. There is not, at least as I write this, anything directly about *Sandman* in this book, but you have this book immediately to hand (if not, I'm sure it's a very interesting backstory), and it's just possible you have had no contact with *Sandman*. The Great Roc is unselective about whom she seizes.

Sandman seems to me a genuine original, an of-its-kind-and-no-other, which is rarer in fantasy than silver-haired people who aren't magicians. Of course it draws from sources, ranging from Greek myth to French history to what your cat is thinking when he is not batting at the catnip mouse or playing *Everquest* on your credit card. And yes, there were other Sandmen; they are all there in the narrative, like inlay fit gapless without glue.

Morpheus is a genuine synthesis of the Dream and the World, the substance of one but intimately coupled to the other, perpetually fascinated and grieved by the events of both. He has a conscience, but that's not the same thing as *being* a Conscience; and like all monarchs with a conscience (there have been a couple of others), knows that the movement of his finger both creates and destroys.

The voting majority of this book is a from-the-field log of Neil's long multinational tour to promote *American Gods*, his exceptional novel of the contemporary world and what lives both alongside and a certain bit inside it. It was originally a Web publication, posted as it happened, or when Neil could catch his breath long enough. There was some discussion in the book's preparation whether to retain material like lists of (then) upcoming appearance dates; they remain, and they are, in fact, part of the narrative. There's something about reading the list of venues and days in succession, working out the compression ratio, that carries a point simply reading the entries at leisure doesn't.

It doesn't quite reproduce the experience some of us had following the log day by day—watching Phileas Fogg being juggled from the hands of one Passepartout to the next, signing books each day in quantities larger than some trade hardcovers are printed, one step ahead of the hired car, two steps away from the sushi bar, and he's so tired—one expects at any moment for Morpheus, in his parallel aspect as Sleep, to reach in and say, 'Mine now.'

Now, there, I have actually introduced the contents of the book. There are more, naturally—poems, introductions, essays on multifarious topics of all shapes and importances. Opals, whirling.

I trust that the benevolent Emperor of this great nation will find my contribution of value. Now I depart, as if borne aloft by the California Street line. As that someone else surely might have said,

Though you've wandered o'er the byre, or the tramways of desire,
From the Thules to the beaches of Grand Cayman,
Chock the tire and cut the wire, stoke the fire a little higher,
You are going on a journey with Neil Gaiman.

—John M. Ford, 2001

MOSTLY INTRODUCTIONS

Eddie Campbell portrayed me, cruelly and inaccurately, in his comic *Bacchus*, as a man imprisoned in a back room whose own life and work had been taken over by the constant interruption of writing blurbs and introductions. It's not true. It's not like that. It's just, some weeks, it can feel like it.

When I get weeks like that I tell the world very loudly that I'm not going to introduce anything ever again, let alone write another blurb, and I mean it too; and the resolution lasts until someone waves something I really like at me. And then comes the urge to tell people. And all too often, I do.

I tried to explain it once, in an appreciation I did of writer-artist Bryan Talbot, in 1994. It began:

> I was one of the Guests of Honour this year at the British Eastercon, in Liverpool. And I tried to make a point of keeping people introduced to each other, as one does. At least one of my fellow guests knew nobody there.
>
> I made some introductions. I like making introductions.
>
> "This is Geoff Ryman," I said. "He's one of Britain's finest writers. His last book, *Was*, was a tour-de-force. He's also one of the nicest people you could hope to meet." I didn't say anything about Geoff being tall, because that was obvious.
>
> "This is Professor Jack Cohen," I said. "He's a leading reproductive biologist with an international reputation, and as a sideline he designs aliens for famous science fiction writers. He also knows more strange and bizarre biological facts than anyone you will ever meet in your life." I said nothing about Jack looking like a real honest-to-goodness crazed professor, because that was obvious.
>
> "This is John Clute. He's the foremost critic of science fiction in the world, and has the finest critical mind and

17

the largest vocabulary of anyone I've ever met." I did not say anything about John's wife Judith being the nicest person I know, and that wasn't obvious because she was in London at the time, but it's true anyway.

And a young lady who was nearby snorted loudly, and said to me "*I* see what you do. You use introductions to *flatter* people." She said this proudly, as if she had deduced, from damning evidence, that I was wanted by the police of several nations.

I tried, and failed, to explain that I wasn't flattering anyone. Jack Cohen is everything I said he was and more; Geoff Ryman is without question one of the finest writers out there; John Clute has the most incisive critical mind I've ever encountered. These are remarkable people, and it gave me pleasure to say so.

Introductions should tell you the important things like this. They should tell you things you didn't know about people. They should avoid the obvious.

(The young lady, incidentally, was Jane Barnett, and I don't think she was more than 15 at the time, and the guest I was introducing around was Barbara Hambly.)

The best thing about introducing things is that it allows you to stop and decide what you think about them. And then it allows you to tell other people about them. It allows you to point to what's good, and to talk about why it's good.

Sometimes it lets you stretch your fingers and actually attempt a short essay.

(I have been told that the H. P. Lovecraft introduction contains several factual errors. This may be true, but my source for them was editor emeritus Julius Schwartz. Julie is old, funny, cranky and knows everybody and everything. "When I was Lovecraft's agent," Julie told me, once, "I sold his only story to *Astounding*." Now, honestly: which version of events would you choose? Julie's, or some reference-book written by someone you don't even know? Exactly.)

These introductions were written over a period of 13 years, in a variety of voices and styles, for a variety of audiences. There are ones written for people who know and love the work they are about to read, and ones written for people who do not have a clue about the book they've picked up. There are pieces to explain why something's important and pieces that exist to give background and to make what they are reading comprehensible. (There's one piece that exists because the author called me up and said "You have to write an introduction, as I've already printed the book-cover and it has your name on the spine." So I sighed and I did. But that trick only works once.)

A few of them aren't introductions. "After They've Brought on the Dancing Girls..." was an afterword for a benefit book done to raise money for artist Reed Waller's medical bills. Reed drew a comic called *Omaha The Cat Dancer*, an anthropomorphic soap opera about an exotic dancer. "300 Good Reasons to Resent Dave Sim" was written, if memory serves, for the *Comic Buyer's Guide* on the occasion of Cerebus achieving some landmark number or other. Dave's within spitting distance of episode 300, his finishing post, as I write this and manages to embody even more contradictions than he did when I wrote the article, ten years ago. The Roger Zelazny piece was an afterword to my story in *Lord of the Fantastic*, an appreciation of Roger.

"The Dark Knight Returns" piece, which I wrote for John Clute when he was editing the SF Foundation's house journal, *Foundation*, is the only piece of full-length criticism I've ever attempted (as opposed to book reviewing, which I did for years). Looking it over now, fifteen years later, I'm no longer sure I agree with its conclusion; but without it, as a thesis, it strikes me that *Sandman* would probably not have taken the shape it did.

FAN LETTER

FAN Magazine recently received the following letter from Neil Gaiman on the set of *Neverwhere*...

(February, 1996)

Dear FAN—

This is being written in a canvas chair, in front of a tiny gas fire, in a high, damp, vaulted cellar lined with brick and corrugated iron, a little way under London.

The vaults are in Clink Street, home of London's original and most famous prison, knocked down these three hundred years, between Southwark Cathedral and the site of the new Globe Theatre.

In the next room along, the 1st Assistant Director just shouted "Turning over! Very quiet please!" and the director said "Action!" and this is what happened:

Through a haze of thick fog, a monk stepped out in front of a huge cathedral door (installed yesterday in an empty vault arch by the art department) and asked the three travelers to state their business.

The monk is tall, and black, and he wears a black robe.

The travelers are an odd bunch: a tall, beautiful, black woman with close-cropped hair, wearing coppery-leather clothes, holding a spear; a small, tangle-haired young woman in a baggy blue-brown coat, with huge eyes, and lips that would make Julia Roberts jealous; and a faintly bemused young man, with a faint resemblance to the young Paul McCartney, who said "we're here for a key," to the monk. The monk eyed him in an unimpressed fashion and then pushed him into the mud.

("Neil, I think that very soon someone very cold is going to need that fire," said Johnny, the 3rd AD. "I'll move," I told him.)

The mud was brought in this morning by the art department. The lady with the spear just came and sat in front of the fire and shivered, while a make-up lady touched up her face.

Down in the vaults there are about fifty people—electricians and camera people, make-up and props and directors and producers: everyone. Most of them have been up since 5:00 am. All of them are cold. Some of them are muddy.

Very soon a number of them are going to be a whole lot colder and an awful lot muddier.

There are little smudge fires of solid paraffin burning through the smoke, and green lights reflecting off sheets of foil glimmering like the light bouncing off an underground river, and (I've moved into the room next door by the way, where a fight is going on even as I write this, because they moved the little gas fire and where it goes, I go) I've got my leather jacket done all the way up, and many layers of clothing beneath it, and sometimes I can't see the keyboard in front of me because of the smoke, most of which comes out of a device called an OPTIMIST, and I think: "This'll teach me to make things up."

In case you were wondering, what I'm doing right now is making some television. Or rather, I'm not making television. Everyone else here is making television. I, on the other hand, am sitting writing this, hoping they won't remember whose idea this was and rend me limb from limb, or at least cover me in cold wet mud. It seemed such a wonderful idea for a scene when I wrote it, a year ago, somewhere that was nice and inside and warm.

I wonder about making a break for it. The actors in particular, I am convinced, must really hate me by now.

Our female lead, whose name is Laura Fraser, just turned to me and grinned and said "Can you believe we're getting PAID for this?"

And then I'm watching the fight scene being filmed, and on the second take ("Remember, be really vicious!" called the director before they started) the actress with the spear, Tania Moodie, all supple in leather and copper, misjudged a swing and broke her spear over her opponent's head: stunt men are not paid enough.

And the mud gets more and more slushed and stomped and slurried, and pretty soon now we'll be filming the takes with them down in the mud, and despite the fact that breathing is becoming impossible and I can't feel my fingers any more, I can't believe I'm getting paid for this either.

Yesterday we were in a house in Chiswick that had once belonged to Hogarth, the engraver and artist, where I got to watch the art department's astonishing interpretation of my request in the script for "A VCR that looked like it was designed and built by Sir Isaac Newton in the 1680s".

The day before we were in the crypt of a church in Paddington watching a dozen monks with Kalashnikovs strapped to their backs walking down a misty aisle. The day before that we were filming someone eating a pigeon in Trafalgar Square.

Tomorrow we'll be in the Freemason's Hall in Great Queen St., which will be doubling for a room in the British Museum, in which an exhibition of angels will be displayed. This means that as I type, an art department crew, plus carpenters and movers, are creating a room filled with angels, a stage and an enormous door into another world; and forty or so extras are delighted to know they'll be working tomorrow...

...sorry for the interruption. They're flailing in the mud. The smoke's a bit thick. I keep getting distracted.

The process of fiction for me is one that requires a certain amount of stillness, of emptiness, of reflection and even boredom. Right now I couldn't be bored if you paid me, and the small still hours in the middle of the night are lost to me and forgotten. I'm up before seven in the morning and home around nine at night, all ready to do last minute *Sandman* stuff, wash the soot off, and stumble bedwards.

So this is by way of being a short letter of apology from a rather exhausted writer.

I wrote the outline for *NEVERWHERE* five years ago, and wrote the scripts over the last five years, and I'm pleased with them. The BBC are having a hard time describing it—"mythic fantasy" and "urban gothic romance" and "in the tradition of *Dr. Who* and *Blake's 7*" and even "the most bizarre journey since *Alice in Wonderland*" are all attempts that have been made by producers and the press office, none of which seem to bear much resemblance to the story I wrote.

It's obviously written by the person who wrote *Sandman*, and it is about a magical other version of London, and it is, I hope, funny and scary and strange and not really like anything else anyone has done.

Comics and prose are both easier than TV—less frustrating, less chilly and an awful lot less muddy. And even the craziest of comics employs fewer people than a TV show—in the case of this show, we've got 40 actors in the cast, will be employing a total of about 500 extras—and then there are the people who actually make the thing... Comics are less compromised, easier. You never lose locations in comics, you don't lose scenes or dialogue, you don't have to stop work after 11 hours or tumble into the money pit of overtime... And the odds of getting good TV seem even lower than getting good comics.

So why do I do television? I dunno. Maybe, like the machine the smoke is coming out of, I'm an optimist.

And truth to tell, I'm having a wonderful time...somewhere under London...

Wish you were here—

Neil

Shameful Secrets of Comics Retailing: The Lingerie Connection

Several years ago, I wrote a scene in a comic (it was *Sandman* 37, the last chapter of the book *A Game of You*) in which a young lady went into a comic shop for the first time to buy a comic. Here are the panel descriptions I wrote back then:

PAGE 20 PANEL 2

BLACK AND WHITE FLASHBACK PANEL. BARBIE'S STANDING IN A COMIC-BOOK STORE. IT'S A REALLY SMALL, DIRTY ONE. SHE'S STANDING LOOKING SLIGHTLY SCARED. ON THE STAND BEHIND HER IS A TYPICAL ASSORTMENT OF EROS-STYLE PORNO COMICS COVERS, SHOWING WOMEN WITH TITANIC BREASTS IN BONDAGE AND SO FORTH; AND, BELOW THAT, WE'VE GOT A WHOLE SHELF OF JUST THE SAME COMIC WITH THE SAME COVER—OR MAYBE A WHOLE SET OF THE SAME COMIC WITH DIFFERENT COVERS. IT'S GOT TO BE CALLED SOMETHING LIKE *THRUST FORCE* #1, AND IT'S YOUR OPPORTUNITY TO PASTICHE—NOT PARODY—A SET OF X-MEN TYPE COVERS. MUSCULAR MEN AND WOMEN WITH TOWERING BOOBS AND NOT MUCH COVERING THEM. MAYBE IN THE BACKGROUND OR AT THE SIDE WE CAN SEE TWO OR THREE FOURTEEN YEAR OLD BOYS, JUST SORT OF STARING AT HER. THIS IS NOT A NICE COMIC STORE—IT'S THE KIND OF PLACE THAT MAKES YOU FEEL OILY AND GREASY, AND MAKES YOU WISH YOU WERE SOMEWHERE ELSE.

Barbie cap: "In order to buy it I had to go into this bizarre little store. I mean, I don't think they'd swept the floor in a decade, and I bet the staff *had* to have taken unhelpfulness lessons."

PAGE 20 PANEL 3

BLACK AND WHITE: WE'RE LOOKING AT BARBIE, FROM BEHIND OR THE SIDE, STANDING AT THE COUNTER. SHE LOOKS VERY SMALL, PHYSICALLY, AND VERY VULNERABLE AND SCARED. WE CAN SEE A FAT, UNSHAVEN GUY IN A SWEAT-STAINED SHIRT, LEERING AT HER AS HE TAKES HER DOLLARS. MORE UNSAVOURY COMICS AND DISPLAYS AROUND; IT'S ALL SEX OR SUPERHEROES.

Barbie caps: "And there was a big *greasy guy* behind the counter who seemed *really* amused that I was like, female, and asking for this comic.

"He said it *wasn't* very collectable. Then he said they didn't normally see breasts as *small* as mine in his store, and all these guys laughed."

The scene was ably and accurately drawn by Shawn MacManus, who depicted the comic shop in question as a claustrophobic, rather dirty place, with a leering and unwashed gentleman behind the counter staring at the discomfited heroine.

We got two different kinds of reaction from that scene, in readers' letters, and afterwards. Three (male) readers wrote in to complain that nothing like this ever happens in life, that the comic shop we had depicted was purely and only the product of Shawn's and my fevered brains, all-too-obviously corrupted by some kind of strange bleeding-heart feminist urge to blacken the public face of comics retailers. And dozens of (female) readers wrote in to say, all of them in more or less the same way, and at the same volume, "That's exactly what it's like. HOW DID YOU *KNOW?*"

The point that the male correspondents seemed to miss was not that *all* comics stores are like that, but that *some* are—some subtly, many not-so-subtly.

There are comics stores out there which are simply boys' clubs, owned or run by people who've never been much good at talking to or being in the presence of women, and, for that matter, have never quite mastered basic woman-friendly skills, like washing, changing their tee-shirts, or sweeping the floor. Women feel as uncomfortable in these places as most men do when inexorable circumstances cause them, blushing, coughing and staring nervously at the floor, to spend any amount of time in the lingerie department of a large department store.

This is not good.

Lingerie departments exist to serve only half the human race (and a small handful of fetishists). The other half of us will only stumble in there more or less at gunpoint, looking for birthday presents (or, worse, accompanying a grandmother on the scent of a pre-war foundation garment), and stare around us desperately, then, unable to meet the eyes of the saleslady, will sidle out embarrassed, somehow managing to convince ourselves that our wives or girlfriends will be just as happy with a power tool (or we sit, drumming our feet and wishing we were elsewhere until elderly female relations have made their purchases).

Comics, unlike lingerie, are not a gender-specific product.

Women, after all, buy more of the books than men do. They like to read. And there is no X-chromosome-linked inability to read comics, either. When I was a boy, in England, I tended to prefer my cousins' and sisters' girls' comics to the blander fare that boys got, because the stories were better. (They may have tended to be about virtuous young ladies being ill-treated by vicious step-families, their only friend the cheerful young stable-boy, but they were *stories,* dammit. They were going somewhere.)

But there were two points that I was making in the *Sandman* panels I mentioned above. One was that, often, the stores themselves are less than women-friendly. The other was that the material on sale often has as little interest for women as the aforementioned lingerie, when not actually being worn by an object of desire, has for most men.

Sometimes comics retailers come over to me, and grin. "I want to thank you for bringing women into my store!" they say, happily.

Sandman was in the minority of comics whose readers, based on whatever unscientific measures one can use to measure these things (in this case, readers' letters and the genders of people turning up for signings), seemed, after the first year or so, pretty much evenly divided between men and women.

When interviewers would ask me why that was, I used to tell them it was because women liked real stories about people, and that was undoubtedly part of it.

The other part of it was probably that the women in *Sandman* (and there were a lot of them) were there neither for decoration nor to appeal to the glandular needs of pubertal readers; they didn't get tied to chairs wearing nothing but their lingerie ("If I were a female comic character," wrote Alan Moore in his 1982 essay *Invisible Girls and Phantom Ladies,* talking about this tendency, "I think I'd be inclined to dress up warm, wear three pullovers at once and never go anywhere without a pair of scissors"); neither were they six-gun-wielding huge-breasted gals who were, in effect, guys in unconvincing drag.

I'm not claiming here that *Sandman* was perfect, or alone in the world of comics in its depiction of women. Obviously neither statement is true. My point is that, given a comic with a story, that was not actually offensive, and comic stores that did not actually drive women away, we soon had a significant, word-of-mouth driven, female readership. And comics retailers were selling comics to an expanded customer base.

Which is good for everyone. At the time I write this, the world of comics is in the kind of depression that tends to provoke comments like "Well, at least it can't get any worse" from people in all branches of the industry, just before it goes and does just that.

This volume, published and compiled by Friends of Lulu, is here to help all of you sell more comics. You are selling people dreams and stories and pictures, and there's never been anything gender-specific about *them*.

You have, after all, nothing to lose but fifty percent of the human race.

June 11, 1997

BUT WHAT HAS THAT TO DO WITH BACCHUS?
(Deadface:An Introduction of Sorts)

I want to talk about Eddie Campbell.

Our word *Tragedy* comes from the Greek, *tragos-ode:* "The song of the goat." Anybody who has ever heard a goat attempt to sing will know why.

A man called Thespis is credited as being "the Father of Tragedy." He was an itinerant player, who travelled from Greek town to Greek town, in a cart, about 535 BC. The cart was both a form of transportation and a stage, and in each town he would recite his poetry, and his actors—a novelty in themselves—their faces "daubed with the lees of wine" (the earliest stage make-up), would entertain the crowd.

As the story goes, until then all songs and performances had been about Bacchus, the god of wine. Thespis first tried to experiment by sticking into the songs little recitations he had written about Bacchus—a remarkable innovation which the people bore nobly, up to a point. Then he decided to experiment further, and began to speak and recite about other things.

This failed miserably.

"What has that to do with Bacchus?" they would ask him, and chastened, he would return to the subject of the god of the vine.

As far as they were concerned, *real* songs, and poems and stories, were about Bacchus.

They would have liked *Deadface* too.

So who was Bacchus?

Like most gods, he accumulated to himself a number of names—amongst them, *Dionysus* "The God from Nyssa," *Bimater* "twice mothered," *Omadios* "Eater of Raw Flesh," *Bromios* "the noisy," *Bacchus* "the Rowdy," and of course *Enorches*, "the betesticled."

He was the son of Zeus and Semele, god of wine and drama, who taught mankind how to cultivate the earth, the use of the vine, the collecting of honey. The fir, the fig, the ivy and the vine were sacred to him, as were all goats (whether they could sing or not). He was the most beautiful of all gods (despite often being represented as having horns), and many of the stories of his life and miracles have remarkable parallels to those of both Jesus Christ (whose biographers may have pinched them) and Osiris (from whose legends they were probably nicked in the first place).

Probably the best and strangest of Euripedes' plays is *The Bacchae*, the story of Bacchus' revenge on Pentheus, King of Thebes, who refused to acknowledge the divinity of this new god. Pentheus gets—literally—torn to pieces by his mother, and his two aunts.

Really shitty things happen to people who piss off Bacchus. It's a tragedy, really.

But what has that to do with Eddie Campbell?

I don't suppose anyone much (except maybe me, and I'm weird about that stuff) cares that mythologically speaking (and any other way of speaking lacks something important) *Deadface* is correct and on the money in every detail, but it is anyway. It's joyful and funny and magical and wise. It is also a tragedy—quite literally. (I was kidding about the goats singing. Actually the singer of the best tragic song got a goat as a prize. I think.) Tragedy tells us of the hero with one tragic flaw, of *hubris* (something between pride and arrogance) being clobbered by Nemesis. For Joe Theseus it's a tragedy. For Bacchus, of course, it's a comedy.

Most things go back to Bacchus.

Within these pages you'll find the old mythology and new. The Eyeball Kid and the Stygian Leech rub shoulders with older gods and heroes. *Deadface* mixes air hijacks and ancient gods, gangland drama and legends, police procedural and mythic fantasy, swimming pool cleaners and the classics. It shouldn't work, of course, and it works like a charm.

But what has that to do with Eddie Campbell?

Well, Eddie Campbell is the unsung King of comic books. While the rest of us toil away on what we imagine, certainly mistakenly, to be Olympus, Eddie is travelling from island to island, thyrsus in one hand, scritchy pen and Letraset in the other, surrounded by short men with hairy ears and women who suckle panthers and eat human flesh, and all of them are drinking far too much wine and having much too much fun. (The Silenus for this tale is Ed Hillyer, who wanders in, in the second half of the book, and inks over Eddie's pencils.)

I hope that this book, along with Eclipse's collection of Eddie's *Alec* stories (which don't have all the fun killing and flying and running about that this one has, but are, in my opinion, probably about as good as comics ever get) and *From Hell* (in Spiderbaby Graphics' *Taboo,* which Eddie's drawing. It's being written by a talented Englishman called Alan Moore—definitely someone to watch if you ask me) will raise his reputation to the heights it ought to be. The man's a genius, and that's an end to it.

If you're one of the lucky ones who read this series when it first came out, you'll need no further recommendation or praise from me: you know how good it is. If you're discovering *Deadface* for the first time, I envy you: you have a treat in store.

But what has this to do with Bacchus? Or Eddie? Or the Eyeball Kid?

Keep reading.

You'll find out.   August 19, 1990, Sussex, England.

BREATHTAKER

Some people look at me enviously when they discover that, as a working professional in the wacky world of comics, I get sent free comics, which is something I've gone far beyond taking for granted or even appreciating, although (hope springing eternal in the human etc.) I still open all the big padded envelopes from the different publishers with the free comics in, well mostly, and sometimes they get even read before they scurry off to the distant recesses of the basement to become a fire hazard.

This is because Sturgeon's Law applies to comics, just like it applies to everything else in the world: 90% of them are crap. Or 99%, I forget the exact wording, and it depends on the day and the pile of comics anyway.

And because hope springs eternal etc., I still read too much of the 90% (or the 99%) looking for the 10% (or the 1%), and I'm still much too frequently disappointed. I don't understand why so many mainstream comics have to be lousy, repetitive, poorly drawn, clumsily coloured, unimaginatively told. I don't understand why so many mainstream comics are bad copies of other comics, ones that weren't that good to begin with anyway.

Sometimes I'm ready to believe that nothing good will ever arrive in the freebie envelopes ever again.

And then once in a while, for a change, you get something like *Breathtaker,* which arrives in a large manila envelope with twenty or thirty other comics and proves itself to be something utterly odd and new. Powerful art, vibrant colouring, a new, quirky story told in a different way. Strong and surprising stuff. It's something that makes free comics worth reading.

It's the story of Chase Darrow (a name that conjures up both fugitives and, more distantly, the trials of evolution), the "breathtaker" of the title, and of The Man (abbreviated, of course, to TM) a sort-of-superhero, licensed product, and all-around psychopath.

It's a story in four parts addressing four subjects close to all of our hearts—either money, sex, god and escape (if you believe the first word in each episode), or love, death, sex and power (if you believe the words on the covers).

29

It's a love affair—a sequence of love affairs—that unravels and reveals the mysteries of Chase Darrow, and explains for us the death (of old age) at the start of the tale of one Paul Raymond (he shares a name with a British porn and property king); and we learn on the way what happened to Chase's mother; we find out what happens to people who make love to Chase Darrow, and we get to decide whether or not it's actually worth it.

The strange thing, in my opinion anyway, about *Breathtaker,* is that it didn't set the world afire on its first appearance.

Maybe people were looking in the wrong direction, looking for more grim&gritty vigilantes, looking for more mutants, more platinum-covered holographic special collectors' editions.

Maybe that's not it at all.

Maybe it's *Breathtaker's* use of all the usual pulp motifs. It has (in a vague and almost dismissive nod of the head to mainstream comics) a brutal, action-style superhero; it has the sinister government plots and secret laboratories of standard pulp fiction; it has a *femme* quite literally *fatale;* it has a posse of vigilantes up against the forces of law and order…

Except that the action hero transcends his caricatured hair-trigger steroid-case status; except that the sinister government plots are pretty much entirely beside the point; and the *femme fatale*—Chase Darrow, human succubus—is a good soul, as much about life as she is about death. The Posse dissolves into well-meaning chaos, the forces of law and order come down on the side of freedom and escape.

Maybe it's the style of the art that was the problem—subtle, expressive, not a line wasted, gently and appropriately coloured. It's a long way from the excesses of many of today's mainstream comics, and it's also a long way from the art styles which, for reasons I have never quite been able to fathom, are seen as being more *realistic.*

(A sidenote here: they say that Picasso was once berated by an American GI in Paris for his cubist art style. "It's not realistic," the GI kept telling him. "Art must be realistic." Later, in a mellower mood, the GI pulled out from his wallet a snapshot of his girlfriend back home. Picasso squinted at it for a moment, then looked up at the GI innocently. "Is she really that small?" he enquired.)

Breathtaker is a more or less seamless work. The team of Mark Wheatley (he wrote this, and also did the painting) and Marc Hempel (design, and drawing and lettering) blends and fuses and works together astonishingly well.

Marc and Mark have redone the final pages of *Breathtaker,* making a sequence that was implicit pretty explicit, but other than that, this is the book that originally appeared in four parts in 1990. It's the story of Chase and The Man.

It's about sex, but the sex is never divorced from love, from need, from pain or from humanity.

It's about love: what we give when we love, and what we take.

I got to read it for free; and for a few months in 1990 it re-established my faith in mainstream comics, and hope once more got to spring eternal in the human etc.: they don't have to be dumb. They don't have to be bad. They don't have to be stale copies of stale copies...

And some of them are so good they can almost take your breath away.

February 1994

BRATPACK
(BY RICK VEITCH)

Shortly before Rick Veitch began *Bratpack,* DC Comics ran a telephone vote on whether or not Robin—Batman's kid sidekick, at that time a youngster named Jason Todd, already the second boy proudly to wear the Robin costume—should be killed.

And, next issue, Robin died in a bomb blast: thousands of fans had voted, and they wanted blood. It made the front pages of newspapers in the real world.

Immediately after that the four issues of *Batman* in which Robin's deathtrap was set up became instantly collectible. I seem to remember that the book in which the kid in the green underwear bought it was trading for over $40 at the height of the craze.

If you're worried by this, let me reassure you: the dead Jason was rapidly replaced by another Robin, Tim Drake. Batman, after all, must have his kid sidekick. The launch of the new Robin was attended by comic-store hype (multiple collectible covers, holograms and the like) and was also much collected.

Two weeks ago Rick Veitch sent me the complete *Bratpack,* the book you're holding.

By a coincidence sent, I assume, by the Little God of Introductions, that was the same week Northstar, a minor Marvel superhero in the *Alpha Flight* team, came out of the closet. While he was by no means the first gay character in comics, nor even the first gay superhero, this for some reason made headline news internationally. Copies of the issue of *Alpha Flight* in which he came out were selling for $25 two days later.

It's worth mentioning that the creators—the writers and artists—saw no part of these grossly inflated prices. Nor did the comic companies. These were short-term profits made by certain comic stores, trading chiefly on the cupidity and foolishness of pubescent males.

Perhaps it's also worth mentioning (although with the caveat that this is no more than hearsay) that in neither case, it is strongly rumoured, was the parent corporate body pleased with the attention the unexpected death and outing attracted. The corporations, after all, own the characters. Remember: Batman isn't simply a comic character: he's a movie star, a lunchbox pin-up, a licensing gold-mine. You mess with Batman and Warner Entertainment gets worried. You screw with Spider-man and watch Revlon get upset.

Collectibles; merchandising; corporate ownership of characters; killing the spandex brigade and bringing them out of the closet; the gullibility of children: all these things should be borne in mind when reading the following tale.

After Rick Veitch had plotted *Bratpack,* but before he began to draw it, he found himself put in a professional position he found untenable, and resigned as the writer of the comic *Swamp Thing,* leaving DC Comics permanently. The issue was one of blasphemy: he told a story in which Swamp Thing, an Earth Elemental spirit, encountered Jesus Christ in the Garden of Gethsemane. While the story itself depicted Christ in a similar manner to many respected quasi-biblical fictions such as *The Robe,* it was deemed to be potentially offensive, and was pulled—most of the way through the production process. That story made the front page of the *Wall Street Journal.*

That blasphemy (if it was a blasphemy) should also be borne in mind when reading *Bratpack.*

Rick Veitch cares deeply about superheroes. He thinks they matter. That they're important. That they tell us things about ourselves. There's a mixture of love and hatred here that's heady, weird, and unique: subtle as a gang-rape, gentle as a crowbar shattering a skull, sweet as a dead boy in a bell tower feeding on pigeons.

Rick Veitch thinks dirty, grotesque, and completely unfair thoughts about costumed crimefighters. He remembers Green Arrow's ward Speedy, and Wonder Woman's protégée Wonder Girl, Captain America's sidekick Bucky, and the 1940s Sandman's assistant Sandy the Golden Boy. He remembers them, and the hundreds of others like them. Innocent kids out there swinging from tall buildings with their vigilante mentors so the kids reading would have someone to identify with, so the heroes could have someone to explain the plot to, and…

Well, yeah. I suppose I'd think it was odd if an adult male's best friend and closest, most constant companion was a twelve-year-old boy. Now you come to mention it.

Rick Veitch is talking about all that stuff.

He's talking about merchandising, about market forces, about censorship. He's talking about blood.

These aren't "superheroes in the real world"; that's been done already, and done well. Slumberg's not Detroit or New York; obviously not—it's the inside of Rick Veitch's head, a landscape as instantly recognisable and as distortedly personal as that of Tex Avery or Heironymus Bosch.

You haven't read this version of *Bratpack* before—not even if you're one of the thousands of people who read it when it came out in periodical form. Rick Veitch has overhauled it, streamlined it, remedied certain errors of judgment. He's rewritten much of it, added new pages, and completely changed the ending. Now it says what he wanted it to say all along. And it's got an important message for us all.

Kill the kids. You'll clean up.

February 1992

ASTRO CITY: CONFESSION
(BY KURT BUSIEK)

Listen, now. Read this carefully, because I am going to tell you something important. More than that: I am about to tell you one of the secrets of the trade. I mean it. This is the magic trick upon which all good fiction depends: it's the angled mirror in the box behind which the doves are hidden, the hidden compartment beneath the table.

It's this:

There is room for things to mean more than they literally mean.

That was it.

Doesn't seem that important to you? Not impressed? Convinced you could get deeper, sager advice about writing from a fortune cookie? Trust me. I just told you something important. We'll come back to it.

There are, in my opinion, two major ways in which superheroes are used in popular fiction. In the first way superheroes mean, purely and simply, what they mean on the surface. In the second kind of fiction, they mean what they mean on the surface, true, but they also mean more than that—they mean pop culture on the one hand, and hopes and dreams, or the converse of hopes and dreams, a falling away of innocence, on the other.

The lineage of superheroes goes way back: it starts, obviously, in the 1930s, and then goes back into the depths of the newspaper strip, and then into literature, co-opting Sherlock Holmes, Beowulf and various heroes and gods along the way.

Robert Meyer's novel *Super Folks* used superheroes as a metaphor for all that America had become in the 1970s: the loss of the American dream meant the loss of American dreams, and vice versa.

Joseph Torcha took the iconography of Superman and wrote *The Kryptonite Kid*, a powerful and beautiful epistolary novel about a kid who believes, literally, in Superman, and who, in a book constructed as a series of letters to Superman, has to come to terms with his life and his heart.

In the 1980s for the first time writers began writing comics superheroes in which the characters were as much commentary upon superheroes as they were superheroes: Alan Moore led the way in this, as did Frank Miller.

One of the elements that fused back into comics at that time was the treatment of some comics themes in prose fiction: *Super Folks* and *The*

Kryptonite Kid, short stories such as Norman Spinrad's "It's a Bird, It's a Plane…," essays like Larry Niven's (literally) seminal "Man of Steel, Woman of Kleenex."

The resurgence that hit comics at this time also surfaced in prose fiction—the early volumes of the George R.R. Martin-edited Wild Cards anthologies did a fine job of re-invoking the joy of superheroes in a prose context.

The problem with the mid-80s revival of interesting superheroes was that the wrong riffs were the easiest to steal. *Watchmen* and *The Dark Knight Returns* spawned too many bad comics: humourless, grey, violent and dull. When the Wild Cards anthologies were turned into comics everything that made them interesting as commentaries upon comics evaporated, too.

So after the first Moore, Miller and Martin-led flush of superheroes (they weren't deconstructed; just, briefly, respected), things returned, more or less, to status quo, and a pendulum swing gave us, in the early 90s, superhero comics which were practically contentless: poorly written, and utterly literal. There was even one publisher who trumpeted *four issues of good writers* as the ultimate marketing gimmick—every bit as good as foil-embossed covers.

There is room to move beyond the literal. Things can mean more than they mean. It's why *Catch-22* isn't just about fighter pilots in the Second World War. It's why "I Have No Mouth, and I Must Scream" is about more than a bunch of people trapped inside a supercomputer. It's why *Moby Dick* is about (believe fifty thousand despairing college professors or not, but it's still true) a lot more than whaling.

And I'm not talking about allegory, here, or metaphor, or even The Message. I'm talking about what the story is about, and then I'm talking about what it's about.

Things can mean more than they literally mean. And that's the dividing line between art and everything that isn't art. Or one of the lines, anyway.

Currently, superhero fictions seem to break into two kinds: there are the workaday, more or less pulp fictions which are turned out by the yard by people who are trying their hardest, or not. And then there are the other kind, and there are precious few of them.

There are two obvious current exceptions—Alan Moore's *Supreme,* an exercise in rewriting fifty years of Superman into something that means something.

And then—and some of you might have thought that I might have forgotten it, given how far we've got into this introduction without it being mentioned, there is *Astro City.* Which traces its lineage back in two directions—into the world of classic superhero archetypes, but equally into the world of *The Kryptonite Kid,* a world in which all this stuff, this dumb wonderful four-colour stuff has real emotional weight and depth, and it means more than it literally means.

And that is the genius and the joy of *Astro City*.

Me? I'm jaded, where superheroes are concerned. Jaded and tired and fairly burnt out, if truth be told. Not utterly burned out, though. I thought I was, until, a couple of years ago, I found myself in a car with Kurt Busiek, and his delightful wife, Ann. (We were driving to see Scott McCloud and his wife Ivy, and their little girl Sky, and it was a very memorable and eventful evening, ending as it did in the unexpected birth of Scott and Ivy's daughter Winter.) And in the car, on the way, we started talking about Batman.

Pretty soon Kurt and I were co-plotting a complete Batman story; and not just a Batman story, but the coolest, strangest Batman story you can imagine, in which every relationship in the world of Batman was turned inside out and upside down, and, in the finest comic book tradition, everything you thought you knew turned out to be a lie.

We were doing this for fun. I doubt that either of us will ever do anything with the story. We were just enjoying ourselves.

But, for several hours, I found myself caring utterly and deeply about Batman. Which is, I suspect, part of Kurt Busiek's special talent. If I were writing a different kind of introduction, I might call it a super power.

Astro City is what would have happened if those old comics, with their fine simplicities and their primal, four-colour characters, had been about something. Or rather, it assumes they were about something, and tells you the tales that, on the whole, slipped through the cracks.

It's a place inspired by the worlds and worldviews of Stan Lee and Jack Kirby, of Gardner Fox and John Broome, of Jerry Seigel and Bob Finger and the rest of them: a city where anything can happen: in the story that follows we have (and I'm trying hard not to give too much away) a crimefighter bar, serial killing, an alien invasion, a crackdown on costumed heroes, a hero's mysterious secret…all of them the happy pulp elements of a thousand comics-by-the-yard.

Except that, here, as in the rest of *Astro City*, Kurt Busiek manages to take all of these elements and let them mean more than they literally mean.

(Again, I am not talking about allegory here. I'm talking story, and what makes some stories magic while others just sit there, lifeless and dull.)

"Astro City: Confession" is a coming-of-age story, in which a young man learns a lesson. (Robert A. Heinlein claimed in an essay in the 1940s, published in Lloyd Eshbach's collection of SF writer essays *Of Worlds Beyond*, that there are only three stories, which we tell over and over again. He said he had thought there were only two, "Boy Meets Girl" and "The Little Tailor," until L. Ron Hubbard pointed out to him that there was also "A Man Learns A Lesson." And, Heinlein maintained, if you add in their opposites—someone fails to learn a lesson, two people don't fall in love, and so on—you may have all the stories there are. But then, we can move beyond the literal.) It's a growing-up story, set in the city in Kurt's mind.

One of the things I like about *Astro City* is that Kurt Busiek lists all of his collaborators on the front cover. He knows how important each of them is to the final outcome: each element does what it is meant to, and each of them gives of their best and a little more: Alex Ross's covers ground each issue in a photoreal sort of hyper-reality; Brent Anderson's pencils and Will Blyberg's inks are perfectly crafted, always wisely at the service of the story, never obtrusive, always convincing. The colouring by Alex Sinclair and the Comicraft lettering by John Roshell are both slick, and, in the best sense of the word, inconspicuous.

Astro City, in the hands of Kurt Busiek and his collaborators, is art, and it is good art. It recognises the strengths of the four-colour heroes, and it creates something—a place, perhaps, or a medium, or just a tone of voice—in which good stories are told. There is room for things to mean more than they literally mean, and this is certainly true in *Astro City.*

I look forward to being able to visit it for a very long time to come.

26 October 1997, Rome

300 Good Reasons to Resent Dave Sim (*Cerebus*)

It's rarely enough in this complex world that one can recognise the sources of things—hologram-covered, die-cut, foil-stamped origin issues notwithstanding. We forget where things begin.

Endings are more memorable than beginnings anyway: we remember where we were when we heard good friends were dead, while our first memories of them are hazy, muzzy things.

Thus it is with a certain amount of pleasure that I find I can recall my first encounter with *Cerebus*. I remember who and how and why I started reading. It went kind of like this:

My friend Roz Kaveney has settled down a lot over the years. When I first met her, however, I was intimidated mightily. She was, and is, several sizes bigger than I am, huge as Thomas Aquinas and just as large as life: all dressed in black leather (Roz, that is, not Thomas Aquinas, who was a Saint), carrying a black leather bag full of manuscripts heavy as bricks, and to top it all she occasionally wears hats.

Roz also knows a lot more than me; and she doesn't believe this, so she has, since I've known her, always assumed I know everything she knows. *Everything.*

A typical conversation with Roz used to go:

Roz: …Of course, he can't *really* be seen as the first of the deconstructionist revisionists, notwithstanding anything the Dickinsons or Frosts may say. Well, you've read the recent translation of the *P'nanok'tian Manuscripts*—you shake your head? Oh dear, silly me, I read an advanced unpublished typescript in the unexpurgated edition that is unlikely to see print in England for the next five years if at all—so, anyway, I pointed this out to Beedle and Twoddy and they said—you do know who Beedle and Twoddy are, don't you?

39

Me: Um. No.

Roz: Ah, well, Beedle is a very close friend of Sammy's—
Sammy knew me when I was at Oxford, and
Twoddy is currently doing 30 years to life for reck-
lessly taking and driving away an ice-cream van...
But then, most of Twoddy's problems date back to
his break-up with Madeleine and Billy... I've told
you about them, haven't I?

Me: Um...

Sometimes Roz would explain stuff, but usually she'd assume I knew
what she was talking about. I had a mental map of Roz's world that was
more or less like listening to an ongoing soap opera of truly operatic pro-
portions (with real valkyries). To be honest it would occasionally be a shock
to meet members of the cast, who were without fail a disappointment:
life-sized people of no particular distinction in whom it was hard to dis-
cern the sacred monsters of Roz's sagas.

So one day at a party we were talking comics, which I thought was
safe territory. She'd discussed fascist imagery in *The Dark Knight Returns*
and the use of the fetish boot as helicopter in *Elektra: Assassin,* and then
she started talking about more people I didn't know.

Roz: ...and of course you saw the Countess. Well, laying
three extra plates for dinner, obviously Lord Julius
is one of the dinner guests, but who are the other
two, we ask ourselves...?

For a brief minute I thought she was talking about more people she
knew that I'd never met, then she said *Cerebus,* and the penny dropped. As
with most conversations with Roz of that vintage, I didn't confess igno-
rance. Instead I made a mental note to find out what I could by our next
conversation. (This method proved the easiest—it was how I discovered
authors such as Peter Ackroyd, who tended to arrive with scurrilous tales
about their private lives before ever I had a chance to read their work.)

So I went off and read a *Cerebus.*

Looking back on it, Roz's friendship proved invaluable in coping with
Cerebus. I had the same sense of being at a party where you don't know
anyone, but everybody else knows everybody else.

In self-defense I went out and bought the six volumes of *Swords of
Cerebus* (this was in the Dark Ages, before the "phone books") and started

getting more of a handle on it all. I wasn't entirely clear on how this little Barbarian Warrior had become Pope, but then, Dave had just brought on Mick and Keef in the regular comic, and he was just about to start his wicked Frank Miller parody…

What was strange, even then (and it's even stranger now), was how far he'd come from the first issues of *Cerebus*. I mean, it all started out as a charming homage to Barry Smith's work on Conan, flat Jane Morris noses and all, with a central conceit—the hero's an aardvark—that didn't seem to amount to more than a couple of jokes (smells when wet, doesn't like granola), combined with a certain deflatory logic applied to comic conventions (the ones we follow, not the ones we go to. They came later).

It was both fascinating and revelatory, how Dave grew, and learned, and kept on growing, and kept on learning; and how what he'd learnt fed back into the work.

Lou Reed (as iconic for me in my way as the Glimmer Twins are for Dave in his) made an album some years back called *Growing Up in Public*. Some of us are lucky, and we do our apprenticeships where no one's watching (I, for example, spent my years learning to write in the disposable world of magazines) and appear in public in adult form. Some of us grow up in public. Dave did.

I met Dave for the first time (a meeting chronicled in one of his *Notes from the President* and in a fax I sent him which he ran in the lettercol) in his suite at the Savoy, back when I was still a starving journalist. (Roz Kaveney, whom I mentioned earlier, was there too. So was *Escape's* Paul Gravett, and my old friend Dave Dickson, a man who has drunk Jack Daniels with Keef Richards and lived to write about the bits he remembered.)

Dave held court (which he does, and very well) and one by one we'd interview him, while the others would munch the Beluga caviar on toast, and drink Dave's champagne (while I drank Dave's scotch diluted with ginger ale).

300 issues, he said. A 300-episode story. It'll happen.

I remember asking him what he'd do if there was something he wanted to write about, something he had to say that didn't fit into *Cerebus*. "I'd use a big hammer," he grinned. "I'd get it in somehow."

That was six years ago. Since then Dave has written (and drawn—with the able assistance of Gerhard, who is one of the nicest people I've met, despite having a really unlikely last name) about eighty issues of *Cerebus*. And the story's still only a fraction over half-way through. That's scary.

(As an aside: I'm typing this on the train, and the man sitting across from me is talking to himself, very clearly, and quite loudly. "Bollocks," he's saying. "My first bloody project. I don't bloody believe it. They can't bloody do this to me. Bollocks. I was going to be a bloody project officer.

Bollocks. Bloody bollocks to the lot of them…" although he isn't actually using the word bloody because this is the *CBG*. The word he's using is the adjectival form of a monosyllabic anglo-saxon word which rhymes with one of our commonest waterfowl.)

300 issues. Think about it. I mean, I think *Sandman*'s daunting, at the roughly 60 plus issues altogether it'll run. And I'm only writing it. (On the other hand I've experienced one thing Dave hasn't: the terrified look in the eyes of people who've just realised that one day there won't be any more. You wait, Dave Sim. In eight or nine years' time twenty thousand people are going to start getting very nervous…)

I've met Dave three times now. Spoken on the phone a few more times. Written a couple of letters and sent a fax. Seems like more than that, but that's all.

Each time he has been, in turns, brilliant, congenial, infuriating, difficult, and, much of the time, right. Often more than one of these at a time. One of the most infuriating things about Dave is that even when you disagree with him, which I frequently do, he's thought about whatever-it-is-I-disagree-about far more deeply and exhaustingly than I have. This is dead irritating. It is even more irritating when I disagree with him utterly, and still suspect he may be right. He also has really good rejoinders.

Dave: Neil, why don't you and Michael Zulli self-publish *Sweeney Todd?* It's easier than stealing candy from blind babies.

Neil: Because both Michael and I are flakes, that's why. I wouldn't trust either of us to manage a lemonade stand, let alone run a comic book company.

Dave: (Proceeds to demonstrate indisputably exactly how you can run a comic-book company and self-publish using only a pencil, a telephone, a small lump of silly putty, and a photograph of Shea Stadium.)

Me: Um…

It's something like that, anyway.

Dave is unique, which is a shame. He's seen how powerful the periodical comic is as a medium, and decided to go the distance: 300 issues of *Cerebus*. In a world in which artists can rise to prominence having drawn a handful of comics, this demands a level of commitment from the readership which is positively unheard of, and it demands a level of commitment from Dave that's positively insane. We're talking rolling huge rocks up impossibly steep hills here: Dave Sisyphus.

Dave Sim is the conscience of comics. It's a lousy, thankless job, and if he wasn't doing it we wouldn't have to invent him. We'd probably just be pleased he wasn't around to bug us. Remember: Jiminy Cricket was squished by a wooden hammer by the end of chapter four in the original Collodi novel of *Pinocchio*. Were there a wooden hammer large enough, and did he not live out in Kitchener, and were there no fear of societal retribution, Dave would probably have been squished long since.

When one talks publishing with Dave, again, he knows what he's talking about. He's published other people; he's been published by other people. He knows the pitfalls, and he tells unpleasant truths. This can be really irritating.

He still hasn't stopped learning. And he doesn't forget what he's learned.

Mothers and Daughters, the new storyline, is a delight for many reasons—one of which, for me, is that he's taken all the techniques he's spent so long honing and he's using them all at once. It's akin to seeing someone write music first for violin, then for oboe, for harpsichord, then for electric guitar. And then, just when you wonder what instrument they'll turn to next, they start to use the full orchestra, with a choreographed display of fireworks somewhere in the background.

I'm rather proud of the fact that my only written-and-drawn comics story was published in a *Cerebus*. I'm just as proud that one of my characters has been misappropriated by Dave for his own purposes. (Note to Dave: treat her well. She enjoys long walks and being taken to saccharine-sweet movies.)

I'm sometimes a good writer. It irks me that Dave is, in my opinion (and when he's firing on all cylinders), as good as, or (okay, I'll say it) better than me, and he's had longer to be good. It also irks me that he's a far, far better artist than I'll ever be, and that he's a better publisher than the majority of us (particularly those of us who really *couldn't* run a successful lemonade stand).

He's offered twice now to put me on the *Cerebus* complimentary list, and each time I've declined. I *like* going into comic book stores, but these days it seems like I buy less and less each time I go in. It's good to have something I can rely on—and which, barring disaster, we all have for more than a decade to come.

Most of us who create comics are mayflies. We come in to the wild wacky world of comics, blaze like little meteors (or not), flitter from one project to the next like small children with access to the TV remote control...

Dave's still there. He's keeping *Cerebus* in print. He's still doing it. He won't shut up and go away.

I'm grateful. Even when I resent it.

There are 300 damn good reasons to resent Dave Sim, and as I write this he's published over 160 of them.

Some time in the next millennium, when the kids coming onto the scene remember Sandman as a dusty old character somebody did a long time ago, like Scribbly or Binky or Jerry Lewis, *Cerebus* 300 will come out, and Dave will stop—or at least, stop *Cerebus*. (I tend to assume he'll go into politics at this point; although the idea of Gerhard as Jean Chrétien is one I find difficult entirely to come to terms with.)

Then, when it's all done, I've promised myself I'll sit down and read the whole thing, start to finish. It may take some time.

300 issues. Hell, that's over 6,000 pages.

Hmmm.

Okay, let's scrap the title we started with. Let's make this *6,000 Good Reasons to Resent Dave Sim*...

TANTRUM
(BY JULES FEIFFER)

There was a Jules Feiffer cartoon in the mid-sixties, in which a baby hardly old enough to walk catalogues the grievances inflicted upon it by its parents, each indignity accompanied by a soothing "Mommy loves baby. Daddy loves baby."

"Whatever that word 'love' means—" says the baby, essaying its first steps, "I can hardly wait till I'm big enough to do it to *them*."

When I first discovered Jules Feiffer I was...what? Four years old? Five, maybe. This was in England, in 1964 or 1965, and the book was a hardback blue-covered edition of *The Explainers*, Feiffer's 1962 collection, and I read it as only a child can read a favourite book: over and over and over. I had little or no context for the assortment of losers and dreamers and lovers and dancers and bosses and mothers and children and company men, but I kept reading and re-reading, trying to understand, happy with whatever comprehension I could pull from the pages, from what Feiffer described as "an endless babble of self-interest, self-loathing, self-searching and evasion." I read and re-read it, certain that if I understood it I would have some kind of key to the adult world.

It was the first place I had ever encountered the character of Superman: there was a strip in which he "pulled a chick out of a river" and eventually married her. I'd never encountered that use of the word "chick" before, and assumed that Superman had married a small fluffy yellow baby chicken. It made as much sense as anything else in the adult world. And it didn't matter: I understood the fundamental story—of compromise and insecurity—as well as I understood any of them. I read them again and again, a few drawings to a page, a few pages to each strip. And I decided that when I grew up, I wanted to do that. I wanted to tell those stories and do those drawings and have that perfect sense of pacing and the killer undercut last line.

(I never did, and I never will. But any successes I've had as a writer in the field of words-and-pictures have their roots in poring over the drawings in *The Explainers,* and reading the dialogue, and trying to understand the mysteries of economy and timing that were peculiarly Jules Feiffer's.)

That was over thirty years ago. In the intervening years the strips that I read back then, in *The Explainers,* and, later, in discovered copies of *Sick, Sick, Sick* and *Hold Me!,* have waited patiently in the back of my head, commenting on the events around me. ("Why is she doing that?" "To lose weight."/ "You're not perfection…but you do have an interesting off-beat color…and besides, it's getting dark."/ "What I wouldn't give to be a non-conformist like all those others."/ "Nobody knows it but I'm a complete work of fiction.")

So. Time passed. I learned how to do joined-up writing. Feiffer continued cartooning, becoming one of the sharpest political commentators there has ever been in that form, and writing plays, and films, and prose books.

In 1980, I got a call from my friend Dave Dickson, who was working in a local bookshop. There was a new Jules Feiffer book coming out, called *Tantrum.* He had ordered an extra copy for me.

I had stopped reading most comics a few years earlier, limiting my comics-buying to occasional reprints of Will Eisner's *The Spirit.* (I had no idea that Feiffer had once been Eisner's assistant.) I was no longer sure that comics could be, as I had previously supposed, a real, grown-up medium. But it was Feiffer, and I was just about able to afford it. So I bought *Tantrum* and I took it home and read it.

I remember, mostly, puzzlement. There was the certainty that I was in the presence of a real story, true, but beyond that there was just perplexity. It was a real "cartoon novel." But it made little sense: the story of a man who willed himself back to two years of age. I didn't really understand any of the whys or whats of the thing, and I certainly didn't understand the ending.

(Nineteen is a difficult age, and nineteen-year-olds know much less than they think they do. Less than five-year-olds, anyway.)

I was at least bright enough to know that any gaps were mine, not Feiffer's, for every few years I went back and re-read *Tantrum.* I still have that copy, battered but beloved. And each time I re-read it, it made a little more sense, felt a little more right.

But with whatever perplexity I might have originally brought to *Tantrum,* it was still one of the few works that made me understand that comics were simply a vessel, as good or bad as the material that went into them. And the material that goes into *Tantrum* is very good indeed.

I re-read *Tantrum* a month ago.

Now, as I write this, I'm in spitting distance of Leo's age, with two children rampaging into their teens: I know what that place is. And I have a two-year-old daughter—a single-minded, self-centred creature of utter simplicity and implacable will.

And as I read it I found myself understanding it—even recognising it—on a rather strange and personal level. I was understanding just why

Leo stopped being 42 and began being two, appreciating the strengths that a two-year-old has that a 42-year-old has, more or less, lost. Leo's drives are utterly straightforward, once he's two again. He wants a piggy-back. He wants to be bathed and diapered and fussed over. As a 42-year-old he lived an enervated life of blandness and routine. Now he wants adventure—but a two-year-old's adventure. He wants what the old folk tale claimed women want: to have his own way.

Along the way we meet his parents, his family, and the other men-who-have-become-two-year-olds. We watch him not burn down his parents' home. We watch him save a life. We watch his quest for a piggy-back and where it leads him. It's sexy, surreal, irresponsible and utterly plausible.

Everyone, everything in *Tantrum* is drawn, lettered, created, at white-hot speed: one gets the impression of impatience with the world at the moment of creation—that it would have been hard for Feiffer to have done it any faster. As if he were trying to keep up with ideas and images tumbling out of his head, trying to capture them before they escaped and were gone.

Feiffer had explored the relationship between the child and the man before, most notably in *Munro,* his cautionary tale of a four-year-old drafted into the US army (later filmed as an Academy Award-winning short). Children populated his Feiffer strip, too—not too-smart, little adult Peanuts children, but real kids appearing as commentators or counterpoints to the adult world. Even the kids in *Clifford,* Feiffer's first strip, a one-page back-up to *The Spirit* newspaper sections, feel like real kids (except perhaps for Seymour, who, like Leo, is young enough still to be a force of nature).

Tantrum was different. The term "inner child" had scarcely been coined when it was written, let alone debased into the currency of stand-up, but it stands as an exploration of, and wary paean to, the child inside.

When the history of the Graphic Novel (or whatever they wind up calling long stories created in words and pictures for adults, in the time when the histories are appropriate) is written, there will be a whole chapter about *Tantrum,* one of the first and still one of the wisest and sharpest things created in this strange publishing category, and one of the books that, along with Will Eisner's *A Contract with God,* began the movement that brought us such works as *Maus,* as *Love and Rockets,* as *From Hell*—the works that stretch the envelope of what words and pictures were capable of, and could not have been anything but what they were, pictures and words adding up to something that could not have been a film or a novel or a play: that were intrinsically comics, with all a comic's strengths.

I am delighted that Fantagraphics have brought it back into print, and, after reading it, I have no doubt that you will be too…

March 1997

THE DARK KNIGHT RETURNS
(BY FRANK MILLER)

"He knows exactly what he's doing, His kind of social *fascist*
always *does.*"
"Then why do you call him psychotic? Because you like to
use that word for any motive that's too *big* for your little mind?
Because he fights crime instead of perpetrating it?"
(Television Debate: *The Dark Knight Returns*, p.34)

The most important dreams, the most manipulable of cultural icons,
are those that we received when we were too young to judge or analyse. The
things that mattered—*really* mattered—when we were too young to dis-
criminate have tremendous power to move us now. Real chunks of junk
culture that can sleep in the back of your mind for decades: Donald Duck
or The Beatles, *Mad Magazine* or the old glass Coca Cola bottles. It's part of
a huge nostalgic undermind that one can ignore, or tap into, or use. Currently in *Watchmen* Alan Moore is taking apart the whole concept of the
"Superhero", using these grotesque childhood wish-fulfillment fantasies to
comment on the state of America and the world.

In *Dark Knight,* American comics auteur Frank Miller reassesses the har-
diest and most mutated of superheroes: Batman. Originally a dark and venge-
ful, almost supernatural, vigilante in the late Thirties, he soon gained Robin
"the Boy Wonder", was appointed an honorary member of the Gotham City
Police Department, and became a bastion of the establishment.

Batman spent much of the Fifties time-travelling and being kidnapped
by aliens; he was a large and good-natured father figure who fought crime
in a Gotham City that differed from New York only in the number of
fully functional giant household objects (pens, typewriters, bottles of milk
etc.) scattered around the city for advertising purposes. He bore little re-
lation to the mysterious night-stalking "Bat-Man" of the original *Detective Comics.*

In the mid-Sixties the *Batman* television series gave Bruce Wayne and
his masked alter ego a new audience: it was a high camp joke, played with a

straight face because that made the joke funnier, a formulated ritual in which a succession of costumed criminals attempted to steal something, left Batman and/or Robin in a death trap…(end of part one. Next episode same Bat-time, same Bat-channel…) from which they duly escaped and won.

Since 1969 an attempt has been made to take Batman back to his roots: Robin was sent to college, artist Neal Adams set a visual standard for Batman of long ears and cloak (not cape) that echoed those early comics, and a variety of writers have attempted to breathe life into him as a good-natured, all-American, obsessed, brilliant, mysterious man who dresses up as a bat and fights crime, chiefly and ultimately with his fists.

This is a more than somewhat silly idea, and, even in a comic-book milieu, difficult to use as a basis for an adult entertainment. But much of what is lovable about Batman is the sheer stupidity and silliness of the trappings that have grown up about him. The television series *couldn't* bring it off for real, and didn't even try, sending it up straightfaced instead.

It is to Frank Miller's credit that he has assimilated into his Batman not only the original conception of the Caped Crusader, but also the others (the television series; Neal Adams' visual reworking) and even managed, perhaps perversely, to bring Superman into a story that is an attempt at creating the first Great American Superhero graphic novel.

Miller's universe is the heart of the DC world, ten years after. The hordes of minor league heroes, villains, oddballs and geeks are sensibly ignored and forgotten, fallen by the wayside, leaving only the most important, the most memorable. Superman works undercover for the Reagan administration, keeping those troublesome South American countries in line. Green Lantern left for space, Wonder Woman went back to Paradise Island, Green Arrow (one of the few DC Superheroes who, one was convinced, voted Democrat) lost his right arm, was sentenced to prison, busted out and is currently anonymously screwing up nuclear submarines. Batman retired. He hung up his cowl, grew a moustache, and went back to being playboy millionaire Bruce Wayne. As the story opens he drinks too much, races fast cars, wants to die.

But the world is getting dirtier, nastier, more violent; Gotham City is a war-zone where yuppie kid-gangs kill babies. The world as Miller perceives it is one that desperately needs heroes, needs people who will Do Something About It, but no longer has any place for them.

Miller's Batman is in his fifties: a square-built giant who is driven by an internal demon—externalised as a bat—to fight crime. For the last ten years he had not been Batman, and he was now emotionally and effectively dead. Seeking death, but still trying to do something about his world, he became a vicious, sadistic monster, totally ruthless as he seeks to save Gotham City and thus America from itself.

Miller gives us a multitude of viewpoints on this, through the ubiqui-tous television screens that dot the pages (laid out on a twelve panel grid—half the size of a normal comics panel—so that the visual impact of the occasional full-page splash can be quite stunning, while the effect of large numbers of tiny panels often rapidly cutting from event to event, gives us the fast-cutting texture found in television show like *Hill Street Blues*). There are the liberal do-gooders, such as the psychiatrist Bartholomew Wolper, whose sole goal in life seems to be to release homicidal maniacs (Two-Face, the Joker) onto the streets. He claims that

> Batman's psychotic sublimative/psycho-erotic behavior pattern is like a net. Weak-edged neurotics, like Harvey (Dent—Two-Face), are drawn into corresponding intersticing patterns. You might say Batman commits the crimes using his so-called vil-lains as narcissistic proxies...

The Left regard Batman as a fascist; the Right sees him as a dangerous vigilante, a criminal, a disturbance to the status quo. It's a post-Bernard Goetz look at the vigilante. However, the device of presenting opposing viewpoints is loaded: the anti-Batman talking TV heads are uniformly unpleasant, while the pro-Batman group, alongside its share of "Hope he goes after the homos next" types, contains a number of right-thinking, obviously *nice* people who are obviously glad that someone is doing some-thing, as in the Lana Lang quote at the head of this review.

The viewpoint that seems to be Miller's own is Lang's, or retiring Commissioner Gordon's, explaining to his successor that the phenom-enon of Batman reminds him of accusations that Roosevelt allowed Pearl Harbor to happen in order to drag America into World War Two...

> "Wasn't proven. Things like that never *are*. I couldn't stop thinking how horrible that would be...and how Pearl was what got us off our duffs in time to stop the Axis. But a lot of innocent men died. But we won the War. It bounced back and forth in my head until I realized I couldn't judge it. It was too big. *He* was too big..."

"I don't see what this has to do with a vigilante..." is Ellen Yindel's response, until she too comes to the conclusion that Batman is simply too big to be judged. After all, he *is* doing something about the problems brought about by a Russian nuclear missile. He is effective.

Miller slowly sheds the trappings of the Batman of years gone by. The blue-clad, long-eared Neal Adams Batman he draws at first transforms into a grey-costumed, short-eared Batman who is visually reminiscent of a mutated Batman of Dick Sprang, square-jawed, with a huge black bat plastered across his chest, a Batman of the late Forties and Fifties. In the same way Miller tears down and builds up each of the familiar aspects of Batman kitsch.

The Batmobile becomes a fifty-foot-long tank.

Dick Grayson, the first Robin, has not spoken to Batman for years.

Jason Todd, the second Robin, is dead. Now Carrie, a thirteen-year-old girl, becomes the third Robin.

The Joker is a sexually ambiguous figure, visually somewhere between Cesar Romero and David Bowie, released from his ten-year coma by his deadly and one-sided love affair with Batman.

Selina (Catwoman) Kyle is now a blowzy middle-aged blonde who runs an escort agency.

Where Miller's achievement is most impressive is in his treatment of these factors, and of the rest of the supporting cast: Alfred the butler, a bitchy gaunt old retainer obviously related to John Gielgud's crusty butler from *Arthur,* convinced that Master Bruce is going through his second childhood; Oliver Queen—Green Arrow—in a scene-stealing cameo as an ageing revolutionary convinced that quiet subversion beats dressing up in a costume and making waves that attract the attention of the establishment; Ronald Reagan, a senile figure whose folksy metaphors and downhome insufferability are handled exactly; and Clark Kent: Superman. Miller first presents us with a Superman seen from Batman's viewpoint: "You always say yes to anyone with a badge…or a flag." "We could have changed the world—now look at us. I've become a political liability, and you…you're a joke…" Wayne and Queen see Superman as "The Big Blue Schoolboy", the ultimate straight, someone who wouldn't even stay up after bedtime. Superman, however is more complex than that. He *doesn't* see the world as a threatening place. He understands that people can be jealous of power, envious of what they don't understand: he functions undercover, invisibly, taking his orders from an obviously senile Reagan.

"They'll kill us if they can, Bruce," he muses at one point. "Every year they grow smaller. Every year they hate us *more.* We must not *remind* them that *giants* walk the earth."

"You were the one they used against us, Bruce. The one who played it *rough.* When the noise started from the Parents' groups and the Sub-Committee called us in for questioning…you were the one who laughed…that scary laugh of yours… '*Sure* we're criminals', you said. 'We've always *been* criminals. We have to be criminals.' "

Kent's viewpoint is essentially optimistic. As long as the planet Earth has not been destroyed, he is winning, he is doing his job. Wayne, on the other hand, is pessimistic: as long as there is one criminal left—as long as, in effect, his parents stay dead—he is losing the fight against crime, his reason for being. They are day and night, and the culmination of the story is the showdown between them. Superman *does* stand for "Truth, Justice and the *American Way*" as he perceives it; Batman stands for Justice, and for revenge.

Miller's future America is obviously his perception of America now: the sf content is limited to a "cloaking" device for helicopters and to a nuclear missile that can cause the kind of nuclear war that doesn't act as anything more than a plot device: an instant American nuclear winter that doesn't last for more than a couple of months, and doesn't do much more damage than to turn the skies grey and the mood sombre for the rest of the story. The kid-gangs are today's yuppie junior nasties, only with better dress sense and worse jargon. The feelings, the obsessions, are those of those parts of America where law and order have broken down and nobody *does* seem to be doing anything about it. Once one has been mugged and burgled a few times the desire for some huge policeman-cum-schoolmaster-cum-vigilante to terrify the muggers into ceasing to mug would begin to make perfect sense.

The book as a whole seems to have some pacing/plotting problems: the showdown with the Joker in the third section, built up gradually in the first two parts, ending with the Joker's killing himself in such a way that Batman will get the blame, seems part of an earlier version of the story. In this story it's almost unimportant to the final outcome—for the amount of time spent on it, and the ultimate Superman/Batman showdown.

Where Miller fails is in trying to play the whole thing for real and still remain within the world of comic-book convention. To, in effect, have his cake and eat it. His interest in the real effects that Batman would have are subordinate to the plot; attempts to produce moral ambiguities result rather in a moral fog.

For example, after Batman's defeat of the Mutants' (kid-gang) leader the gang splits into a number of factions. One of these, the self-styled "Sons of the Bat", commit atrocities on minor criminals. Muddying the conventions, Batman—Bruce Wayne—is then seen taking them under his cloak, using them to keep law and order in nuclear-wintered Gotham, and following Batman's "death" taking them to form the basis of the army with which he will move out and "bring sense to a world plagued by worse than thieves and murderers."

Initially the balance seems maintained; one is allowed to make up one's own mind about Batman's behaviour. He is a vigilante, but he seems necessary. The later images, however, tend to be the ones that linger: images from the final book, of the Batman on his black horse, leading a pack of kids on a mission to keep Gotham from falling into post-nuclear anarchy; of Bruce Wayne planning his assault on the world. It's one strong and determined man restoring civilisation to a world gone rotten, reminiscent of the Lieutenant in Hubbard's *Final Blackout*. But while the Lieutenant was in effect a superhero of the Thirties with the strict code of conduct that entailed, Miller's Batman is a product of the Eighties, a driven creature ultimately as dark as the world he is fighting.

What, then, is Miller offering?

The final vision is colourful (Lynn Varley's painted naturalistic colours are one of the chief factors that take this away from the four-colour world of comic books, establish mood, and, by the last section, could almost carry the book on their own). The comic-book story-telling draws on many influences, including Japanese and European comics, and Miller's artwork is strong and impressive, occasionally stunning.

Where Miller succeeds is in the romance, in the telling of a high adventure, in taking superhero comics as far as they can go and still be superhero comics. He captures the magic of the Batman—and not just the Batman that he carves out for himself, a huge and grinning gargoyle Doing Something About a World Gone Rotten, but also a multiplicity of earlier Batmans, the Batman of Bob Kane, Bill Finger and Dick Sprang, the Batmans of Infantino and Adams and Rogers, even the Batman of Adam West: all of them are visually echoed in something that is uniquely Miller's. The texture is there in the text as well: the narration is all internal monologue, the dialogue and scenes shift rapidly from scene to TV screens and back, all rapid cutting and tight panel control. The romance of Batman, the figure of the night, the scourge of evildoers, is allied to the romance of the Vigilante—the original charm of Batman, which is the charm of Dirty Harry, of anyone who sets himself above the law: something which only works, as Miller correctly perceives, if the law is seen as doing nothing, as condoning crime.

But credibility, both in the political sense, and as "suspension of disbelief", begins to break down when the story gets too large: Batman vs Gotham City is credible and gripping. Batman vs Superman, vs Nuclear Winter, vs the United States, simply isn't. We're back into the comic-book land of "When Titans Clash!" again, in which men in leotards hit each other and no-one ever dies for real. And that's a pity. Miller has dragged Batman into the 1980s, without a doubt. His overall achievement is quite remarkable; the story is Batman's last stand, an old man coming out of retirement to fight his last battle.

But he should have died for real.

September 1986

STARCHILD: CROSSROADS
(BY JAMES A. OWEN)

Firstly, I would like to go on record as stating that I am writing this introduction entirely of my own free will, and not under duress of any kind… The merest suggestion that James Owen might, for example, have, say, kidnapped any of my children or domestic animals in order to obtain this introduction is obviously arrant, libelous nonsense of the worst kind, which will be prosecuted to the full extent of the law by Coppervale International's lawyers, who are tall gentlemen in expensive suits with very thin briefcases and even thinner watches and they know where you live, so don't even think about it.

Secondly, I would like to explicitly state, in case anyone is wondering, that I am writing this myself and it is not being dictated by Coppervale International's Head of Enforcement, Big Ronald. Furthermore I am not currently tied up in a basement of indeterminate location, and I have not been promised that I will only see daylight again on satisfactory receipt of this introduction. Nor will I under any circumstances go to the police.

Mr. Owen asked me to write this introduction because he is very tired of people telling him that he stole a bunch of characters and ideas from me, people with names like Titania and Oberon and Thomas the Rhymer, and I am writing this introduction of my own free will just because I feel like it and not because I am worried about whether I will ever see my kids or cats again.

(They like *Meow Mix,* the brand cats ask for by name. The cats that is. The kids'll eat anything. Except lima beans, spinach, liver, mushrooms, cabbage, onions or…well, you're probably safe with hamburgers. Or pizza. Actually, the cats like pizza too. Pizza's probably a safe call all around.)

Mr. Owen and the executives, staff, enforcement and legal division of Coppervale International would like to say that these unfounded and unwarranted rumours of character theft have caused them a great deal of needless and unwarranted distress, not to mention their having precipitated the recent sharp tumble in the price of Coppervale International shares on the Hong Kong exchange.

Therefore I would like to make this following statement:
What writers do is this: we borrow, and we invent, and we embroider.

When Shakespeare named his Fairy King Oberon, he was taking the name of a 'humpty dwarf', the son of Julius Caesar and half-brother to Alexander the Great, who ruled Fairyland in the fifteenth-century French tale of 'Huon of Bordeaux'. And perhaps that Oberon began life as Alberich, the Scandinavian king of the dwarfs (it comes from the Old German for 'Elf Ruler' after all).

We build upon what went before.

Literature teems with queens of Faerie. Shakespeare was the first we know of to name her Titania, a name previously used for the goddess Diana (Mab, or Maeve, were commoner names for the Fairy Queen in Shakespeare's time), but Titania stuck as a name ever since.

We loot and pillage and we hone and we shape.

We tell stories about stories. We take characters from literature and from ballad and from folk tale and from song, and we use them in our stories, just as Shakespeare did, and Chaucer, only nowhere near as well.

There are only a handful of tales, it has been said. But there are an infinite number of voices in which these tales can be told, and an infinite number of ways to tell them.

A story is a journey; and no two journeys are ever alike, though you start and finish your journey in the same place. You see different things upon your way.

We never start nor finish in a vacuum, or alone.

Of course we tell tales in inns. On the one hand, people have been telling stories in inns in stories since well before a group of fictional pilgrims gathered in the *Tabard* in Southwark, a little south of London Bridge, and on the other hand, people *do* tell stories in pubs, and all of them, I was assured, were quite true, for they happened to a friend of a friend of the person who told me the tale.

And the tales you will find in *Crossroads* are James Owen's tales. And the journey he will take you upon, and the company that you will encounter on the way, is uniquely his own.

Written entirely of my own volition, not tied to a chair or anything, on the ninth of December in the Year Nineteen Hundred and Ninety Seven.

by
Neil Gaiman

and not at all by
Big Ronald

Dear Dick and Kim,

Here's the Thintwhistle introduction for you; it's about a thousand words of late Victorian balderdash, and was a joy to write.

Hope it's what you wanted. I'm afraid I didn't fit any of the High History of the Thintwhistle background saga in, so you may want to bung that into an afterword or something.

Drop me a line when you get it, and let me know if it meets with your approval,

best

Neil.

PROFESSOR THINTWHISTLE AND HIS AETHERIC FLYER
(BY LUPOFF AND STILES)

My Dear Lupoff,

your letter, having been conveyed across the wide Atlantic by packet steamer, arrived today at a most salutary moment. Indeed, I was breaking my fast this morning and pondering the wondrous miracles that progress brings us, year in, year out; the sun shone brightly on my eggs and toast, and outside the window I could hear the merry voices of the street people and costermongers raised in raucous joy as they twitted each other with the catch-phrases of the day: "Twopence more, and up goes the donkey!" they called, one to another, and "Has your mother sold her mangle? Ho, call again tomorrow, Vicar, and we'll have a crusty one!"; and it was at that moment that the housemaid brought me your missive, and the parcel of illustrated text you enclosed with it.

Is it not a remarkable world we live in, in which you can write a letter in California, and a mere matter of months later, it arrives at my door, here in the British Isles?

To answer your question—and indeed, to put you out of the miseries you must now be going through even as you read this—the answer is *yes;* I would indeed be delighted to pen a brief introductory note for your remarkable fictional tale of Professor Thintwhistle, and his Aether Flyer. Indeed, should you so wish, you might consider publishing *this very letter,* as a preamble to your fine work.

As to what I think about Thintwhistle? Sir, I think three things, which I shall list here.

Firstly the tale is scientifically educational and of much worth. I rejoice to think how many young minds (both young men, and if one may presume, perhaps even some *bluestockings*) may be awakened to the delights of scientific advancement by such a palatable introduction to the concepts of the Properties of the Aether, of Phlogiston, even of the rarified mysteries of Gravitational Attraction, through your tale.

Secondly it is inspiring: who can but thrill at the achievements of the Learned Professor, of Clarence, his noble protégé, as they make their way into the sky? What heart of stone could gaze up into the summer sky having read this tale, and remain unmoved by the possibility that one day a human foot—clad, I would venture to presume, in the sturdy leather footwear of a Briton or American—will make its imprint upon the dusty surface of fair Luna?

Thirdly it is morally instructing. The youth of today, alas, tends toward the cheap and meretricious delights of the Penny Dreadful, morally void and sensational works which debase and degrade the reader. If but *one* impressionable child is drawn away from the lure of *Varney the Vampire,* or *Her Guilty Secret,* then, my dear Lupoff, you will have done humanity a great service. Incidentally, I must say I find your technique of combining words with pictures one that has great merit, and one that may indeed, as you Americans so quaintly say, "catch on." It is to be regretted that Mr Charles Dickens passed away before this nascent medium was birthed; who knows what strange and magnificent fruits could have grown of the collaboration between the Great Man and the estimable Mr Stiles? Do you have a name for this unique mode of graphic literature?

On the evidence of *Thintwhistle,* I do not feel it is overstating matters to suggest, stout fellow, that you may well be the equal—nay, the superior—of our young English writer, Mr Wells, or of Verne, the Frenchman, in your imaginings; that you stand now poised at the apogee of this triumvirate of scientific romancers.

On a lighter note, I have taken the liberty of showing your tale to my good friend (and member of the Royal Society), Professor M_____ , and I must tell you that he questioned the scientific plausibility of the Aether Flyer: he maintains that a vehicle of the nature you posit here would need far more coal than you illustrate to make a voyage to a destination as remote as the Moon, and that your Professor would need to take an entire Welsh Mining Village with him, were he to travel to, let us say, examine close at hand proud Saturn's beauteous rings. But (you will be pleased to learn) he opines that the Thintwhistle Aether Flyer would be far more practical than firing a craft to the sky from the barrel of a gun, as Verne himself suggested.

M_____ was also dismayed by the pictorial representation of Selena, the Queen of the Moon; but as I explained to him—forcefully, as you may tell from my language— "Dash it all, M_____, it is no more than one can see hanging in the Tate Gallery, or carved from finest marble in the vasty halls of the British Museum," and he was forced to agree. But his is a scientific mind, and not an artistic one. Mr Stiles and yourself handle these matters with tact and discretion, and should Mrs Grundy cavil, we can but say, "Humbug, Ma'am!" and leave her to her Philistinism.

I trust that you are in good health. Please reassure Messrs Groth and Thompson, your publishers, that I desire no honorarium for penning these *pensees;* after all, it is enough to know that I am, in my own small way, helping to keep the flame of progress burning, as we head inexorably toward the bright and splendid dawn of the *Twentieth Century*—and towards waiting wonders that, I suspect, not even your Professor Thintwhistle could imagine.

Let us all dream of a world in which Mankind may harness the power that hides itself in the heart of a nugget of common house-coal and travel to the most distant stars!

Yours as ever,

Neil Gaiman esq.

OF TIME, AND GULLY FOYLE
(ALFRED BESTER)

You can tell when a Hollywood historical film was made by looking at the eye makeup of the leading ladies, and you can tell the date of an old science fiction novel by every word on the page. Nothing dates harder and faster and more strangely than the future.

This was not always true, but somewhere in the last thirty years (somewhere between the beginning of the death of what John Clute and Peter Nicholls termed, in their *Encyclopedia of Science Fiction,* "First SF" in 1957 when *Sputnik* brought space down to earth and 1984, the year that George Orwell ended and William Gibson started) we lurched into the futures we now try to inhabit, and all the old SF futures found themselves surplus to requirements, standing alone on the sidewalk, pensioned off and abandoned. Or were they?

SF is a difficult and transient literature at the best of times, ultimately problematic. It claims to treat of the future, all the what-ifs and if-this-goes-ons; but the what-ifs and if-this-goes-ons are always founded here and hard in today. Whatever today is.

To put it another way, nothing dates harder than historical fiction and science fiction. Sir Arthur Conan Doyle's historical fiction and his SF are of a piece—and both have dated in a way in which Sherlock Holmes, pinned to his time in the gaslit streets of Victorian London, has not.

Dated? Rather, they are of their time.

For there are always exceptions. There may, for instance, be nothing in Alfred Bester's *Tiger! Tiger!* (1956 U.K.; republished in the U.S. under the original 1956 *Galaxy* magazine title, *The Stars My Destination,* in 1957) that radically transgresses any of the speculative notions SF writers then shared about the possible shape of a future solar system. But Gully Foyle, the obsessive protagonist who dominates every page of the tale, has not dated a moment. In a fashion which inescapably reminds us of the great grotesques of other literary traditions, of dark figures from Poe or Gogol or Dickens, Gully Foyle *controls* the world around him, so that the awkwardnesses of the 1956 future do not so much fade into the background as obey his obsessive dance. If he were not so intransigent, so utterly bloody-minded, so unborn, Gully Foyle could have become an icon like Sherlock Holmes. But he is; and even though Bester based him on a quote—he is a reworking of the Byronesque magus Edmond Dantes whose revenge over his oppressors takes a thousand pages of Alexandre Dumas's *The Count of Monte Cristo* (1844) to accomplish—he cannot himself be quoted.

When I read this book—or one very similar; you can no more read the same book again than you can step into the same river—in the early 1970s, as a young teenager, I read it under the title *Tiger! Tiger!* It's a title I prefer to the rather more upbeat *The Stars My Destination*. It is a title of warning, of admiration. God, we are reminded in Blake's poem, created the tiger too. The God who made the lamb also made the carnivores that prey upon it. And Gully Foyle, our hero, is a predator. We meet him and are informed that he is everyman, a nonentity; then Bester lights the touchpaper, and we stand back and watch him flare and burn and illuminate: almost illiterate, stupid, single-minded, amoral (not in the hip sense of being too cool for morality, but simply utterly, blindly selfish), he is a murderer—perhaps a multiple murderer—a rapist, a monster. A tiger.

(And because Bester began working on the book in England, naming his characters from an English telephone directory, Foyle shares a name with the largest and most irritating book shop in London—and with Lemuel Gulliver, who voyaged among strange peoples. Dagenham, Yeovil, and Sheffield are all English cities.)

We are entering a second-stage world of introductions to SF. It is not long since everyone knew everybody. I never met Alfred Bester: I never travelled to America as a young man, and by the time he was due to come to England, to the 1987 Brighton Worldcon, his health did not permit it, and he died shortly after the convention.

I can offer no personal encomia to Bester the man—author of many fine short stories, two remarkable SF novels in the first round of his career (*The Demolished Man* and the book you now hold in your hand); author of three somewhat less notable SF books in later life. (Also a fascinating psychological thriller called *The Rat Race,* about the world of New York television in the 1950s.)

He began his career as a writer in the SF pulps, moved from there to comics, writing Superman, Green Lantern (he created the "Green Lantern Oath"), and many other characters; he moved from there to radio, writing for *Charlie Chan* and *The Shadow.* "The comic book days were over, but the splendid training I received in visualization, attack, dialogue, and economy stayed with me forever," he said in a memoir.

He was one of the only—perhaps the only—SF writers to be revered by the old-timers ("First SF"), by the radical "New Wave" of the 1960s and early 1970s, and, in the 1980s, by the "cyberpunks." When he died in 1987, three years into the flowering of cyberpunk, it was apparent that the 1980s genre owed an enormous debt to Bester—and to this book in particular.

The Stars My Destination is, after all, the perfect cyberpunk novel: it contains such cheerfully protocyber elements as multinational corporate intrigue; a dangerous, mysterious, hyperscientific McGuffin (PyrE); an amoral hero; a supercool thief-woman...

But what makes *The Stars My Destination* more interesting—and ten years on, less dated—than most cyberpunk, is watching Gully Foyle become a moral creature, during his sequence of transfigurations (keep all heroes going long enough, and they become gods). The tiger tattoos force him to learn control. His emotional state is no longer written in his face— it forces him to move beyond predation, beyond rage, back to the womb, as it were. (And what a sequence of wombs the book gives us: the coffin, the *Nomad*, the Goufre Martel, St. Pat's, and finally the *Nomad* again.) It gives us more than that. It gives us:

Birth.

Symmetry.

Hate.

A word of warning: the vintage of the book demands more work from the reader than she or he may be used to. Were it written now, its author would have shown us the rape, not implied it, just as we would have been permitted to watch the sex on the grass in the night after the Goufre Martel, before the sun came up, and she saw his face...

So assume it's 1956 again. You are about to meet Gully Foyle, and to learn how to jaunte. You are on the way to the future.

It was, or is, or will be, as Bester might have said, had someone not beaten him to it, the best of times. It will be the worst of times...

March, 1996

CONCERNING
DREAMS AND NIGHTMARES
(H. P. LOVECRAFT)

If literature is the world, then fantasy and horror are twin cities, divided by a river of black water. The Horror place is a rather more dangerous place, or it should be: you can walk around Fantasy alone.

And if Horror and Fantasy are cities, then H. P. Lovecraft is the kind of long street than runs from the outskirts of one city to the end of the other. It began life as a minor thoroughfare, and is now a six-lane highway, built up on every side.

That's H. P. Lovecraft, the phenomenon. H. P. Lovecraft, the man, died at the age of forty-seven, over fifty years ago...

The man: thin, ascetic, an anachronism in his own time.

There's a World Fantasy Award sitting on my stairs; I pat its head as I walk past: a Gahan Wilson sculpture of Howard Phillips Lovecraft (1890-1937). It's a portrait of a thin-lipped man, with a high forehead, a long chin, and wide eyes. He looks vaguely uncomfortable, vaguely alien, an Easter Island statue of a man.

He was a solitary individual, an inhabitant of Providence, Rhode Island. He communicated with the outside world through letters, some of them the length of short novels.

He wrote for the pulps: disposable fiction for publications like *Weird Tales,* its covers showing vaguely arty lesbian bondage scenes. He ghost-wrote a Houdini story, rewrote the work of aspiring writers; he sold one tale—"At The Mountains of Madness"—to John W. Campbell's *Astounding Science Fiction.*

He was a believer in unpleasant doctrines of racial superiority, and an Anglophile. He was a student of horror. There is an abundance of conjectures as to the circumstances of his life and death, the roots of his fiction, but they remain theories.

In his lifetime, he wasn't a major writer. He wasn't even a minor writer. He was a minor pulp writer, as forgettable as any of his time (quick! can you name five other writers for *Weird Tales* in the twenties and thirties?). But there was something there which, like Lovecraft's own Cthulhu, did not die.

(Poor Robert E. Howard, creator of Conan and of King Kull, is one of the other *Weird Tales* authors who's still remembered, when Seabury Quinn and many of the rest of them have blown away into the footnotes. Howard killed himself at the age of thirty, in 1936, when he heard of his mother's impending death. Then there's Robert Bloch, who, at the age of 18, published his first professional short story in *Weird Tales,* and went on to a long and distinguished career.)

Some of the influence of Lovecraft was immediate. His correspondents and fellow writers, including Bloch, Fritz Leiber, Manly Wade Wellman, and others, played with the mythos he created: a world in which we exist in a tiny fragment of space-time, in which space, inner and outer, is vast, and inhabited by things that mean us harm, and by other things to which we matter less than cosmic dust. Much of Lovecraft's influence on fiction, however, would not really be felt for fifty years after his death.

His fiction was not collected while he lived. August Derleth, Wisconsin author, co-founded with Donald Wandrei the small press publisher Arkham House, in order to publish Lovecraft's fiction: and Derleth first collected Lovecraft's prose in *The Outsider and Others,* two years after Lovecraft's death. Since then Lovecraft's stories have been collected and re-collected internationally, in many anthologies, in many permutations.

This anthology is about dreams.

Dreams are strange things, dangerous and odd.

Last night I dreamed I was on the run from the government, somewhere in middle Europe—the last hold-out of a decayed communist regime. I was kidnapped by the secret police, thrown in the back of a van. I knew that the secret police were vampires, and that they were scared of cats (for all vampires were scared of cats, in my dream). And I remember escaping from the van at a traffic light, running from them through the city, trying to call several unresponsive city cats to me: grey and sleek and skittish, they were, unaware that they could save my life...

It is possible to go mad, looking for symbolism in dreams, looking for one-to-one correspondences with life. But the cats are Lovecraft's. And the vampiric secret police, in their own way, are his too.

Lovecraft got better as he went on.

That's a polite way of putting it.

He was pretty dreadful when he started out: he seemed to have no ear for the music of words, no real sense of what he was trying to do with stories. There's no feeling in the earliest material of someone putting their life, or even the inside of their head, down on paper; instead, we watch Lovecraft in the beginning, copying, pastiching awkwardly—here's a dash of Poe, there's a little Robert W. Chambers—and over and above all the other voices of Lovecraft's early days, the awkward Anglophilic imitation of the voice of Lord Dunsany, the Irish lord and fantasist, whom Lovecraft admired more, perhaps, than was good for his fiction.

Dunsany was one of the great originals. His prose voice resonated like an oriental retelling of the King James Bible. He told stories of strange little gods of faraway lands, of visits to dream-lands, of people with odd, but perfectly apt names: always with a slight amused detachment. Many of the stories you'll find in this anthology, like "Hypnos," or "The Quest of Iranon," are vaguely Dunsanyish in tone.

Somewhere in there, however, as time passed, Lovecraft's own voice began to emerge. The writing became assured. The landscape slowly becomes the inside of Lovecraft's head.

It was September 1983, at the New Imperial Hotel in Birmingham, in the English Midlands: I had come to Birmingham for the British Fantasy Convention, to interview authors Gene Wolfe and Robert Silverberg for English magazines.

It was my first convention of any kind. I went to as many panels as I could, although I remember only one panel. The panelists were, if memory serves, authors Brian Lumley, Ramsey Campbell, and the late Karl Edward Wagner, and Irish illustrator Dave Carson.

They talked about the influence of Lovecraft on each of them: Campbell's hallucinatory tales of urban menace, Lumley's muscular horror, Wagner's dark sword and sorcery and modern, slick tales: they talked about the psychology of Lovecraft, the nightmarish visions, how each of them had found something in Lovecraft to which he responded, something that had inspired him: three very different authors, with three very different approaches.

A thin, elderly gentleman in the audience stood up and asked the panel whether they had given much thought to his own theory: that the Great Old Ones, the many-consonanted Lovecraftian beasties, had simply used poor Howard Phillips Lovecraft to talk to the world, to foster belief in themselves, prior to their ultimate return.

I don't remember what the panel's response was to that. I don't recall them agreeing with it, though.

Then they were asked why they liked Lovecraft. They talked of the huge vistas of his imagination, of the way his fiction was a metaphor for everything we didn't know and feared, from sex to foreigners. They talked about all that deep stuff.

Then Dave Carson, the artist, was handed the mike. "F— all that," he said happily, having drunk a great deal of alcohol, dismissing all the erudite psychological theories about Lovecraft and cutting to the chase: "I love H.P. Lovecraft because I just like drawing monsters."

Which got a laugh from the audience, and a bigger laugh when Dave's head gently touched down on the table a few seconds later, and then Karl Edward Wagner took the microphone from Dave's fingers, and asked for the next question. (And, now, a decade later, Dave Carson's still with us, last heard of fishing off the pier at Eastbourne, probably fishing up strange Lovecraftian beasties he draws so well from the depths of the English Channel, but the bottle carried away poor Karl.)

It's true, though. Lovecraft's influenced people as diverse as Stephen King and Colin Wilson, Umberto Eco and John Carpenter. He's all over the cultural landscape: references to Lovecraft, and Lovecraftian ideas, abound in film, television, comics, role-playing games, computer games, Virtual Reality...

Lovecraft is a resonating wave. He's rock and roll.

I'm introducing a collection here that takes us through the dream-fiction of H. P. Lovecraft, weaving it into a huge tapestry that drives from Fantasy to Horror and back again. Here's the tale of "Pickman's Model"— pure horror, and vintage Lovecraft—and then there's Richard Upton Pickman, creeping through "The Dream Quest of Unknown Kadath"... The chronological arrangement of stories forms odd patterns. Dreams and nightmares, too. Vampires and cats.

There's something about Lovecraft's fiction, about his worlds, that is oddly alluring for a writer of fantasy or horror. I've written three Lovecraftian stories: one obliquely, in *Sandman*—a quiet, dream-like story (it's the first story in the *Worlds' End* collection. You can tell it's Lovecraftian, because I use the word "cyclopean" in it); one a hard-boiled Maltese Falcon variant with a werewolf as hero (in Steve Jones's fine anthology *Shadows over Innsmouth*), and a third, when I was much younger, that was an awkward attempt at humour, an extract from Cthulhu's autobiography. If I go back to Lovecraft again (and I'm sure I shall, before I die), it will probably be for something else entirely.

So what is it about Lovecraft that keeps me coming back? That keeps any of us coming back? I don't know. Maybe it's just that we like the way he gives us monsters to draw with our minds.

If this is your first excursion into H.P. Lovecraft's world, you may find the way a little bumpy at first. But keep going.

You'll soon find yourself driving down a road that will take you through the twin cities, and off into the darkness beyond.

If literature's the world.

And it is.

THE EINSTEIN INTERSECTION
(BY SAMUEL R. DELANY)

Two misconceptions are widely held about that branch of literature known as science fiction.

The initial misconception is that SF (at the time Delany wrote *The Einstein Intersection* many editors and writers were arguing that Speculative Fiction might be a better use of the initials, but that battle was lost a long time back) is about the future, that it is, fundamentally, a predictive literature. Thus *1984* is read as Orwell's attempt to predict the world of 1984, as Heinlein's *Revolt in 2100* is seen as an attempted prediction of life in 2100. But those who point to the rise of any version of Big Brother, or to the many current incarnations of the Anti-Sex League, or to the mushrooming power of Christian fundamentalism as evidence that Heinlein or Orwell was engaged in forecasting Things To Come are missing the point.

The second misconception, a kind of second-stage misconception, easy to make once one has travelled past the "SF is about predicting the future" conceit, is this: SF is about the vanished present. Specifically SF is solely about the time when it was written. Thus, Alfred Bester's *The Demolished Man* and *Tiger! Tiger!* (vt. *The Stars My Destination*) are about the 1950s, just as William Gibson's *Neuromancer* is about the 1984 we lived through in reality. Now this is true, as far as it goes, but is no more true for SF than for any other practice of writing: our tales are always the fruit of our times. SF, like all other art, is the product of its era, reflecting or reacting against or illuminating the prejudices, fears, and assumptions of the period in which it was written. But there is more to SF than this: one does not only read Bester to decode and reconstruct the 1950s.

What is important in good SF, and what makes SF that lasts, is how it talks to us of our present. What does it tell us *now?* And, even more important, what will it always tell us? For the point where SF becomes a transcendent branch of literature is the point where it is about something bigger and more important than Zeitgeist, whether the author intended it to be or not.

The Einstein Intersection (a pulp title imposed on this book from without—Delany's original title for it was *A Fabulous, Formless Darkness*) is a novel that is set in a time after the people like us have left the Earth and *others* have moved into our world, like squatters into a furnished house, wearing our lives and myths and dreams uncomfortably but conscientiously. As the novel progresses, Delany weaves myth, consciously and un-self-consciously: Lobey, our narrator, is Orpheus, or plays Orpheus, as other members of the cast will find themselves playing Jesus and Judas, Jean Harlow (out of Candy Darling) and Billy the Kid. They inhabit our legends awkwardly: they do not fit them.

The late Kathy Acker has discussed Orpheus at length, and Samuel R. Delany's role as an Orphic prophet, in her introduction to the Wesleyan Press edition of *Trouble on Triton*. All that she said there is true, and I commend it to the reader. Delany is an Orphic bard, and *The Einstein Intersection,* as will become immediately apparent, is Orphic Fiction.

In the oldest versions we have of the story of Orpheus it appears to have been simply a myth of the seasons: Orpheus went into the Underworld to find his Eurydice, and he brought her safely out into the light of the sun again. But we lost the happy ending a long time ago. Delany's Lobey, however, is not simply Orpheus.

The Einstein Intersection is a brilliant book, self-consciously suspicious of its own brilliance, framing its chapters with quotes from authors ranging from de Sade to Yeats (are these the owners of the house into which the squatters have moved?) and with extracts from the author's own notebooks kept while writing the book and wandering the Greek Islands. It was written by a young author in the milieu he has described in *The Motion of Light in Water* and *Heavenly Breakfast,* his two autobiographical works, and here he is writing about music and love, growing up, and the value of stories as only a young man can.

One can see this book as a portrait of a generation that dreamed that new drugs and free sex would bring about a fresh dawn and the rise of *homo superior,* wandering the world of the generation before them like magical children walking through an abandoned city—through the ruins of Rome, or Athens, or New York: that the book is inhabiting and reinterpreting the myths of the people who came to be known as the hippies. But if that were all the book was, it would be a poor sort of tale, with little resonance for now. Instead, it continues to resonate.

So, having established what *The Einstein Intersection* is not, what is it?

I see it as an examination of myths, and of why we need them, and why we tell them, and what they do to us, whether we understand them or not. Each generation replaces the one that came before. Each generation newly discovers the tales and truths that came before, threshes them, discovering for itself what is wheat and what is chaff, never knowing or caring or even understanding that the generation who will come after them will discover that some of their new timeless truths were little more than the vagaries of fashion.

The Einstein Intersection is a young man's book, in every way: it is the book of a young author, and it is the story of a young man going into the big city, learning a few home truths about love, growing up and deciding to go home (somewhat in the manner of Fritz Leiber's protagonist from "Gonna Roll the Bones," who takes the long way home, around the world).

These were the things that I learned from the book the first time I read it, as a child: I learned that writing could, in and of itself, be beautiful. I learned that sometimes what you do not understand, what remains beyond your grasp in a book, is as magical as what you can take from it. I learned that we have the right, or the obligation, to tell old stories in our own ways, because they are our stories, and they must be told.

These were the things I learned from the book when I read it again, in my late teens: I learned that my favourite SF author was black, and understood now who the various characters were based upon, and, from the extracts from the author's notebooks, I learned that fiction was mutable— there was something dangerous and exciting about the idea that a black-haired character would gain red hair and pale skin in a second draft (I also learned there could be second drafts). I discovered that the idea of a book and the book itself were two different things. I also enjoyed and appreciated how much the author doesn't tell you: it's in the place that readers bring themselves to the book that the magic occurs.

I had by then begun to see *The Einstein Intersection* in context as part of Delany's body of work. It would be followed by *Nova* and *Dhalgren*, each book a quantum leap in tone and ambition beyond its predecessor, each an examination of mythic structures and the nature of writing. In *The Einstein Intersection* we encounter ideas that could break cover as SF in a way they were only beginning to do in the real world, particularly in the portrait of the nature of sex and sexuality that the book draws for us: we are given, very literally, a third, transitional sex, just as we are given a culture ambivalently obsessed with generation.

Rereading the book recently as an adult I found it still as beautiful, still as strange; I discovered passages—particularly toward the twisty end— that had once been opaque were now quite clear. Truth to tell, I now found Lo Lobey an unconvincing heterosexual: while the book is certainly a love story, I found myself reading it as the story of Lobey's courtship by Kid Death, and wondering about Lobey's relationships with various other members of the cast. He is an honest narrator, reliable to a point, but he has been to the city after all, and it has left its mark on the narrative. And I found myself grateful, once again, for the brilliance of Delany and the narrative urge that drove him to write. It is good SF, and even if, as some have maintained (including, particularly, Samuel R. Delany), literary values and SF values are not necessarily the same, and the criteria—the entire critical apparatus—we use to judge them are different, this is still fine literature, for it is the literature of dreams, and stories, and of myths. That it is good SF, whatever that is, is beyond question. That it is a beautiful book, uncannily written, prefiguring much fiction that followed, and too long neglected, will be apparent to the readers who are coming to it freshly with this new edition.

I remember, as a teen, encountering Brian Aldiss's remark on the fiction of Samuel R. Delany in his original critical history of SF, *Billion Year Spree:* quoting C. S. Lewis, Aldiss commented that Delany's telling of how odd things affected odd people was an oddity too much. And that puzzled me, then and now, because I found, and still find, nothing odd or strange about Delany's characters. They are fundamentally human; or, more to the point, they are, fundamentally, us.

And that is what fiction is for.

October 1997

THE SWORDS OF LANKHMAR
(BY FRITZ LEIBER)

It is too often a sad and unwise thing to go back and read a favourite book.

Favourite books are the treasure-chests of memory: just thinking of the book evokes the place you read it, the circumstances under which it was read, the music you were listening to, and, most importantly, the person you were, when you read the book first.

Some of these books should not be revisited. It is not wise. A book is a place, after all, particularly when one is young: somewhere to which one goes while one is reading. And, like all places from one's childhood, the action of revisiting is one fraught with strangeness and danger.

Some places shrink ("I used to walk along that wall. And I was scared of falling off. But it's only a foot high"); some places change ("That tree wasn't there when I was growing up, was it…?"); some places simply aren't there any more, taken by time or distance or decay (quiet meadows in which I lay and read as a boy are now covered with row after row of identical houses).

It's the same with the books you remember. They shrink, some of them. Or they change ("I don't remember that chapter at all," you mutter to yourself, puzzled). And worse: as you grow up you carry with you, for example, the memory of our heroes' terrified flight through the forest that awful night, the way the wind whipped and howled through the oak trees, the way the rain soaked through their clothes; you remember the water dripping from their faces as they urged their poor exhausted horses on through the night, the twigs that slashed and cut their terrified faces, the steam that rose from the horses' flanks… And then you go back to the book, years later, and you discover that the whole sequence was a sentence along the lines of: *"It's jolly wet tonight," said Bill to Bunty, as they urged their horses through the dark woods. "I hope they don't catch us."* You did the rest of it yourself. Those are the ones to which you wish you never had gone back.

And then there are books that, when you try to go back and reread them, just aren't there at all. (Sometimes the book is out of print, or unidentifiable. In the saddest cases they took your book and rewrote it, edited it or heavily abridged it—a dreadful and pernicious practice. I'm still looking for an original version of Noel Langley's *The Land of Green Ginger*.)

Some books, however, like some places, are safe to return to. They welcome you back. They aren't as good as you remember: they're better. You appreciate them in ways you never could have done when you were younger. I first read *The Swords of Lankhmar* at the age of thirteen. I found a battered paperback copy in a dusty glass-fronted cabinet at the back of Mr Wright's English classroom. The cover painting was the sea-serpent rider (much later I saw the American covers, by Jeff Jones, and realised that mine had been a poor re-painting of his cover). I read it for a day, and learned from it (during this time I suspect I was meant to have been learning other things). And I was hooked. I was entranced.

It was not my first encounter with Fritz Leiber's work. (That was an astonishing story called "The Winter Flies," in Judith Merril's anthology *SF 12*.) It was not even my first encounter with Fafhrd, the huge, hearty and hairy, and his friend, partner, and occasional adversary, the Grey Mouser (that was in, of all places, a *Wonder Woman* comic, written by, of all people, Samuel R. Delany). But *The Swords of Lankhmar* changed the way I saw the world, and changed what I demanded of my fantasies.

I've read it several times since—the last time almost a decade ago. Over the last few weeks I've been rereading it once again; slowly, savouring it like a fine liqueur, making it last as long as I could.

And it's a different book to the one I read when I was thirteen.

Now, an admission: I find it harder and harder to read fiction for pleasure. I have spent too long wandering around behind the scenes in the place where fictions are created. Like a stage magician at a magic show, I may appreciate the skill with which the trick is done, but I'm unlikely to find myself worrying whether the young lady has really been sliced in half. I'm a professional storyteller: I find it hard to be a member of the audience.

Reading this book, I was a member of the audience once more. It was every bit as fine as I remembered.

I found myself noticing material I hadn't noticed before: the way the book is pervaded gently by alcohol, for example; the way the Mouser's elegant sado-masochistic games with Hisvit counterpoint Glipkerio and Samanda's grosser pleasures; that Leiber's citing of James Branch Cabell's novel *Jurgen* in his Author's Note is more than just a conceit (which is why, I suspect, Fafhrd gets such short shrift in a novel in which he and the Mouser share top billing. Fafhrd, unlike Cabell's Jurgen or the Mouser, is not convinced that he is "a monstrous clever fellow"). I appreciated the deftness with which each character gets what he or she really wants, delighted in the prose, and in the ironies, and in Frix's stage directions.

And, having finished the rereading, I was delighted to discover that this was still one of my very favourite books.

The Swords of Lankhmar glitters and shimmers and dances. It cheerfully plays with the conventions of genre (a genre, Sword and Sorcery, that the stories of Fafhrd and the Mouser helped to create and to name), it toys with them as a cat plays with a terrified mouse. The book contains swordplay and dragons, dead gods and magical transformations, wise wizards and brave heroes and beautiful women—the trappings of routine fantasy, but all handled with an ironic elegance that leaves this novel with the same relationship to the usual supermarket fantasy that a black panther does to a stray kitten: it's the same class of thing, to be sure, but still…

It's one of the true originals. If you enjoy it (as I have no doubt you will, being a person of taste and discernment), you will be delighted to know there are other stories of Fafhrd and the Grey Mouser: they span Leiber's writing career, and an amazing and a remarkable writing career it was too.

So, preamble over with and done, I would like to introduce you to one of my very favourite books, by one of my very favourite authors, starring two of the most delightful characters in the history of fantastic literature. It's an enchanting confection of magic and adventure, funny, and witty and sane. Perhaps it will become one of your favourite books also, one you can return to, from time to time, in the future, each time finding something new to delight you in Leiber's splendid tale of a city which, like Hamelin in Browning's tale of the Pied Piper, had a little trouble with rats.

And now, with no more ado, I suggest you turn the page, and you shall find yourself transported, in the company of a couple of the finest rogues you will ever meet, to the End Gate of the City of Lankhmar, which is the oldest and greatest of all the cities on the world of Nehwon, which is a world on the inside of a fleeting bubble, floating forever, with all the other world- and star-bubbles, through the oceans of night…

THE SCREWTAPE LETTERS
(BY C. S. LEWIS)

Clive Staples Lewis put it best in his preface to the original book—of which the volume you are holding is an illustrated abridgement. "*There are two equal and opposite errors into which our race can fall about the devils,*" he said. "*One is to disbelieve in their existence. The other is to believe, and to feel an excessive and unhealthy interest in them.*" And with that he began his story of redemption, moral advice and good digestion, subtitled "letters from a senior to a junior devil," written originally as a series of essays in the *Guardian* newspaper at the time of the outbreak of World War II.

Wormwood, the junior devil, is diligently tempting, as best he can, an unnamed young everyman, and reporting Downstairs in a sequence of epistles—that we are never shown. Screwtape's replies, which make up the body of the book, are a series of advices, remonstrances, thoughts and occasional memoirs concerning the road to Hell, and the more difficult road to Another Place (about which Screwtape finds it uncomfortable to think). Screwtape is, make no mistake, a demon, and a very good one. Screwtape would find it amusing that people think he and his ilk spend time recording messages on rock and roll albums, and recording them backwards at that. They have much better things to do—as you'll find out in the pages that follow.

The late C. S. Lewis is probably best known today for his series of seven novels set in and around the country of Narnia, on a far world inhabited by giants (both the really big, stupid kind, and the smaller ones, who eat people), not to mention fauns, fallen stars, amazingly wicked witches and talking animals; a world in which Father Christmas rubs shoulders with Greek gods, and boys undergo Pauline conversions when transformed into Dragons. (I occasionally wonder what he'd make of the current tendency amongst certain groups of people who consider themselves Christians to condemn all fantastic literature as a demon-inspired plot to distract people from what Screwtape so derisively refers to as "real life." But then we're probably back to that "excessive and unhealthy interest" I mentioned earlier.)

I first read *The Screwtape Letters* when I was nine years old—I bought it from the school bookshop, a pre-teenage Narnia addict—and was relieved on rereading it recently to find it as fresh and delightful and even as wise as I found it then, and would urge anyone who enjoys this book to hunt down the original (still in print after all these years), which is longer and has even more of Screwtape's counsel in it, and the subsequent volume *Screwtape Proposes a Toast and Other Pieces.*

The world Screwtape gives us is one of battle between the flesh and the spirit, in which Hell is purely spiritual and Heaven has the loathsome (to Screwtape) advantage of having once been incarnate. As a writer, with a regrettable tendency to stumble into theological terrain, I find Screwtape, via Lewis, a source of delight—as much for the questions he leaves unanswered as for what he tells us: I find myself wondering if Screwtape—and Wormwood, and Glubose, Toadpipe, Slubgob and the rest of the Lowerarchy—have voices that whisper to them, too. I wonder whether angels write each other letters, and, for that matter, what angels feed on...

But I fear I stray from the task in hand, which is that of introducing you to the entertaining and educational material which follows.

So, ladies and gentlemen, it is with great pleasure that I hand you over to His Abysmal Sublimity Under-Secretary Screwtape, T.E., B.S., etc., and his sage advice...

THE KING OF ELFLAND'S DAUGHTER
(BY LORD DUNSANY)

It has on occasion been a source of puzzlement to me that there are a number of otherwise sensible people, many of them old enough to know better, who maintain, perhaps from some kind of strange cultural snobbery, that William Shakespeare could not have written the plays that bear his name, and that these plays must, obviously, have been written by a member of the British aristocracy, written by some Lord or Earl, some grandee or other, forced to hide his literary light under a bushel.

And this is chiefly a source of puzzlement to me because the British aristocracy, while it has produced more than its share of hunters, eccentrics, farmers, warriors, diplomats, con-men, heroes, robbers, politicians and monsters, has never been noted in any century or era for the production of great writers.

Edward John Moreton Drax Plunkett (1878-1957) was a hunter, and a warrior, and a chess champion, and a playwright, a teacher and many another thing besides, and he was a member of a family that could trace its lineage back to before the Norman Conquest; he was eighteenth Baron Dunsany, and he is one of the rare exceptions.

Lord Dunsany wrote small tales of imaginary gods and thieves and heroes in distant kingdoms; he wrote tall stories based in the here and now and retold, by Mr Joseph Jorkens, for whisky in London clubs; he wrote autobiographies; he wrote fine poems and more than 40 plays (at one point, reputedly, he had five plays being staged on Broadway at one time); he wrote novels of a vanished and magical Spain that never was; and he wrote *The King of Elfland's Daughter*, a fine, strange, almost forgotten novel, as too much of Dunsany's unique work is forgotten, and if this book alone were all he had written, it would have been enough.

To begin with, the writing is beautiful. Dunsany wrote his books, we are told, with a quill pen, dipping and scritching and flowing his prose over sheets of paper, and his words sing, like those of a poet who got drunk on the prose of the King James Bible, and who has still not yet become sober. Listen to Dunsany on the wonders of ink: "...how it can mark a dead man's thoughts for the wonder of later years, and tell of happenings that are gone clean away, and be a voice for us out of the dark of time, and save many a fragile thing from the pounding of heavy ages; or carry to us, over the rolling centuries, even a song from lips long dead on forgotten hills."

For secondly, *The King of Elfland's Daughter* is a book about magic; about the perils of inviting magic into your life; about the magic that can be found in the mundane world, and the distant, fearful, changeless magic of Elfland. It is not a comforting book, neither is it an entirely comfortable one, and one comes away, at the end, unconvinced of the wisdom of the men of Erl, who wished to be ruled by a magic lord.

For thirdly, it has its feet well-planted on the ground (my own favourite moments are, I think, the jam-roll that saved the child from going to Elfland, and the troll watching time pass in the pigeon-loft); it assumes that events have consequences, and that dreams and the moon matter (but cannot be trusted or relied upon), and that love, too, is important (but even a Freer of Christom should realise that the Princess of Elfland is not merely a mermaid who has forsaken the sea).

And finally, for those who feel that they need historical accuracy in their fictions, this novel contains one historically verifiable date. It is in chapter 20. But there are, I suspect, few who will have got that far in the book who will need a date to establish the veracity of the story. It is a true story, as these things go, in every way that matters.

Today, Fantasy is, for better or for worse, just another genre, a place in a bookshop to find books that, too often, remind one of far too many other books (and many writers writing today would have less to say had Dunsany not said it first); it is an irony, and not entirely a pleasant one, that what should be, by definition, the most imaginative of all types of literature has become so staid, and, too often, downright unimaginative. *The King of Elfland's Daughter,* on the other hand, is a tale of pure imagination (and bricks without straw, as Dunsany himself pointed out, are more easily made than imagination without memories). Perhaps this book should come with a warning: it is not a comfortable, reassuring, by-the-numbers fantasy novel, like most of the books with elves and princes and trolls and unicorns in, on the nearby fantasy shelves: this is the real thing. It's a rich red wine, which may come as a shock if all one has had experience of so far has been cola. So trust the book. Trust the poetry and the strangeness, and the magic of the ink, and drink it slowly.

And, for a little while, perhaps you too shall be ruled, like the men of Erl would have been, by a magic lord.

December 1998

CURIOSITIES: *LUD-IN-THE-MIST*
(BY HOPE MIRRLEES)

Hope Mirrlees only wrote one fantasy novel, but it is one of the finest in the English language.

The country of Dorimare (fundamentally English, although with Flemish and Dutch threads in the weave) expelled magic and fancy when it banished hunchbacked libertine Duke Aubrey and his court, 200 years before our tale starts. The prosperous and illusion-free burghers of the town swear by "toasted cheesecrumbs" as easily as by the "Sun, Moon, Stars and the Golden Apples of the West." Faerie has become, explicitly, obscenity.

But fairy fruit is still being smuggled over the border from Fairyland. Eating it gives strange visions and can drive people to madness and beyond. The fruit is so illegal that it cannot even be named: smugglers of fruit are punished for smuggling silk, as if the changing of the name will change the thing itself.

The Mayor of Lud-in-the-Mist, Nat Chanticleer, is less prosaic than he would have others believe. His life is a fiction he subscribes to, or would like to, of a sensible life like everyone else's—and particularly like the dead that he admires. His world is a shallow thing, though, as he will soon learn: without his knowledge, his young son, Ranulph, has been fed fairy fruit.

Now the fairy world—which is also, as in all the oldest folk tales, the world of the dead—begins to claim the town: a puck named Willy Wisp spirits away the lovely young ladies of Miss Crabapple's Academy for young ladies, over the hills and far away; Chanticleer stumbles upon the fruit smugglers, and his life takes a turn for the worse; Duke Aubrey is sighted; old murders will out; and, in the end, Chanticleer must cross the Elfin Marches to rescue his son.

The book begins as a travelogue or a history, becomes a pastorale, a low comedy, a high comedy, a ghost story and a detective story. The writing is elegant, supple, effective and haunting: the author demands a great deal from her readers, which she repays many times over.

The magic of *Lud-in-the-Mist* is built from English folklore—it is not such a great step from Aubrey to Oberon, after all; Willy Wisp's *Ho-ho-hoh* is Robin Goodfellow's, from a song they say Ben Jonson wrote; and it will not come as a surprise to the folklorist that old Portunus says nothing and eats live frogs. The "lily, germander and sops in wine" song is first recorded in the 17th century, under the name of *Robin Good-Fellow or, the Hob-Goblin*.

I have seen editions of *Lud-in-the-Mist* which proclaim it to be a thinly-disguised parable for the class struggle. Had it been written in the 1960s it would, I have no doubt, have been seen as a tale about mind-expansion. But it seems to me that this is, most of all, a book about reconciliation—the balancing and twining of the mundane and the miraculous. We need both, after all.

It is a little golden miracle of a book, adult, in the best sense, and, as the best fantasy should be, far from reassuring.

FROM THE END OF THE TWENTIETH CENTURY
(BY JOHN M. FORD)

Concerning Speculative Engineering, with notes on Exploration, the Scattered Oeuvre of John M. Ford, and an Unreliable and Vaguely Scatalogical Anecdote about Freud or Someone Like That.

...and here we gather to celebrate John M. Ford (b. 1957 and still very much alive)—not the Elizabethan playwright John Ford (1586-1639), nor the film director John Ford (real name Sean O'Feeney) (1895-1973), although they frame him as they framed several of his early novels, but the late twentieth-century writer of that name—and the immediate metaphor that keeps coming to mind, embarrassingly, is entirely defecatory.

It's a half-remembered anecdote about Freud or Jung or one of those brainy big-bearded German bods who was, at least in the anecdote, asked by some aspiring young man how he (the aspiring young man that is, not the big-brained German bod) could become famous in his field.

And Freud, or Jung, said, "You shit all in the same place."

Which is something that comes to mind when we stop to puzzle why Mike Ford (the John is silent, as in M. John Harrison) is not as well-known as lots of other writers who are a damn sight less able and thousands of times less good.

This is a man who has written a World Fantasy Award-winning novel of alternate history, *The Dragon Waiting;* who wrote the best hard sf juvenile since Heinlein stopped doing juveniles, *Growing Up Weightless;* who wrote my favourite modern spying and intrigue and Christopher Marlowe too novel, *The Scholars of Night;* who wrote not one but two astonishingly brilliant "Star Trek" novels—one, *The Final Reflection,* a first contact novel from the Klingon perspective, the other, *How Much for Just the Planet?* a genuinely funny musical farce—each book responsible for setting new parameters to the "Star Trek" Franchise, mostly consisting of "He got away with it because we hadn't thought to make rules against it, and now he's done it no-one else is going to do it again," who has written award-winning poems—one of his Christmas cards won a World Fantasy Award as Best Short Story; who published a cyberspace novel, prefiguring *Neuromancer, Web of Angels,* when he was 23, in 1980.

79

You begin, I trust, to see what one of those beardy German bods I mentioned earlier would probably refer to as "zer problem." And if you don't, read this book.

It's like dipping into a kaleidoscope, or receiving mailings from far-flung departments of the Library of Babel—or talking to Mike Ford.

Mike Ford in person has been my friend for over a decade: he is a warm, brilliant man, with an habitually slightly quizzical expression which dissolves into a delighted, almost schoolboyish grin when he makes a connection no-one has made before, which is pretty often. He is one of the few people who genuinely has no snobbish considerations about high and junk culture: he speaks both languages, and can translate between them. (He once took a typo on an invitation to my annual bonfire party as the starting point for a short [and, incredibly, performed] musical drama—somewhere between Rodgers and Hammerstein, and Sellars and Yeatman.)

Examine the goodies here assembled, from over 15 years of writing:

Essays include "Rules of Engagement"—a delightful study of how readers relate to texts (using Ford's own contentious *How Much for Just the Planet?* as a case in point); "From the End of the Twentieth Century", in which he talks about The Naming of Trains and fantasy and the theatre, and also offers us a key to opening the fiction of John M. Ford:

"The artistic task is to present things clearly, approachably, while still leaving space for them to mean more than their literal existence," he tells us, exactly and wisely.

Of course it is. And like a slack-rope walker, a master-baker, or the original "Mission: Impossible" team, he makes it look so easy.

Prose tales in this collection include the new story "Here to Get My Baby Out of Jail", which turns out not to be a new story at all, but one of the oldest stories; "Intersection" and "Mandalay," two (of the four) *Alternities* stories, which make one wish he would write the other three; "Walkaway Clause," which is a love story; "Waiting for the Morning Bird," which is, as the author points out, non-fiction, even the parts that are made up.

And there are songs—proper lyrics, capable of being sung. One caveat though—while most of Ford's anagrams and references are capable of being resolved by anyone with a *Brewer's Dictionary of Phrase and Fable,* a good dictionary and a little luck, I must confess myself still utterly baffled by the identity of Ilen the Magian, who sang "Monochrome" in *How Much for Just the Planet?* Lord, but it's a fine song nonetheless.

When the weather gets colder and the nights get shortest, then, addressed in a fine and calligraphic hand, the postman brings me Speculative Engineering's latest production, part Christmas card, part chapbook, always limited (one is informed) to one hundred unnumbered copies. And one counts oneself fortunate, never quite knowing what one is going to receive. For example:

A prose-poem meditation on the dreams of satellites, moving and transcendent, very high over Milk Wood.

A tour of Shakespeare's histories, presented by a number of dead playwrights, doing a Dick deBartolo with a nod to Gilbert and Sullivan and Frank Loesser, along with the odd villanelle.

A delving into mythic engineering—the engineering of myth, and the engineers of myth—with Daedalus and his son, Lefty.

And what this next holiday season will bring, no man but one can say. Several of these pamphlets have been assembled here for your delight.

Clear evidence that John M. Ford is not an author who confines himself to one small area, piling it high in one place.

But then...

Reading the materials (and not just "Mandalay") that comprise this book put me in mind of another writer whose output spanned short stories—mainstream, SF, fantasy and adventure, novels, poetry, songs, parodies, and children's fiction—the author of "The Married Drives of Windsor", a Shakespearian caprice about cars, starring all of good Will's main characters, as the high point of "The Muse Among the Motors", his collection of poems about motoring, written in the styles of great poets of history. For there is something of Kipling in John M. Ford: the restlessness, and the willingness to play, to explore formal verse and formal stories, the urge toward parody, and the ability to tug unashamedly on the heartstrings. Like Ford, he was all over the place, but his core subject was people, and what went on inside them—inside all of us. Look at "Walkaway Clause" or "Waiting for the Morning Bird."

And reflecting on what happened to Kipling, it is comforting to observe that sometimes the big-brained anecdotal German bods are, to put it bluntly, full of shit.

For John M. Ford is not just a writer, but a writer's writer. We are lucky to have him. And while some writers are content to sit in their own small rooms, repeating themselves for an audience who knows just what it wants (*id est*, whatever it heard and liked, last time), John M. Ford seeks out new lands, like an Elizabethan sea captain, or a Western pioneer, or the man in Kipling's poem "The Explorer" who heard "a voice as bad as Conscience"...

On one everlasting Whisper day and night repeated—so:
"Something hidden. Go and find it. Go and look behind the Ranges—
Something lost behind the Ranges. Lost and waiting for you. Go!"

And who went to see.

Winter 1996

JONATHAN CARROLL

"All poets and story tellers alive today make a single brotherhood; they are engaged in a single work, picturing our human life. Whoever pictures life as he sees it, reassembles in his own way the details of existence which affect him deeply, and so creates a spiritual world of his own."
Haniel Long, *Notes Toward a New Mythology*.

There are millions of competent writers out there. There are hundreds of thousands of good writers in the world, and there are a handful of great writers. And this is me, late at night, trying to figure out the difference for myself. That indefinable you-either-got-it-or-you-ain't spark that makes someone a great writer.

And then I realise that I'm asking myself the wrong question, because it's not good writers or great writers. What I'm really wondering is what makes some writers *special*. Like when I was a kid on the London Underground, I'd stare at the people around me. And every now and again I'd notice someone who had been drawn—a William Morris beauty, a Bernie Wrightson grotesque—or someone who had been written—there are lots of Dickens characters in London, even today. It wasn't those writers or artists who accurately recorded life: the special ones were the ones who drew it or wrote it so personally that, in some sense, it seemed as if they were creating life, or creating the world and bringing it back to you. And once you'd seen it through their eyes you could never un-see it, not ever again.

There are a few writers who are special. They make the world in their books; or rather, they open a window or a door or a magic casement, and they show you the world in which they live.

Ramsey Campbell, for example, writes short stories that, read in quantity, will re-form your world into a grey and ominous place in which strange shapes flicker at the corners of your eyes, and a patch of smoke or a blown plastic shopping bag takes on some kind of ghastly significance. Read enough R. A. Lafferty and you will find yourself living in a quirky tall-tale of a world in which the people have all stepped out of some cosmic joke, if it is not a dream.

Jonathan Carroll's a changer. He's one of the special ones, one of the few. He paints the world he sees. He opens a window you did not know was there and invites you to look through it. He gives you his eyes to see with, and he gives you the world all fresh and honest and new.

In a bookstore universe of bland and homogenised writers and fictions, the world that pours from Carroll's fountain pen is as cool, as fine and as magical as a new lover, or cool water in the desert. Things matter. You can fall in love with his women, or his men, worry when they hurt, hate them when they betray or fall short, rejoice when they steal a moment of magic and of life from the face of death and eventual nothingness.

I had dinner with Jonathan Carroll, with Dave McKean and with some friends, about eight years ago: what I still remember is not the meal nor even the conversation (although I do recall Jonathan telling us some incidents of his life that I would later encounter in *Kissing the Beehive*): what I recall was the process of becoming a Jonathan Carroll character among Jonathan Carroll characters. We were witty and wise and lucent; intelligent and beautiful men and women; artists and creators and magicians, we were.

It was a couple of days before I noticed that I had become a mundane grey person once more.

Writing fiction is not a profession that leaves one well-disposed toward reading fiction. One starts out loving books and stories, and then one becomes jaded and increasingly hard to please. I read less and less fiction these days, finding the buzz and the joy I used to get from fiction in ever stranger works of non-fiction, or poetry. But a new book by Jonathan Carroll is still, as they used to say on the back of the book jackets, a cause for celebration.

He has the magic.

His most successful books and tales defy genre categorisation. They've more life, more balls, are more *true* than pretty much anything else you'll encounter out there. They call some fantasies "Magical Realism" to try and lend them respectability, like a whore who wishes to be known as a lady of the evening. Jonathan Carroll's tales, however, have every right to parade under the banner of magical realism, if you have to call them something.

I call them Jonathan Carroll stories, and leave it at that. He is one of the handful, and one of the brotherhood. If you don't believe me, pick up *Outside the Dog Museum*, or *A Child Across the Sky*, or *Sleeping in Flame* or *The Panic Hand*, or any of his other works (you'll find a list of them within, I have no doubt) and find out for yourself.

He'll lend you his eyes; and you will never see the world in quite the same way ever again.

Roger Zelazny

I first met Roger Zelazny in 1990, at a convention in Dallas, Texas. We were signing books at the same time, at the same table. This had excited me when I had heard about it: I imagined that I would get to talk to him, and Roger had been a hero of mine since, at the age of 11, I had read *Lord of Light*. Actually, we both sat and signed books for a line of people, and all I managed to do was mumble something about being an enormous fan of his, and I thrust a copy of the Sandman collection *The Doll's House* at him, saying something about the Sandman being one of Roger's illegitimate godchildren.

We did not talk for another year, and then, in 1991, at a World Fantasy Convention in Tucson, Arizona, my friend Steve Brust sat me down in the bar with Roger, and the three of us spoke about short story structure for most of the evening. When Roger spoke Steve and I listened.

"Many of my better short stories," said Roger, pulling on his pipe, explaining how to write short stories, "are just the last chapters of novels I did not write."

The next time I saw Roger he was a guest of honour at the 1993 World Fantasy Convention, in Minneapolis. I was toastmaster, and we were both working hard, doing panels and readings and whatever else one does at conventions. We bumped into each other in the book dealers room, and exchanged books: I gave him a copy of *Angels and Visitations,* the miscellany of my work that had just been published, and he gave me a copy of his novel, *A Night in the Lonesome October.*

I got the impression that it was the first novel he had written in some time that he felt had worked as he had wanted it to. Or at least, that it had been as much of a surprise to him as to his readers.

I remember how tired I was that night, and I remember planning only to read the first few pages of *A Night in the Lonesome October.* I read them and I was hooked, unable to stop reading, and I read until I fell asleep.

I loved a number of things about the book—the delight in a story told from the wrong point of view (Jack the Ripper's dog), the fun in assembling a cast out of stock characters (including Sherlock Holmes and

Larry Talbot), and the sense of Lovecraftian nastiness as a sort of a dance, in which everyone knows the moves they should make and in which the door to permit the Great Old Ones in to eat the world is, always, ultimately, opened a crack, but never all the way.

I wrote this story in February of 1994, and sent it to Roger to read. It was directly inspired by what he had done in *A Night in the Lonesome October*, although my Larry Talbot was no more Roger's than he was the original Wolfman of the movies, or Harlan Ellison's marvellous Talbot in "Adrift Just off the Islets of Langerhans: Latitude 38°54' N, Longitude 77°00'13" W." I was inspired in the way Roger inspired you: he made it look like so much fun, you wanted to do it too, and do it your own way, not his.

It's the last chapter of a novel I haven't written.

It was the only time I had ever sent Roger a story (this was, after all, a man who had written five or six of my favourite short stories in all the world). And he liked it, which is why, when I was asked for a story for this book, this was the only one it could have been.

We saw each other—were on a panel together, and spent part of an evening on a roof beside a swimming pool, talking to Mike Moorcock—in New Orleans at World Fantasy in 1994. We spoke again, on the phone, early in the New Year, following the birth of my daughter, Maddy. Roger had sent her a dreamcatcher, from New Mexico, a web of cord and feathers and beads, to hang above her bed and catch any bad dreams, letting only the good dreams through, and I phoned him to say thank you. We spoke for an hour, about fiction, and stories, and promised each other that sooner or later we would make the time to see each other properly, for a visit. There was, after all, plenty of time.

We did not speak again.

The dreamcatcher hangs there still, above my daughter's bed.

At Roger's memorial in Santa Fe, shortly after his death, we sat on the floor, and on the chairs, and we stood, crowded together in the Saberhagens' front room, remembering Roger. I forget much of what I said, but one thing I do recall is pointing out that Roger Zelazny was the kind of writer who made you want to write too. He made it look so damned fun, and so damned cool. There are many of us who would not have begun to write, if we had not read Roger's stories: the bastard writer-children of Roger Zelazny are a huge and motley group, with little else in common.

I'm proud to be one of them.

November 1996

THE BEAST THAT SHOUTED LOVE AT THE HEART OF THE WORLD
(BY HARLAN ELLISON)

I've been reading Harlan Ellison since I was a small boy. I have known him as long, although by no means as well, as his wife, Susan—we met in Glasgow in 1985 at the same convention at which he first met and wooed his better half.

I interviewed him then for *Space Voyager,* a magazine for which I had written for the previous two years, and which had, until that point, appeared perfectly healthy. The issue of the magazine that was to contain my interview with Harlan went to press…and the publishers pulled the plug on it, with the magazine half-printed, and fired the editor. I took the interview to an editor at another magazine. He paid me for it…and was fired the following day.

I decided at that point that it was unhealthy to write about Harlan, and retired the interview to a filing cabinet, in which it will sit until the end of the world. I cannot be responsible for the firing of any more editors, the closing of any more magazines.

There is no one in the world in any way like Harlan. This has been observed before, by wiser and abler people than me. This is true, and it is quite beside the point.

It has, from time to time, occurred to me that Harlan Ellison is engaged on a Gutzon Borglum-sized work of performance art—something huge and enduring. It's called Harlan Ellison: a corpus of anecdotes and tales and adversaries and performances and friends and articles and opinions and rumours and explosions and treasures and echoes and downright lies. People talk about Harlan Ellison, and they write about Harlan, and some of them would burn him at the stake if they could do it without getting into too much trouble and some of them would probably worship at his feet if it weren't for the fact he'd say something that would make them feel very small and very stupid. People tell stories in Harlan's wake, and some of them are true and some of them aren't, and some of them are to his credit and some of them aren't…

And that is also quite beside the point.

When I was ten I had a lisp, and was sent to an elocution teacher called Miss Webster, who, for the next six years, taught me a great deal about drama and public speaking, and, incidentally, got rid of the lisp somewhere in year one. She must have had a first name, but I've forgotten it now. She was magnificent—a stumpy, white-haired old theatrical lesbian (or so her pupils assumed) who smoked black cigarillos and was surrounded at all times by a legion of amiable but rather stupid scotty dogs. She had huge bosoms, which she would rest on the table while she watched me recite the tongue-twisters and dramatic pieces I had been assigned. Miss Webster died about fifteen years ago, or so I was told by another ex-pupil of hers I met at a party some years back.

She is one of the very small number of people who have told me things for my own good that I've paid attention to. (There is, needless to say, a very large number of people—including, now I come to think of it, Harlan— who've told me perfectly sensible things for my own good that I've, for one reason or another, ignored completely.)

Anyway: I got to be fourteen years old and, one day, after a particularly imaginative interpretation of a Caliban speech, Miss Webster leaned back in her chair, lit a cigarillo with a flourish, and said, "Neil, dear. I think there's something you ought to know. Listen: to be eccentric, you must first know your circle."

And I—for once—heard, and listened, and understood. You can fuck around with the rules as much as you want to—*after* you know what the rules are. You can be Picasso after you know how to paint. Do it *your* way; but know how to do it *their* way first.

I've had a personal relationship with Harlan Ellison for much longer than I've known him. Which is the scariest thing about being a writer, because you make stories up and write stuff down and that's what *you* do. But people read it and it affects them or it whiles away a train journey, whatever, and they wind up moved or changed or comforted by the author, whatever the strange process is, the one-way communication from the stuff they read. And it's not why the stories were written. But it is true and it happens.

I was eleven when my father gave me two of the Carr-Wollheim *Best SF* anthologies and I read "I Have No Mouth and I Must Scream" and discovered Harlan. Over the next few years I bought everything of his I could find. I still have most of those books.

When I was twenty-one I had the worst day of my life. (Up to then, anyway. There have been two pretty bad days since. But this was worse than them.) And there was nothing in the airport to read but *Shatterday,* which I bought. I got onto the plane, and read it crossing the Atlantic. (How bad a day was it? It was so bad I was slightly disappointed when the plane touched down gently at Heathrow without bursting into flames. That's how bad it was.)

And on the plane I read *Shatterday,* which is a collection of mostly kickass stories—and introductions to stories—about the relationship between writers and stories. Harlan told me about wasting time (in "Count the Clock That Tells the Time"), and I thought, fuck it, I *could* be a writer. And he told me that anything more than twelve minutes of genuine personal pain was self-indulgence, which did more to jerk me out of the state of complete numbness I was in than anything else could have done. And when I got home I took all the pain and the fear and the grief, and all the conviction that maybe I *was* a writer, damn it, and I began to write. And I haven't stopped yet. *Shatterday,* more or less, made me what I am today. Your fault, Ellison. And again, quite beside the point.

So: *The Beast That Shouted Love at the Heart of the World,* to which I bid you welcome.

My copy's the 1979 Pan (U.K.) edition: On the cover of this paperback, Blood's a purple thing that looks like a house-cat; Vic, behind him, is apparently a boy in his forties, and is, I think, hopping about on one leg. Still, most of Harlan's British covers had spaceships on them, so I mustn't grumble. And the back cover calls Harlan "the chief prophet of the New Wave in science fiction," attributing the opinion to *The New Yorker.*

Definition time, primarily for those of you born after 1970. "The New Wave": a term almost as unproductive as "Cyberpunk" would be fifteen years later on, used to describe a motley bunch of writers working in the latter half of the Sixties, loosely orbiting but not exclusively confined to *New Worlds* magazine in the Moorcock era and the original *Dangerous Visions* anthology, edited by the author of this collection. (If you want more information than that, go and find a copy of the Clute-Nicholls *Encyclopedia of Science Fiction,* and check out the New Wave entry.)

Harlan may well have been "a prophet of the New Wave," but his foremost prophecy seems to have consisted of pointing out, in the introduction to this volume, that there was no such thing, just a bunch of writers some of whom were pushing the edge of the envelope.

I never noticed the New Wave as anything particularly distinct or separate, when it was happening. It was Stuff to Read. Good stuff to read, even if it sometimes skirted the edge of incomprehensibility. I read it as I read all adult fiction, as a window into a world I didn't entirely understand: found Spinrad's *Bug Jack Barron* a lot of fun, Moorcock's *A Cure for Cancer* addictive and curious. Ballard was distant and strange and made me think of stories told over the tannoy in far-off airports. Delany showed me that words could be be beautiful, Zelazny made myths. And if they were the "New Wave" I liked it. But I liked most things back then. ("Yeah, that's your trouble, Gaiman," said Harlan, when I chided him recently for suggesting that someone I like should be sprinkled with sacred meal and then sacrificed. "You like everyone." It's true, mostly.)

I've digressed a little.

Fiction is a thing of its time, and as times change so does our take on the fiction. Consider the Reagan section of "Santa Claus vs S.P.I.D.E.R."; consider Reagan's final smile "like a man who has regained that innocence of childhood or nature that he had somehow lost." Scary, in a way Harlan never intended, writing about the pompadoured Governor of California. Yet in another few years Reagan and his smile will have begun to lose meaning. He'll lose significance, become a name in the past for the readers, an odd historical name (I'm *just* old enough to know why the Spiro Agnew gag was funny), just as the who and the what and the why of the SF New Wave fade into the black. In a couple of his books James Branch Cabell footnoted the famous of his time—something that was viewed as (and was perhaps partly) an ironic comment—after all, who, today, would bother with an explanatory footnote of John Grisham[1] or John Major[2] or Howard Stern[3]? But Cabell's ironic footnotes are now useful information. Time passes. We forget. The bestselling novel in 1925 was (I am informed by Steve Brust) *Soundings* by A. Hamilton Gibbs. Huh? And who? Still, "Santa Claus..." works, and will keep working as long as there are B-movie spy plots to deconstruct; and as long as there is injustice.

It's true of the rest of the tales herein. They remain relevant; the only thing in the anthology that feels dated is the Introduction, as Harlan grooves to Jimi Hendrix and points to Piers Anthony as an underground writer. But hell, no one reads introductions anyway. (Admit it. You're not reading this, are you?)

And along with Spiro Agnew and A. Hamilton Gibbs and Howard Stern, the anecdotes and tales and the Legend in his Own Lifetime stuff about Harlan (most of which is, more or less, true-ish) and all the Gutzon Borglum stuff (and I ought to have given Gutzon, who carved presidential faces into Mount Rushmore, his own footnote) will also be forgotten.

But the stories last. The stories remain.

"To be eccentric," says Miss Webster, dead for fifteen years, in the back of my head, her voice dry, her elocution perfect, "you must first know your circle." Know the rules before you break them. Learn how to draw, then break the rules of drawing, learn to craft a story and show people things they've seen before in ways they've never seen.

That's what these stories are about. Some of them are quite brilliant, and they sparkle and glitter and shine and wound and howl, and some of them aren't; but in all of them you can see Harlan experimenting, trying new things, new techniques, new voices; craft and voices he'd later refine

---

[1] Author of legal-based thrillers, popular in the early 1990s.

[2] British Conservative member of Parliament. Succeeded Margaret Thatcher as prime minister of England in 1991.

[3] I'm not quite sure. I think he's something on radio.

into the calm assurance of *Deathbird Stories,* his examination of the myths we live by; into the stories of *Shatterday,* in which he took apart, hard, the cannibalistic relationship between the writer and the story; or the bitter elegies of *Angry Candy.*

He knew his circle; and he dared to go outside it.

Being preamble to Harlan is a strange and scary business. I take down the battered and thumbed and treasured paperbacks from the bookshelves amd look at them and there's Harlan on the back cover, with a pipe or a typewriter, and I wonder at how young he looks (it would be foolish to remark that Harlan is the youngest a-whisker-away-from-sixty-year-old I've ever met—it's patronizing and implies that it's a wonder that he's still in full possession of his faculties and capable of telling the Mah-jongg tiles apart; but he has a sense of wonder that's been beaten out of most people by the time they hit their twenties, and a certain cyclonic energy that puts me in mind of my eight-year-old daughter Holly, or of a particularly fiendish explosive device with a ferocious sense of humour; and more than that, he still has convictions and the courage of them): and I then realize the company I'm in, and I reread Stephen King's introduction to *Stalking the Nightmare* and watch Steve making the same points I'm trying so haltingly to make, that it's not about the personality, or the tales about Harlan, or even about Harlan the person. It's not about the pleasure it gave me to hand Harlan the World Fantasy Award for Life Achievement, nor is it about the stunned expressions on the faces of the assembled banquetters, as they listened to his humble and gracious acceptance speech. (I lie through my teeth. Not humble. Not even gracious. Very funny, though. And they *were* stunned.)

Really, all it's about is a shelf of books, and a pile of stories, written as well as he could write them when he wrote them, which is not besides the point; which is, in fact, the whole point.

And Harlan continues to write well and passionately and fiercely. I commend to your attention his story, "The Man Who Rowed Christopher Columbus Ashore" in the *1993 Best American Short Stories* collection— every bit as experimental as anything produced in the wildest excesses of the New Wave and entirely successful. He knows his circle. He is willing to explore outside it.

So, twelve stories follow.

These are not stories that should be forgotten; and some of you are about to read them for the first time.

Prepare to leave the circle with a more-than-capable guide.

I envy you.

December 1993

BANGING THE DRUM
FOR HARLAN ELLISON

Harlan Ellison, sir? Lor' bless you. Of course I remember Harlan Ellison. Why if it wasn't for Harlan Ellison, I doubt I'd even be in this line of work.

I first met Harlan Ellison in Paris in 1927. Gertrude Stein introduced us at one of her parties. "You boys will get on," she said. "Harlan's a writer. Not a great writer, like I am. But I hear he makes up stories."

Harlan looked her in the eye, and told her exactly what he thought of her writing. It took him fifteen minutes and he never repeated himself once. When he finished, the whole room applauded. Gertie got Alice B. Toklas to throw us out into the rain, and we stumbled around Paris, clutching a couple of wet baguettes and a half-a-bottle of an indifferent Bordeaux.

"Where are the snows of yesteryear?" I asked Harlan.

He pulled out a map from an inside pocket, and showed me.

"I would never have guessed that was where they end up," I told him.

"Nobody does," he said.

Harlan knew all kinds of stuff like that. He was braver than lions, wiser than owls, and he taught me a trick with three cards which, he said, would prove an infallible method of making money if I was down on my luck.

The next time I saw Harlan Ellison was in London, in 1932. I was working in the Music Halls, which were still going fairly strong, though they weren't what they used to be. I had worked up a mentalist's act, in a small way. I wasn't exactly bottom of the bill—that was Señor Moon and his Amazing Performing Budgerigar—but I was down there. That was until Harlan came along. He found me at the Hackney Empire vainly trying to intuit the serial number on a temperance crusader's ten-shilling note. "Give up this mentalism nonsense, and stick with me, kiddo," he said. "You've got a drummer's hands, and I'm a man needs a drummer. Together we'll go places."

We went to Goole and Stoke Poges and Ackrington and Bournemouth. We went to Eastbourne and Southsea and Penzance and Torquay. We were

91

doing literature: dramatic storytelling on the seafront to move and entertain the ice-cream-licking multitudes, wooing them away from the baggy-trousered clowns and the can-can girls, the minstrel shows and the photographer's monkey.

We were the hit of the season wherever we went. I'd bang my drum to gather the people around, and Harlan would get up there and tell them one of his stories—there was one about a fellow who was the Paladin of the Lost Hour, another about a man who rowed Christopher Columbus ashore. Afterwards I would pass the hat around, or simply take the money from the hands of the stunned holidaymakers, who would tend simply to stand there when Harlan had finished, their mouths agape, until the arrival of the Punch and Judy man would send them fleeing to the whelk stall in confusion.

One evening, in a fish and chip shop in Blackpool, Harlan confided his plans to me. "I'm going to go to America," he told me. "That's where they'll appreciate me."

"But Harlan," I told him, "we've got a great career here, performing on the seafronts. That new dramatic monologue of yours about the chappie who had no mouth but had to scream anyway—there was almost thirty bob in the hat after that!"

"America," said Harlan. "That's where it's at, Neil."

"You'll have to find someone else to work the seafronts of America with, then," I told him. "I'm staying here. Anyway, what's America got you won't find in Skegness, or Margate, or Brighton? They're all in a hurry in America. They'll not stand still long enough for you to tell them one of your stories. That one about the mindreading fellow in the prison, why it must have taken you almost two hours to tell."

"That," said Harlan, "is the simplicity of my plan. Instead of going from town to town, I shall write down my stories, for people to read. All across America they'll be reading my stories. America first, and then the world."

I must have looked a little dubious, for he picked up a battered saveloy from my plate and used it to draw a map of America with little arrows coming out of it on the table, using the vinegary tomato catsup as paint.

"Besides," asked Harlan, "where else am I likely to find true love?"

"Glasgow?" I suggested bravely (for I "died" once as a mentalist at the Glasgow Empire), but he was obviously no longer listening.

He ate my battered saveloy and we headed back to the streets of Blackpool. When we got to the seafront I banged my little drum until we had gathered together a small crowd, and Harlan proceeded to tell them a story about a week in the life of a man who accidentally telephoned his own house, and he answered the telephone.

There was almost fifty shillings in the hat at the end of that story. We split the proceeds, and Harlan caught the next train to Liverpool, where he said he thought he could work his passage on a steamer, telling stories to the people on board. There was one about a boy and his dog he thought would go over particularly well.

I hear he's doing all right in the New World. Well, here's to him. And as an occasional toiler in the fields of literature myself, I often have cause to remember, with pleasure, all the things I learned back then from Harlan Ellison.

I'm still using them now.

Anyway, sir. Three cards. Round and round and round they go, and where they stop, nobody knows. Are you feeling lucky, today? D'you think you can find the lady?

AFTER THEY'VE BROUGHT ON THE DANCING GIRLS

Some Thoughts on Friendship, Healthcare, Cats and Sex

Introductions are not afterwords, which was why I was pleased when Kate told me Harlan would be up at the front, working the crowd. Introductions need fanfares and drum rolls, spotlights sweeping the stage. It's that old razzamatazz, and razzle-dazzle, when the curtain rises and everyone applauds and they bring on the dancing girls to sparkle and shimmer and flash.

Afterwords are different.

Afterwords are later, when the show's almost over and the curtain's ready to come down, and all the dancing girls have already gone home. Afterwords are post-coital, hanging in those endless black dangerous seconds between orgasm and life's return. Afterwords are the last act on the stage in darkened, smoky bars, about the time that the guy behind the bar starts asking whether or not you people have homes to get to? They're cheap comperes swaying in front of the dim footlights with the important things they had to tell you written safely on a napkin somewhere. Drive safely. Use a condom. Don't wake the neighbours as you leave.

Look, we're almost done. Order yourself one final drink. Get comfortable. It's at times and in places like this that intimacies are exchanged, dark secrets revealed.

I have a weird relationship with nightclubs. I remember once wandering through London on a weird evening. It had started off as a literary party for somebody or other, like P. J. O'Rourke or Spaulding Gray or someone, and afterwards there was me and a number of publicists and a prominent magazine's literary editor, and we all got drunk until they closed down and threw us out. Then we went to someplace else and did the same, and by this time there were only three or four of us left, and the editor pointed out that I was kind of drunk and would I like to sleep on her sofa rather than trek back the 40 miles from London, and I said sure. And then eventually we're wandering out on the streets of London because that place had shut too, and it's only us left, and she says, "How come you can't get a drink in London at four in the morning?"

And I said, hey it's easy, and knocked on a door, and a man came out and looked at us, and I said, It's okay, we're friends of Lemmy's, and he

94

said, Lemmy's downstairs, and let us in. This part of the anecdote is more impressive when you stop and realise a) I had no clue as to where we were, it just kind of looked like an after-hours kind of door, and b) previous times in Soho I'd noticed that Lemmy of Motorhead could often be seen playing fruit machines in strange establishments late at night, so I figured he had to be a good name to drop, but it was kind of weird that he was down there. I went over to him (he was playing the fruit machine) and I said, Hi, I used your name to get in, and he said no problem.

Anyway, so we have a really expensive drink or so, then we go back to her place, and I have a splitting headache, and it turns out she doesn't actually have a sofa, so I explain that I'm married, and she gets kind of pissed off and says she doesn't sleep with married men, and I point out I hadn't actually planned to sleep with her, I just wanted to take up her offer of a non-existent sofa, and things get rather frosty and she gives me the number of a cab and gives me a pain-killer and I go home. But a few weeks later she runs a pretty nice review of a book I'd written, and I figure maybe we're still friends, and, oddly enough, it turns out we actually are still friends, and we've been friends ever since.

Recently she asked me how to get back to that particular club. I had to confess I didn't have a clue as to the address: I told her probably the only way I could find it would be turned adrift in Soho at 3:00 am and at a certain level of intoxication it would manifest wherever I happened to be, Lemmy, fruit machines, and all.

Another late night memory, from a different time in my life: an anonymous blue door in Dean Street, locked. Me and the editor of *Penthouse* were looking for a drink at 4:00 am, and he pulled me up in front of the door, and knocked, 1-2-1, like in a prohibition movie. The door opened, and an impassive face stared down at us. "We're friends of Harry's," said the editor. "I don't know any Harry." "Come on, man, don't give us that shit," said my friend (and I thought, I could never put this into a story, it's a living cliché) and we found ourselves ushered down steep steps to a small bar far below street level, smoky and comfortable: only the suits the men wore were too expensive, and they were doing quiet and earnest business, and the women were pale and fragilely decorative and didn't smile; and in the toilets, on the white-tiled wall, was a patch of still-drying blood with a few long blonde hairs in it, at eye-level. We left soon.

That was back when I was writing mostly for British soft-core porno magazines, doing celebrity interviews. It was kind of educational: I remember talking to my first nude model—Marie, a sharp northern blonde—and asking how she felt about posing nude, about being masturbated over by thousands of men each month. "It beats working the night-shift in a Bradford biscuit factory," she explained. There were two of them at the shoot, accompanying an interview I was doing with a stick-insect-thin junkie poet. Marie and her friend Sherry. The last I saw of Marie she was hanging out with junior Kray-types and TV directors, and the last I saw of Sherry she was sad and stoned and on her way down. I ran into her in a London Bondage nightclub on which I was doing an article, long time ago. (Called *La Maitresse*. Closed down by the police for good about a month later, at which point that scene sort of split into Bondage and Pain on one side and Looking Good In Rubber n' Leather on the other.) And Sherry came over and told me that she'd been dancing nude in Stringfellows all night for Japanese businessmen and was coked out of her head and that her boyfriend didn't love her any more and that I had wonderful eyes, she knew I had wonderful eyes if only I'd take off the fucking shades, and that no one cared if she lived or died. A friend of hers came over and she took her back to the little knot of party girls glittering at the bar.

I've been out of that world for a long time, now, but word travels. Marie's doing fine (still alternately living with gangsters and TV directors; I presume that one day she'll meet a homicidal TV Director who's just come out of Sing Sing and settle down, finally satisfied). Sherry's been missing for a long time; presumed dead. But maybe she's just gone quiet and suburban and got married to this nice guy who doesn't have a clue about her colourful past, and she's really happy, which is why no one's heard from her in years. Only sometimes she dreams of spinning around and around naked on a dance floor with everyone looking admiringly and cheering and waving and laughing, and the glamour, and the glitz…

I hope so. But the last time I saw her she didn't look good, and I'm probably being kind of optimistic.

Later that same night, 4:00 am, in La Maitresse, after pretty much everyone had gone home, the DJ put on the Velvet Underground's *Venus in Furs* and these three school-aged leatherettes began bopping around on the empty dance floor to it, and then started getting kind of carried away, and I sat in the corner, waiting for my disreputable friends, and watched the three girls performing the rock video the V.U. never made for that song, with no one watching or caring but me. And when they finished I stubbed out my cigarette and abandoned my drink, and found my friends to say goodbye, and I went home.

Introductions should be to the point. Afterwords can go all over the show. Even so, I know there were a few things I planned to say, back when I started.

I've got it written down somewhere, on a napkin. You ready? Okay.

The US healthcare system stinks; friendship's important; sex is never that simple; and cats do whatever the fuck they want to.

That's all. Thank you, drive safely, use a condom. Don't make too much noise leaving.

Goodnight.

POETRY

There's poetry, and then there's "poetry", and then there's *poetry*.

And then there's the stuff in this section, which is none of the above. This section is a small ragbag of what might be called occasional verse, if it weren't for occasional verses all over the world writing in to complain.

One day I'll collect together all the real poetry I've written. The stuff that got awards and made it into Year's Best collections. The immortal, deathless words I'm proud to have penned.

None of them are here (well, except possibly for "A Writer's Prayer"). This is the other kind.

This section includes a thank-you letter, a couple of useful poems I wrote for my children ("How To…" guides to writing, respectively, sonnets and Hiawatha. The how-to-write-a-limerick limerick is lost to posterity, I'm afraid, for which posterity is probably grateful), a pantoum done to teach myself how to write pantoums, and a prayer I sent out as a Christmas Card a couple of years ago.

A Writer's Prayer

Oh Lord,
let me not be one of those who writes too much.
Who spreads himself too thinly with his words
diluting all the things he has to say
like butter spread too thinly over toast,
or watered milk in some worn-out hotel.
But let me write the things I have to say
and then be silent, till I need to speak.

Oh Lord,
let me not be one of those who writes too little.
A decade man between each tale. Or more.
Where every word accrues significance
and dread replaces joy upon the page.
Perfection is like chasing the horizon.
You kept perfection, gave the rest to us.
So let me earn the wisdom to move on.

But over and above those two mad spectres of
parsimony and profligacy,
Lord, let me be brave.
And let me, while I craft my tales, be wise.
Let me say true things in a voice that's true,
and, with the truth in mind, let me write lies.

April 24, 1999

Neil's Thankyou Pome
(*Hexwood*)

There's a kitten curled up in Kilkenny was given a
    perfect pot of cream
And a princess asleep in a thornwrapped castle who's
    dreaming a perfect dream
There's a dog in Alaska who danced with delight on a
    pile of mastodon bones
But I got a copy of *Hexwood* (dedicated to me) by
    Diana Wynne Jones

There's an actress who clutches her Oscar (and sobs,
    with proper impromptu joy),
There's a machiavellian villain who's hit on a wonderf'lly
    evil ploy,
There's wizards in crystal castles and kings on their
    golden thrones
But *I* got a copy of *Hexwood*—dedicated—to me!—by
    Diana Wynne Jones

There are fishermen out on the sea today who just
    caught the perfect fish,
There's a child in Luton who opened a genie-filled
    bottle, and got a wish,
There are people who live in glass houses have managed
    to outlaw stones
But I've got a copy of *Hexwood*…
Dedicated to me…
By Diana Wynne Jones

SONNET

This is a **sonnet**, just like Shakespeare wrote,
Iambic, which means *pumpty pumpty pum,*
Pentameter, which is, I'll have you note,
A word that can intimidate the dumb
but only means: five *"pumpties"* on a line
(*penta* means five, and *meter* means the beat).
A sonnet, like this one I write for you,
has only fourteen lines, that's always true,
and ends in a rhymed couplet. Not a feat
too far beyond these meagre skills of mine
(I rhymed the first four lines A-B-a-b
The latter six C-D-E-e-d-c).
I hope this little lesson was no bother;
tomorrow: limericks, and Hiawatha.

HOW TO WRITE
LONGFELLOW'S *HIAWATHA*

Yesterday we did iambics
Now today your education
Carries on with *Hiawatha.*
Longfellow, the man who wrote it,
Stole it from the "Kalevala"
(Famous poem, comes from Finland).
Strong beats first and after weak ones
And eight beats in every line which
Mostly talk of Hiawatha,
Or his girlfriend Minnehaha
(Indian for "Laughing Water").
Soon the thing is second nature:
Not Iambic, it's trochaic
Which means DUM-dum-DUM-dum-DUM-dum
Does it rhyme? Not Hiawatha,
For a rhyme would be redundant
But a little repetition
Every now and then is welcome.
(Just a little bit is welcome.)

When I was the age of Maddy
I'd a *Children's Hiawatha*
Which, at night, my mother read me,
And the rhythms still stay with me.
Till the end, those lines stay with me:
"By the mighty Gitchee-Gumee
By the Shining Big Sea Water
Stood the wigwam of Nokomis…"
That's the bit that I remember.
It began the Children's version.

Now you can write *Hiawatha.*

THE OLD WARLOCK'S REVERIE:
A PANTOUM

Shrieking shapes that stalk the night,
I can hear them scream and moan:
Fox or wolf, they love or fight,
And I wait here on my own.

I can hear them scream and moan:
Clench my nails into my palms—
And I wait here on my own,
Pondering forgotten charms.

Clench my nails into my palms.
—*Where's the girdle made of pelt?*
Pondering forgotten charms:
—*Where's my lycanthropic belt?*

Where's the girdle made of pelt?
Did she burn it, steal it, hide it?
Where's my lycanthropic belt?
(Never knock it till you've tried it.)

Did she burn it, steal it, hide it?
—Pour myself more wormwood gin—
Never knock it till you've tried it;
Trying too much does you in.

Pour myself more wormwood gin,
Blessed drunkenness eludes me.
Trying too much does you in,
True, but just a little soothes me.

Blessed drunkenness eludes me.
Once, beneath the moon, we ran,
True, (but just a little soothes me)
Wolf or fox or cat or man.

Once, beneath the moon, we ran.
That was then. She has not aged.
Wolf or fox or cat or man,
Shapes in which our love we waged…

That was then, she has not aged,
And the pale moon discovers
Shapes in which our love we waged—
Now she shares with other lovers.

And the pale moon discovers
Shrieking shapes that stalk the night.
Now she shares, with other lovers,
Fox or wolf, they love, or fight.

FLASH GIRLS

I love writing songs. But, given all the other things to do, I don't write them unless there is some kind of chance that someone might perform them, and once I got over the age of about 23 I decided it wasn't going to be me any longer.

Luckily, Lorraine Garland (who is, in real life, my long-suffering assistant. She knows where I put things down) and Emma Bull (writer, and a good one) formed a very small girl group called the Flash Girls, so when I write songs now they have somewhere to go.

The sleeve notes of their first album, "The Return of Pansy Smith and Violet Jones" got an honorable mention in the Year's Best Fantasy and Horror, which amused me then and still does. It's reprinted here, along with a few lyrics. You'll need the CDs to find out the tunes, of course. And lyrics are not poems. They do different things, of necessity.

"Banshee" started as an attempt to write a song that was also a pantoum, but then it reconfigured into a new form, all of its own.

"All Purpose Folk Song" was written while watching the Flash Girls perform at a Renaissance Fair. I had heard too many traditional folk songs being sung by too many people that day, and I decided that it was time for a song that included them all. I wrote the first line and the rest of it came tumbling out. It's funnier to listen to than to read, of course.

In Re:
Pansy Smith and Violet Jones

I'm talking to Emma Bull and Lorraine Garland beside the campfire, which takes the edge off the chill night air, maybe too much so, as I wind up edging forward to get warm, edging backward to cool off again while the fire lights their faces from below, like flickering witch-women in orange and yellow.

Now and again an Autumn leaf spins crazily down from the oak trees above us, into the firelight and out again, and Emma and Lorraine talk, and argue, and discuss, and interrupt, and talk once more.

A guitar case is open on the ground beside them, an open folder inside it (resting on Emma's other guitar, the fibre-glass one that she can play in the rain) which contains several photographs, a video, some cassettes, and sheaves of dog-eared photocopies.

Emma has the photographs now, shuffles through them in the firelight, hands one to me, says, "Look. See? That's her. That's Violet."

I stare at the image. The flames dance and make the grey people move and flicker. "The tall one in the front?"

"No, behind her. In the corner. She's looking away from us. See?"

"I'm not sure."

"Well, that's Violet. I'm almost sure that's Violet. And if it is, it's the earliest photograph of her we have."

"Where did you find the photograph?"

She doesn't answer. Lorraine hands me a photograph of a small peasant cottage, one glassless window staring out at us blindly, a low door, a teetering chimney.

"Let me guess. The house where Pansy was born?"

She shakes her head. "I don't think so. But it was probably one like this. Somewhere down near Bantry Bay it was. Her father played the fiddle too, we think. Look."

She pulls something else from the folder in the guitar case. A playbill advertising a concert in Schull, County Cork, another in Ballydehob and a third in Skibbereen. Old printing, yellowed paper. She stabs with a finger. "There. See? And there."

Whistling Gimpy Smith, the Fiddling Wonder. It was printed insect-small near the bottom of the playbill, even under the dog act and the man who could croak like a raven. "Was he her father, then?"

Lorraine shrugs. "Who knows? But the towns are local, and the name's the same."

"So you think he came from Schull?"

"Skull," says Emma, "It's pronounced Skull." She reaches into the guitar case. "Here. Take a look at these."

These are old, old ten-inch records, in ripped brown-paper sleeves. I think *vinyl*, then realise these were pressed long, long before vinyl. "Seventy-eights?"

Emma nods. I read the titles out loud. "*Let's Sit on the Porch and Canoodle, Bertie. Flopsy With the Mopsy on Top. I'll Be Your Borzoi Baby if You Tell Me How to Woof Woof Woof. I Never Said I'd Never Be Your Hotsy-Totsy Girl...*"

"Stop laughing." Emma takes the records away from me, points with one long finger to a name, written by nib pen in faded brown ink, on the brown-paper record sleeve. "See?"

The last name is undoubtedly Jones. The first name is harder to make out. It might conceivably be Violet, I suppose. It might just as conceivably be William, or Urquhart, or Noel.

Emma leans close, so she's staring straight at me, eye to eye. "She left home. She was little more than a child when she left home. She was forced to leave home. She was singing songs like these ones, in public, with a guitar. Her parents thought..." She trails off, stares into the fire. "Can you imagine what it was like for her, a sixteen-year-old girl, making her way across America alone?"

The wind comes up, rustling the papers, freezing us, pushing the fire up into a blaze. I edge back into the darkness and the cold.

"How did she get to Europe, then?"

"Stowed away. On the *Brummagem Maid*, New York into Liverpool."

"You know this for sure?"

She's quieter now. "I don't know anything for sure."

Lorraine picks up her fiddle, plays something that sounds like a funereal jig.

"So what's that?"

Lorraine shakes her head, continues to play. Emma says, "Something of Pansy's, we think. It's from a BBC Archives tape. That was when it was still the British Broadcasting Company, before it was the British Broadcasting Corporation. It was taped at a tea dance in Sloane Square."

"So they got together, when?"

Emma again. "On the Orient Express, we think. They were busking."

Lorraine puts down the violin, shakes her head. "I think it was in Berlin, in a nightclub."

Will Shetterly, who has come over to the fire with an armful of logs, says, "There's a school of thought that claims they never met at all. That it was another couple of women entirely, with the same names. Like who wrote Shakespeare, that stuff." He puts the logs on the fire and walks away, stopping just before he leaves the circle of light, where he turns, and stands, and stares at me.

Lorraine passes me some photocopies of old newspapers, lines of type highlighted in red. A review from the *Preston Sentinel* of a performance at the Alhambra Theatre in Preston, Lancashire— *"Also on the bill were...two young Ladies;"* another from *The Daily Telegraph*, reviewing a performance at The London Piccodrome—*"Two ladies...were also...playing instruments and singing...competently..."*

"Pansy and Violet?"

Emma and Lorraine nod, together, like one person. Lorraine passes me a videotape from the guitar case. Handwritten on the side are two movie titles—*Broadway Gold-Diggers of 1932* and *She Done Him Bad.*

I laugh at this. "*She Done Him Bad?*"

Lorraine stares at me. "It was a very famous film in its day. MGM. It starred Myrna Carlton and Harold 'Buster' Brake."

"Who?"

She just stares at me. "Pansy and Violet sing a song in it. I think they're meant to be hookers or something."

"You can't tell?"

"The picture's a bit fuzzy. We taped it off the television one night. But it's definitely them. They're doing *I Think It Must Be Something I Ate.* You know." She sings: *"This is not my kind of June, even birds sing out of tune..."*

"That's one of their songs?"

"Definitely," says Emma.

"Probably," says Lorraine.

Will Shetterly, standing behind Emma, now, staring into the fire, catches my eye, shakes his head vigorously.

"So do you have any, uh, tapes, or anything, of their performances?"

Emma: "Not as such. But you can reconstruct them."

Lorraine: "We're not the only fans of theirs. Not at all. They were going to be on *This Is Your Life,* in the fifties. They were going to reunite them after all this time."

"Did they?"

Emma laughs, as if I just asked a very stupid question. Lorraine tosses her head, covering her face with hair, and looks away.

"Lorraine? What's wrong? Did I say something wrong?"

"Nothing," she says. "Nothing's wrong."

"So. Pansy Smith and Violet Jones. When did you two get interested in them? In their music?"

"When I was a girl," says Emma. "I had a great-aunt who thought she'd seen them perform in River's Bend, the year of the bad storms. She said you could never forget them. She said that they *had* something."

Lorraine's still looking away from me. She says, "All my life," very quietly.

Emma stirs the contents of the guitar case with her hands, stirs the tapes and the papers and the photographs.

I try again. "Isn't there anything *certain* about them? Are they still alive? Are there any contemporary records? Anything you can show me? I mean, you can't ask me to write an article about them for this CD of yours and then give me, I don't know, nothing…"

Will, standing behind them, is making "zip-it" movements with his hand across his mouth. I try to ignore him. "I mean, from what you're both saying now, it sounds like you've devoted your lives to recreating the musical achievements of two women who might not even have existed."

Emma stirs the fire with a stick. She smiles, but it's a pitying smile, as if I just don't get it and probably never will. "I suppose when you put it that way it does sound a little odd," she says, amused.

Lorraine has picked up her violin, and is cradling it, like a child. "Emma? Make him go away," she whispers. "Make him go away."

Will's making "wrap it up" gestures. I shrug. I don't care. I thought I was trying to do them a favour.

It's getting cold again. I stand up and begin to walk back to the house.

That's when the music starts. I turn around: Emma and Lorraine are playing in the firelight, something odd and funny and strange, and dancing as they play, round and round the flickering pile of burning wood.

Will is taking the papers, the photographs, even the old 78 records, from the guitar case, and, one by one, he is dropping them onto the fire.

BANSHEE

And if you touch me I shall die
And if you want me you are always where I am
Asleep at night I hear your cry
The darkened echoes in the hallways of the damned

And if you want me you are all
Your skin is whiter than a cloud that hides the moon
The darkened echoes in the hall
I hear your voice it isn't loud it is my doom

Banshee
You know I want to see
Banshee
And just a little bit of me
Banshee

Your skin is whiter than a cloud
I heard you singing on the day my brother died
I hear your voice it isn't loud
It tells me things about me way down deep inside

I heard you singing in the day
I'll hunt you down I'll scream and yell across the moor
You tell me things about my way
And when the mists arise, in Hell, that open door

Banshee
When you going to call?
Banshee
Any time at all
Banshee

I hunt you down I scream and yell
For living breathing talking lovers leave me cold
And when the mists arise in Hell
I pray you come down from above I'm here to hold

For living breathing talking love
Is not the same as one who screams when people die
I pray you come down from above
I pray you'll walk into my dreams where spirits lie

Banshee
Anything you want
Banshee
Anything you aren't
Banshee

It's not the same as one who screams
And if you touch me I will die but I don't care
I pray you'll walk into my dreams
Asleep at night I hear your cry, but you're not there

Banshee
Who you want to be
Banshee
Anything you see
Banshee

And if you touch me I will die
And if you touch me I will die
And if you touch me I will die

POST-MORTEM ON OUR LOVE

I've been dissecting all the letters that you sent me,
Slicing through them looking for the real you
Cutting through the fat and gristle of each tortuous epistle
Trying to work out what to do

I've laid the presents that you gave me out upon the floor
A book with pages missing, and a bottle, and a glove.
Now outside it's chilly autumn, I'm conducting a post-mortem
On our love.

I'm conducting a post-mortem on our love.
An autopsy to find out what went wrong.
I know it died.
I just don't know how, or why.
Maybe its heart stopped.

There's an eyeball in a bottle staring sadly at the morgue
There's a white line on the sidewalk silhouetting where it fell
In the dark I am inspecting all the angles of trajectory
of Hell.

Was it suicide, or murder, or an accident, or what?
Though I cut and slice and saw and hack it won't come back to life
And I'm severing the label of each organ on the table
With a knife…

I'm conducting a post-mortem on our love.
An autopsy to find out what went wrong.
I know it died.
I just don't know how, or why.
Maybe its heart stopped.

PERSONAL THING

Tracing your face in the way it all started
Eyes like assassins, we cried when we parted
Shimmy and slip like the mists of December
I close my eyes and I try to remember

Now I need you here like a kite needs a string
I need more than I need anything
I want you back but I'm too proud to say it out loud
—It's a personal thing

Starlight and moonlight and madness and heaven
You made me all that I am: you're forgiven
The touch of your hand or the feel of your finger
Memories cut through my heart and they linger on…

I need you here like a bird needs to sing
I need you more than I need anything
I want you back but I'm too proud to say it out loud
—It's a personal thing

Every cold mile between us is painful
All of the words we could never unsay in full
Moments are magical, pain universal,
Frozen like ice, and it's just too damn personal

I need you here like a dream needs a wing
I need you more than I need anything…
I want you back but I'm too proud to say it out loud
—It's a personal thing.

ALL PURPOSE FOLK SONG (CHILD BALLAD #1)

There's a ship a-sort of sinking in the harbour
And my lover is come down from the sea
Or fens, or heather
Fair maid, he sings, oh show me to your chamber door
Or arbor,
And he means me well
Or ill
Or he ignores me altogether.

Ah, my love he is a knight so bold,
Impressive in his ardour
Or a minstrel or a pirate
With his thighs and arms so firm
With a mandolin or an angry grin and a dead wife in the larder
And somewhere around this point in the song someone
normally gets transformed into a loathly worm.

Sing dum-a-diddle, dum-a-diddle, dum-a-diddle dee
I'm singing of the forests or the tavern or the sea
Sing dum-a-diddle, dum-a-diddle, dum-a-diddle die
You can cross out or forget about the bits that don't apply.

Well, I sent my love a message as they led me to the pyre
But he'd shipped off with Prince Charlie to be a buccaneerio
And the pipes of Faerie skirled and the cows were in the byre,
And we drank good English ale until we felt a little queerio.

Oh, I care not nothing for your goose feather crotch
And I know you by the feathers in your you-know
And we bantered and we badinaged, and then she stole me watch
Then we sang and danced and lost our way all under the autumn moon.
  Oh.

Sing dum-a-diddle, dum-a-diddle, dum-a-diddle doot
No one's really listening and no one gives a hoot
Sing dum-a-diddle, dum-a-diddle, dum-a-diddle die
You can cross out or forget about the bits that don't apply.

A Girl Needs a Knife

I have bought myself a new knife
It is steel and horn, and it glints
like a star in the sun
I have bought myself a new knife,
I hold it and stare at the line of
my knife, and I think about
things that it's done.

a girl needs a knife
a girl needs a knife
a girl needs a knife
And I've got mine

I have bought myself a new knife
I bought it from an old man selling
silver in the street
When I held it I knew it was my new
knife
I heard it hiss my name in the
whisper it made when I pulled the
blade out of the sheath

a girl needs a knife
a girl needs a knife
a girl needs a knife
And I've got mine

I have bought myself a new knife
It has a channel down the side for
the blood to run
Everything is different,
now I own a new knife
In the twilight, I reach out and I
test the blade of my knife with my thumb

a girl needs a knife
a girl needs a knife
a girl needs a knife
And I've got mine

I have bought myself a new knife
You'd be surprised at what my knife
can do.
Guns can jam; bombs are complex.
Sometimes bombs can fail to
explode.
You better listen — this is true.
My knife is simple: part of it I hold.
The other part of it's for you.

a girl needs a knife
a girl needs a knife
a girl needs a knife
And I've got mine

AMERICAN GODS WEB LOG

I've never managed to keep a diary, although I love reading them.

What follows is probably the nearest I've come to a diary: eight months in the life of an author and a book. It's an online journal, a weblog (or blog). I'm still keeping it up, over at neilgaiman.com, but without the sense of mission I had with this one.

I wanted to take people backstage.

When you write a book in fiction, it's all very easy. You type the words "The End" at the bottom of your manuscript, and then, in the next scene, the publisher is on the phone to say that you're on the *New York Times* list.

In reality, typing "The End" marks the point where much of the work starts. That's what this journal is about. The copy-editing, promotion and publication of one book.

I don't like showing my first draft material to the world. The stuff in here, on the other hand, would be happy if it ever made it to first draft. It's a mixture of author's journal, diary, bulletin board, advertising hoarding, backstage tour, stream of consciousness and Pooterish wittering, punctuated and interrupted by incomprehensible sentences that once contained web-links.

You'll learn stuff about books from it, though. How they're made, how they're edited, how they're promoted. How to survive a book tour. You'll learn why Sandboys are happy. And, on the entry for May 31, 2001, you'll get the single best piece of advice I have ever been able to offer the world.

And to answer the question I seem to get asked most, yes, I really did eat all that sushi. (The best was probably in Victoria, in British Columbia. The worst was a gift of ready-made supermarket sushi—but seeing it was all I got to eat that evening, I ate it anyway, with enthusiasm.)

So what follows is a mixture of stuff and nonsense. Good luck...

AMERICAN GODS
WEB LOG
(February to September 2001)

Friday, February 09, 2001

June the 19th 2001 is the publication date of *American Gods*, a book which despite the many shelves in this office filled with books with my name on the spine, feels an awful lot like a first novel. (Perhaps because it was the first long work I've done without any collaborative input from anyone, and that wasn't first something else.) And this, in case you were wondering, is the occasional journal on the americangods.com website. I thought the journal could count us down to publication, and see us through the US and the UK publication and tours for the book in June and July.

I first suggested we do something like this to my editor, the redoubtable Jennifer Hershey, about a year ago, while the book was still being written (a process that continued until about 3 weeks ago). She preferred to wait until the book was on the conveyor belt to actual publication, thus sparing the reading world lots of entries like "Feb 13th: wrote some stuff. It was crap." and "Feb 14th: wrote some brilliant stuff. This is going to be such a good novel. Honest it is." followed by "Feb 15th: no, it's crap." and so on. It was a bit like wrestling a bear. Some days I was on top. Most days, the bear was on top. So you missed watching an author staring in bafflement as the manuscript got longer and longer, and the deadlines flew about like dry leaves in a gale, and the book remained unfinished.

And then one day about three weeks ago it was done. And after that I spent a week cutting and trimming it. (I'd read Stephen King's *On Writing* on the plane home from Ireland, where I'd gone to do final rewrites and reworkings, and was fired up enough by his war on adverbs that I did a search through the manuscript for "_____-ly," and peered at each adverb suspiciously before letting it live or zapping it into oblivion. A lot of them survived. Still, according to the old proverb, God is better pleased with adverbs than with nouns...)

Today I wrote a letter to go in the front of a Quick & Dirty reading edition Harper will put out—taken from the file I sent them, so it'll be filled with transatlantic spelling, odd formatting errors and the rest, but it'll be something to give to the buyers from bookstores and to people who get advance manuscripts so they can see what kind of book this is.

I have no idea what kind of book this is. Or rather, there's nothing quite like it out there that I can point to. Sooner or later some reviewer will say something silly but quotable like "If J.R.R. Tolkien had written *The Bonfire of the Vanities...*" and it'll go on the paperback cover and thus put off everyone who might have enjoyed it.

This is what I wrote about it in the letter in the Quick & Dirty proof:

> *American Gods* is the most ambitious book I've written. It took longer to write, was a harder and stranger beast than anything I've tried before.
>
> It's a thriller, I suppose, although as many of the thrills occur in headspace as in real life, and it's a murder mystery; it's a travel guide, and it's the story of a war. It's a history. It's funny, although the humour is pretty dark.
>
> It's the story of a man called Shadow and the job he is offered when he gets out of prison.

When I finish a project, I sometimes like to go back and look at the original outline—see how far the project came from my first thoughts. When I finished *American Gods,* in January 2001, I looked, for the very first time in two and a half years, at the letter I wrote to the publisher describing the book I planned to write next. (I wrote it in a hotel room in Iceland in June 1998.) The outline ended like this:

> If *Neverwhere* was about the London underneath, this would be about the America between, and on-top-of, and around. It's an America with strange mythic depths. Ones that can hurt you. Or kill you. Or make you mad. *American Gods* will be a big book, I hope. A sort of weird, sprawling picaresque epic, which starts out relatively small and gets larger. Not horror, although I plan a few moments that are up there with anything I did in *Sandman,* and not strictly fantasy either. I see it as a distorting mirror; a book of danger and secrets, of romance and magic.
>
> It's about the soul of America, really. What people brought to America; what found them when they came; and the things that lie sleeping beneath it all.

And, oddly enough, that seemed to describe the book I'd written pretty well.

And the other thing I'm doing (you'd think I'd have people who would do this for me, but no, it's just me) is sending out the e-mails to music publishers telling them I'd like to quote their song at the start of a chapter, and then waiting for their reply. There's no commonly agreed scale of pricing on this—$150 is pretty usual (as the author is paying), but some publishers ask for a whole lot more. If they ask for too much more I say sod it and go and find a good public domain quote that does the same thing.

So, there. Journal entry #1 done. & now back to my day job (which currently mostly involves writing *Death: The High Cost of Living*).

posted by Neil Gaiman 12:45 PM

You know, this web site is like a new office, with white walls and bare desks. It needs things to make it feel more homey. More pictures, for a start. (Remind me to tell you about the Author Photos some time.) I'm planning some fun things for it. Well, that's not true. I only have one fun thing planned, which is an area which won't go live until the book is out, and may even be passworded in some way that would mean you'd need to have read the book to access bits of it. It would be an area of annotation and background information. Mostly mythic…The other stuff will be pretty obvious—we'll put up the signing tour dates as we get them (for the US and for the UK), we'll probably have a place people can leave questions and comments. And every now and again when I run out of ideas for things to write, I'll do a sweep through the questions, and answer them.

I thought about putting links up to the various chain stores online, places where you could pre-order *American Gods*. And then I thought, well, you have plenty of time before it comes out, there's no rush: the next time you walk past your local bookshop, why not go in and tell them to make sure they get a copy in for you?

posted by Neil Gaiman 8:50 PM

Sunday, February 11, 2001

A little over a year ago, I was asked to do a thing over at The Well's inkwell.vue area. I had a topic and people could ask questions, and it just quietly became a sort of combination of occasional diary and place I could mention things. It was only meant to go for a few months, but these things sometimes have a life of their own, and it's become the topic that hasn't died. Or rather it has just died, as, with over 1900 postings in it, they've frozen the topic and started a new one, Countdown to *American Gods*. It's at http://engaged.well.com/engaged engaged.cgi?c=inkwell.vue&f=0&t=104

And I just went in and posted a little blurb about the book, and the covers and such. Once I'd finished typing it, it struck me that it would probably serve as a pretty good journal entry for here, as well. So here you are. Me introducing *American Gods*.

It's a big fat book about America, and about a man called Shadow, and the job he is offered when he gets out of prison. It's kind of a thriller, I suppose, if you can have mythic thrillers. I suppose it could be considered SF or fantasy or horror, depending on where you stand, and I'd not argue with anyone who considered it such. My former publisher, Lou Aronica, read it and said it was a slipstream novel, using Bruce Sterling's term for (as I understood it) books that give you the same buzz you got as a kid from genre stuff but that aren't published as genre.

The US cover shows a road and a lightning bolt. The UK cover shows a motel sign, a telegraph pole, and a lightning bolt.

This is not actually an example of parallel evolution. Scarily, the US cover for *American Gods* was designed before I started writing the book, over two years ago, and the cover was simply based on a two or three page letter to the publisher about the kind of book I thought I'd write next. I'd called the book *American Gods* in the letter as a kind of placeholder name, until I came up with something better, and then they sent me a cover mock-up, and it looked so definite I never had the heart to even try to come up with another title. And the image they'd sent me really did look like the cover of the book I was writing.

When they'd read the first half of the book, the UK publishers, Headline, called and said they hadn't a clue what to put on the cover. So I sent them a photocopy of the US cover, and they took the lightning bolt idea and added a wonderful motel sign (for the "Stardust Motel" which must have amused somebody).

We're four months away from publication here, at a point in the process that's usually a lot further down the road (we're compressing the usual eight months-plus between handing in a manuscript and publication into about half the time).

Then again, my scary children's novel *Coraline* was handed in in June 2000, and won't reach bookshops until May 2002. (Although Harper Audio may release an audio version of it in December 2001/January 2002.)

posted by Neil Gaiman 12:03 PM

Wednesday, February 14, 2001

So…permissions are in on Greg Brown's song "In the Dark With You" (which starts Chapter Fourteen) and Stephen Sondheim's "Old Friends" (which starts Chapter Thirteen). I decided that I'd start Chapter Six with the public domain "Midnight Special" rather than Iggy Pop's "Sister Midnight," but that was more because it was slightly more appropriate than because of the public domainness or otherwise of the thing. I've also, with a little regret, changed an Alan Moore song-quote into a Ben Franklin *Poor Richard* quote, because it said the same thing and fitted the theme slightly better on several counts. And because Ben said it first. No word yet on "Please Don't Let Me Be Misunderstood," or on the Robert Frost, e.e. cummings or Yeats quotes. (The Yeats is from "The Second Coming," which I almost consider public domain these days, considering it's been quoted to the point of cliché—which is why the character who quotes it, quotes it when he does—but I thought it polite to ask.) I'm waiting to see how much "Please Don't Let Me Be Misunderstood" comes in at before I start negotiating with the Tom Waits people over a couple of lines of "Tango Till You're Sore."

There are probably more than 20 chapters in the book, but all the rest of the chapter headers are from dusty and out of print books.

Incidentally, I'm trying to decide whether to put a bibliography in the back of *American Gods*, or whether it might be more fun to put it up online here (when we open that wing of the website).

posted by Neil Gaiman 10:55 AM

So strange and organic changes are happening to the website. Which I for one find fascinating, so I went and played with everything. I signed up to get the first chapter of *American Gods*. And I even clicked on all the weblinks to order *American Gods,* to find out what was what.

The results were: the Amazon.com link took me to the book; the Barnes and Noble link took me to the book; the Borders link didn't take me to the book, but a hasty search brought it up. And booksense.com was, well, quite bizarre.

I did a search for the book. Nothing. I did a search for any books by me and this was all I got:

"Search Results Page 1 of 1"
Neil Gaiman by Gaiman, Neil
Format: Hardcover Price: $19.95 Published: Westhampton
House, 05/01/2001 Inventory status: Not yet published.

Leading us to all sorts of mysterious questions about this eponymous book. Why did I write a book called Neil Gaiman? Who are Westhampton House? I suppose we'll all find out on May the first.

posted by Neil Gaiman 12:24 PM

Thursday, February 15, 2001

Mystery slightly solved—the Neil Gaiman thing is the video of the Comic Book Legal Defense Fund Reading I did at the Aladdin Theatre in Portland last year (the real title is something like *Live at the Aladdin*). This seems faintly cursed—when Amazon initially listed the video they gave it the ISBN and information of a book on the history of pro wrestling.

Still doesn't explain why no Minneapolis area Booksense store has any other book by me, including *American Gods,* but I assume it's just a glitch in the system. (I tried it on Booksense with a New York zip code and it worked just fine.)

I started a journal entry today that turned into a 1500 word rambling essay on the start of *American Gods,* how it began, how the characters got their names, and why, in my opinion, some books and some stories have genders. So I've put it aside and will look at it tomorrow to see if it makes any sense or not…if it does I'll post it here. If not, consider yourselves lucky to have been spared it…

posted by Neil Gaiman 8:48 PM

Friday, February 16, 2001

Yes, I know this is an *American Gods* website, and an *American Gods* journal, and I really ought to write about *American Gods* here. (And I'm just about to try a draft of the dustjacket copy—I felt the first round might have given too much away.) But I thought I'd mention that my spooky children's book *Coraline* (which will come out in hardback from Harper about the time *American Gods* comes out in paperback) is being adapted by Henry Selick (who directed the *Nightmare Before Christmas, James and the Giant Peach* and *Monkeybone*). You can read more about it at

http://www.scifi.com/scifiwire/art-main.html?2001-02/15/14.00.film

posted by Neil Gaiman 2:55 PM

There's coin magic in *American Gods,* of the conjuring kind. And just as I ran the medical parts (and the post mortem parts) past a doctor, I ran the coin magic past a top coin magician—Jamy Ian Swiss, better known as a card magician. (I met him some years ago, at a Penn and Teller gig in Las Vegas I attended—P&T had just guest-starred in the *Babylon 5* episode I'd written, "The Day of the Dead".)

Jamy sent me a terrific professional's-eye critique of the coin magic, and I can make some subtle changes in the copy-editing (which I think will start tomorrow, Wednesday, at least on the US version—I've been told I'll get the copy-edited manuscript by lunchtime). (And there's always a little nervousness in receiving a copy-edited mss. One never knows what kind of copy editor one will have got. On *Stardust* I had a lovely one, who even made sure that the UK spelling *grey* rather than *gray* held throughout, because she thought it more appropriate. On the book before that I had a copy editor who, it seemed at the time, repunctuated practically every sentence for no good reason, leaving me muttering "Look, if I'd wanted a comma there I would have bloody well put a comma there" too often for comfort.)

But I was talking about coin magic, not copy editing. Sorry.

This is from my last e-mail to Jamy Ian Swiss, who was grumbling about the depiction of stage magic in most forms of fiction. And I thought it might be interesting for you, hypothetical journal reader.

> One reason I wanted the coin magic in *American Gods* to be good magic, was to ground the whole thing in reality, and to introduce a world in which nothing you are being told is necessarily reliable or true, while still playing fair with the readers.
>
> I know what you mean about stage magic in fiction though: too often it seems to read as if the writer hasn't done anything magical since getting the magic set aged 11.
>
> I think part of the reason that fiction has problems with stage magic is that the compact the magician makes with the audience is twofold: "I will lie to you" and "I will show you miracles", and fiction tends only to grasp the second half of that.

Now back to writing the jacket blurb. (Or at least, doing a draft of the plot bit that the publisher may or may not use. When it comes to the "Neil Gaiman writes good stuff" bits of the blurb they are on their own.)

posted by Neil Gaiman 10:37 PM

Friday, February 23, 2001

I'd post more, but there's nothing in the world as dull as an author going over a copy-edited manuscript. I finished chapter eight today. The copy editor's done a very solid job. Occasionally I wish that he'd queried things instead of just fixed them. (Mad Sweeney, for example, who claims when drunk to be Irish and a leprechaun, says "fucken" a lot. The copy editor has carefully gone through and carefully changed every "fucken" to "fuckin", figuring, I suppose, that I just didn't know how it was spelled.)

When you see things fixed that weren't broken, you write STET in the margin in green pencil. Mostly, you just nod and are happy that someone caught your goofs before it went to press. You'd be astonished at the number of different ways I'd managed to spell McDonald's in one small book. Well, one quite big book, actually, but the point holds.

posted by Neil Gaiman 6:38 PM

Friday, March 02, 2001

One longish, quite funny, entry on the mechanics of copy editing was eaten by Blogger a couple of days ago, and I was too busy copy editing the novel to re-enter it. And then February did that thing that February does, where it stops suddenly just as you were getting the hang of it, and the time allotted by the publisher to copy editing was done. I spent one last day trying to input all of the major and minor revisions to the computer, so I had a file that was more or less the same as the version that was to be printed, and then had to drive at silly speeds down icy country roads to make it to the FedEx drop-off in time, which (deep sigh of relief here) I did.

And the manuscript is safely at HarperCollins, and now I just have to figure out the best way of doing the UK copy edit for the Hodder edition (as I discovered when they sent me their list of queries, the biggest problem with sending electronic files of books around the world rather than printouts is that page numbers change depending on things like your default font size and the type of paper you're using—so my sending them a list of changes of the "delete comma after the word of on page 16 line 12" variety would be somewhere beyond useless).

The strangest thing about doing a copyedit is how much you learn. About the world, and about writing. Before I start I grab a pile of dictionaries, English and American, and a bunch of books on usage— Fowler's, and the *Harper Dictionary of Contemporary Usage,* and Bill Bryson's lovely *Penguin Dictionary of Troublesome Words*—and the *Chicago Manual of Style,* and wade in.

Is blowjob one word or two? Judgement or judgment? Wintry or wintery? Why has the copy editor crossed out "hessian" and replaced it with "burlap"? Aren't they two different fabrics?—twenty minutes of research and I figure out that they may be two different fabrics in the UK, but they stopped using the word hessian for rough hairy sack-type jute or hemp cloth in the US about two hundred years ago. Good…

I'd written "none of the passengers were hurt" and the copy editors changed it to "none of the passengers was hurt"—*Fowler's English Usage,* the *American English Usage,* Harpers and Bill Bryson all agree that the idea that "None" is a singular noun is based on the misconception that it's a contraction of no one, which it isn't, and tell me it's plural if I want it to be. Good. I do.

Now, when I write dialogue I try and punctuate it to give some kind of indication of the rhythms of speech. As far as I'm concerned "Hi, Mike" and "Hi Mike" are two different things. The copy editor likes the first, and assumes that wherever I've put the second, it's because I've forgotten the comma. And I like to spell out "mister" if it occurs in dialogue. I just do. He's replaced them all with "Mr." and I *stet* each one back the way it was, and fix a few that I've forgotten...

He's changed dumpster to Dumpster. Check. Yup, it's a trade-mark. Good call. Okay. He's changed the one occurrence of 'whisky' to 'whiskey'. Nope, it's a good scotch (Laphroaig), and that's how they spell it. Leave it. And here's Diet Coke changed to diet Coke. Is that right? Yup. Good man.

He's changed a sixteen wheeler to an eighteen wheeler in a metaphor but not when there are a cluster of them parked outside a strip club. I add another two wheels to the ones parked outside THE BEST PEAP SHOW IN TOWN...

Why has the copy editor changed "it's the objective case" to "it's the dative case" in a (very) short conversation about 'who' vs 'whom'? Do we even have a dative case in English? My schoolboy Latin, Greek and German are of little use, but none of the reference books seems to think that there's anything other than subject and object going on here, and I write STET.

And on, and on, for six hundred and fifty pages. And if all this seems pedantic, on the copy editor's part or on mine...well, yes. That's the point. He's paid not to see the wood for the trees. Actually he's paid to look up at the wood now and again, but mostly to keep track of all the leaves, and especially to make sure that Missy Gunther on page 253 isn't Missie Gunther when she returns on page 400.

(And as I type this, looking down to my assistant Lorraine's Xena mouse pad, I've just noticed that the copy editor corrected Xena: Warrior Princess to Xena the Warrior Princess, and I let it pass as I assumed that was the official trademark, but nope, I was right originally—quick phone call to HarperCollins "in chapter five, just before the bank robbery, there's a Xena: Warrior Princess harem doll in the bankrupt stock store—can you fix it back the way it was?")

Meanwhile, there's a list of queries in from the UK, only one of which is the same as the US copy edits (a twenty-five minute long half an hour I'd managed to create. Don't ask).

I decide to lose the quote from a Blur song ("Magic America") (which doesn't say very much, but which was in my head when I started the book, along with Elvis Costello's "American Without Tears") and replace it with a quote from Lord Carlisle written just after the War of Independence about the hugeness of America and the way even their losses and disasters occurred on a massive scale...

And now it's over and done. For three weeks, anyway, when the galleys will come back and I'll read it through a microscope for the second time, making sure that every comma is where it's meant to be...

posted by Neil Gaiman 7:35 AM

So the post today brought a copy of *American Gods*—a book, and a cover—from the UK. It's the Hodder uncorrected proof, and it is lovely. I was completely thrilled, mostly I think by the bookness of it. I also really liked the back cover copy, although it doesn't bear a whole lot of resemblance to the book it describes, having been written from my original outline and not from the text. So some of the facts are off, but the mood and the pitch and the tone are just right.

You can see the cover image at http://images-eu.amazon.com/images/P/0747274231.02.LZZZZZZZ.jpg

Although they've now put a lot more silver on my name, and distressed the title letters, and the whole looks smashing.

All of a sudden, it's starting to feel like something very real—a book, not just something I've been writing for a few years.

posted by Neil Gaiman 3:05 PM

And in case you were wondering—Permissions: still waiting to hear from Warner Chappell about "Please Don't Let Me Be Misunderstood," and from all the poets. Permissions in from Greg Brown (for his song "In the Dark with You"), agreement reached with Sondheim's people (for "Old Friends")...

posted by Neil Gaiman 4:20 PM

Monday, March 05, 2001

Permissions...well, good news, bad news. According to the copyright office website:

> Therefore, the U. S. copyright in any work published or copyrighted prior to January 1, 1923, has expired by operation of law, and the work has permanently fallen into the public domain in the United States. For example, on January 1, 1997, copyrights in works first published or copyrighted before January 1, 1922, have expired; on January 1, 1998, copyrights in works first published or copyrighted before January 1, 1923, have expired. Unless the copyright law is changed again, no works under protection on January 1, 1999 will fall into the public domain in the United States until January 1, 2019.

Which means that two of the poems I needed to quote from are public domain.

The third, unfortunately, isn't...and the request originally went to the wrong people. So I've just re-sent it to the right people. Keep your fingers crossed for me.

So, today, apart from Permissions emergencies, is trying to fix the UK and the US blurbs. The UK blurb feels just right, but is factually wonky; the US one has all its facts right, but doesn't quite feel like the book yet (as someone who read it said, "It could be about a war between rival clans of elves in the

US"—which, I hasten to add, it isn't). So I need to try and get the UK jacket copy closer to the events of the book, and the US jacket copy closer to the weirdness of the book. And I ought to do it before close of play today...

posted by Neil Gaiman 1:31 PM

Wednesday, March 07, 2001

Let's see...well, the old entries are dropping off the bottom of the site, so we're setting up an archive. There are US quick & dirty proof copies of the book going out to booksellers and authors-for-blurbs right now; I'm doing as many cover letters as I can to them. (It'll be interesting to see how quickly they start showing up on eBay, and how much they go for.) We've finalised the jacket copy in the US, and got permission to use a line from an e-mail as a blurb on the back of the book. (It was something Teller, of Penn and Teller fame, and a very fine writer in his own right, wrote to me, when he read it, which, I thought, described the book I was trying to write perfectly.)

posted by Neil Gaiman 1:32 PM

One of the best things about finishing a book, is there are things you haven't been able to read that now you are.

When I'm writing a book—or even, when I know that one day I'm going to be writing a book—any fiction in possibly a similar area becomes taboo.

If my next book were to be a fictional life of Marco Polo, I'd not read any fiction to do with Marco Polo or Kublai Khan (and would probably have stopped reading it about five years ago): partly because I don't want to see how someone else did that idea, and partly because if someone did do the same thing that I was going to do, I don't want that route closed off because someone else has taken it already. It just keeps things simple.

It doesn't mean you won't be accused of plagiarism. I've still never read Christopher Fowler's *Roofworld,* although I love Chris Fowler as a writer, and have had a copy of *Roofworld* on my shelves since before it came out (they sent me a proof). But I knew I wanted to do a magic city under London novel, and *Roofworld* looked too close to what I planned to do for comfort. I left it unread, as I left Mike Moorcock's *Mother London,* and several other good books. Books I know I'd like I haven't read (and still haven't, since I want to go back to London Below one day).

One of the joys of finishing *American Gods* is that there are books I can read, and books I can reread. John James's *Votan,* for example. A book I read almost twenty years ago, and that I've wanted to reread for ages but didn't dare to, as I knew it had a scene I was going to have to do in *American Gods.* And when I finally read it, last week, I was pleased that the two scenes didn't resemble each other in any real way, and more pleased that twelve years spent getting as deeply into Norse stuff as anyone who doesn't do it for a living had left me with an enormous appreciation for the brilliance of James's novel. (It's about a wily second century Greek trader in Germany who becomes Odin—Votan—and to whom all the Norse myths happen, or at least, the stories that will become the Norse myths. Hilarious, moving and, along with its sequel, *Not For All the Gold in Ireland,* the best mythic-historical fiction out there, apart from Gene Wolfe's *Soldier in the Mist* sequence, and maybe some Robert Graves.)

And now I'm reading a book I've wanted to read for five years, Martin Millar's *Good Fairies of New York*. I read the back jacket copy when I bought the book, and ruled it off limits as it might have strayed into *American Gods* territory. Reading it in the bath today, it doesn't. It's just delightful Martin Millar, as funny and wise and solidly written as he gets at his best.

posted by Neil Gaiman 7:15 PM

Thursday, March 08, 2001

Hey. I'm nominated for a Nebula, for best screenplay. Isn't that fun? http://www.sfwa.org/awards/

(I'm not sure that my part in *Mononoke* was screenplay-worthy, and if it did get it, Jack Fletcher, the English language voice director, deserves as much of it as I do. But still, it's always fun to be nominated for things.)

posted by Neil Gaiman 5:45 PM

Friday, March 09, 2001

The good news is that a box of quick and dirty proof copies of *American Gods* arrived today. The bad news is that the last chapter is missing. And all I can say is thank heavens it's just these early proofs, where we can make sure anyone who gets them also gets a printout of the last chapter rather than the finished book on the shelves missing its last chapter. (It's happened, and worse, and weirder. For that matter I have on my shelves the only extant copies of a UK printing of *The Sandman: Book of Dreams* with Stephen King's name on the cover as author of one of the stories. Luckily I got my author copies before they left the warehouse to go anywhere else. And I called HC UK and said "But he doesn't have a story in the book. You printed it in hardback last year and he didn't have a story in there." And they said "Oops," and trashed the print run.)

posted by Neil Gaiman 11:49 AM

Wednesday, March 14, 2001

So I've spent the last two days doing the UK (Headline Books) galleys of *American Gods*. (Galleys are the output pages of what will be typeset to form the book that will be on sale. They are unbound, at this stage—500 numbered sheets of paper.) It was a strange and gently maddening experience as I got to discover how inconsistent I am when I write. *Aging* AND *ageing, 10:00 am* AND *10:00am., jeweller* AND *jeweler*...and so on. And while I didn't mind my favourite version being in there I found it most trying that I hadn't been consistent. So I reminded myself that a something or other consistency is the hobgoblin of tiny minds and went back to the galleys.

I am getting faster, though.

And I was pleasantly surprised that the book seemed to hold my interest as a reader for the umpteenth time through it. Normally about this point in the equation I cannot even look at it again.

(There was one edition of one of my books, quite some years ago, where the galleys arrived for a paperback edition, and I looked at them and said "They had better be right, for I don't think I can read past page one without screaming." And for all I know, they were.)

So some time in the next few weeks it'll be time to do the US galleys. But for now the UK galleys have been inspected, corrected, several pages have been rescued from a swimming pool and dried out (it was windy), and I found a postal service place to UPS them—all 7 lbs of paper—back to London.

The lady who ran the postal place was somewhat woozy. She spoke like Tracey Ullman's Ruby Romaine character, and had a great deal of trouble focussing on things, like small print, or quite large print, or solid objects. She said she'd been an exotic dancer until her back got bad, but that was some years ago now. She told me it would cost $95 to send the galleys to London. I said that she was looking at the wrong page, and that I was not trying to import anything to the US collect. She moved the book around and squinted a lot. I asked if I could help, and took the book, and found the cost of sending the package and the price and everything. I gave it back to her. She decided that I had the wrong page. She phoned head office. They told her the price code. It was the one that I'd found for her. She came back to tell me about it. An ant started sauntering across the counter top. She kept hitting it ("I know they're all god's creatures but that's a goddamn bug on my counter.") and kept missing it, her fist always slamming down just behind where it had been. It wasn't walking that fast. Then the ant vanished entirely. She looked around for it, muttering, "Where the hell did it go?" I picked it off her forearm, and dropped it into the bin. She told me that she'd be able to focus a lot better after her pharmaceutical break.

And I left her the galleys, hoping against hope that they will actually arrive at the offices of Headline Books on Monday, and that she won't absent-mindedly have sent them to India or somewhere.

Which reminds me...

Currently there's no real mechanism for sending questions about *American Gods* here yet. So if any of you do have questions for me about *American Gods*, go and take a look at the Well's inkwell.vue area (http:// www.well.com/conf/inkwell.vue/). You can e-mail Linda or Jon or any of the guys who run the inkwell (there's a link to them at the bottom of that first page) and they'll post the questions on the inkwell topic—104— and I'll answer them there and here.

And the US part of the signing tour is more or less decided. I'll post it as soon as it's set in stone. It'll be June 19th –29th. Then there will be a UK tour in early July and a short Canadian tour in late July.

And the first *American Gods* proof has surfaced on eBay. It's one of the UK proofs, so it has a nice cover and isn't missing the final chapter. But I was saddened to see that it's "unread"—there aren't many of these proofs (they're few enough that Headline is having to say "no" to people who want them now), and the whole point of sending them out is so that people—booksellers or journalists—can read them, not so that they can make a quick buck off them.

posted by Neil Gaiman 9:24 PM

Thursday, March 15, 2001

By the way, for those who read the archives (or just have good memories) and wondered what happened to the journal entry that turned into an essay on things like whether books have genders and how *American Gods* grew from a bean, I've tidied it up and given it to my editor at HarperCollins to pass on to Powells.com, who wanted an essay for their website. So, when it's up, you'll have to go there and read it.

posted by Neil Gaiman 1:12 PM

Saturday, March 17, 2001

So, I was just starting to get up to speed on the *Death: The High Cost of Living* script when this morning brought with it from HarperCollins the US galleys. So I rolled up my sleeves, took out my pen (the instructions they send say pencil, but I don't have a pencil here) and started in on them. Now it's just little things, and occasionally fixing things I was too tired to fix the last time they went through (HarperCollins hyphenates or doesn't hyphenate on a system all of their own…why, I wonder, would *face up* become one word *faceup?*) and sometimes fixing things I'm pretty sure I did fix last time around but that weren't acted upon (dammit, I like *blond* for boys and *blonde* for girls). The scary point in proofreading is that odd moment when suddenly, the marks on the paper become nothing more than marks on the paper. This is my cue to go and make a cup of tea.

Normally they've fixed themselves and become marks that mean something when I get back. In this case, I decided that doing a journal entry (while the tea brews) might encourage them to head back into wordhood.

Not sure if I mentioned this before, but the Amazon.com entry for *American Gods* has the first draft of the jacket copy up. (It's at http://www.amazon.com/exec/obidos/ASIN/0380973650)

The one on the book jacket is, I think, a little more oblique.

Changing the subject, I keep thinking about the Coen brothers, who proudly announced when they released the directors cut of *Blood Simple* that far from adding any new material, they had managed to cut several minutes from it. I keep thinking about this in context of the book, this blogger journal, and the *American Gods* website. There is stuff I'm very happy to have cut from the manuscript. One story stands alone (I sent it out as a Christmas card this year) but there are some oddments that I cut out because they interrupted the flow of the story, and it was just a little leaner and worked a little better without them. I can imagine in ten years' time rereading *American Gods* and proudly cutting out several paragraphs.

So I think I may post a few here and there. There's one lecture from a character who never really even made it into the first draft, that I keep meaning to transcribe from my notes and put up. The rest of them are full scenes or bits...

Here's a little one.

> "I suppose I need a library card," he said. "And I want to know all about thunderbirds."
>
> The woman had him fill out a form, then she told him it would take a week until he could be issued with his card. Shadow wondered if they spent the week sending out despatches to ensure that he was not wanted in any other libraries across America for failure to return library books.
>
> He had known a man in prison who had been imprisoned for stealing library books.
>
> "Sounds kind of rough," said Shadow, when the man told him why he was inside.
>
> "Half a million dollars worth of books," said the man, proudly. His name was Gary McGuire. "Mostly rare and antique books from libraries and universities. They found a whole storage locker filled with books from floor to ceiling. Open and shut case."
>
> "Why did you take them?" asked Shadow.
>
> "I wanted them," said Gary.
>
> "Jesus. Half a million dollars worth of books."
>
> Gary flashed him a grin, lowered his voice and said, "That was just in the storage locker they found. They

never found the garage in San Clemente with the really good stuff in it."

Gary had died in prison, when what the infirmary had told him was just a malingering, feeling-lousy kind of day turned out to be a ruptured appendix. Now, here in the Lakeside library, Shadow found himself thinking about a garage in San Clemente with box after box of rare, strange and beautiful books in it rotting away, all of them browning and wilting and being eaten by mold and insects in the darkness, waiting for someone who would never come to set them free.

posted by Neil Gaiman 11:33 AM

Ah, and another proof of *American Gods* has hit eBay, I see. This time it's the US edition, so is missing the last chapter…

posted by Neil Gaiman 12:15 PM

Monday, March 19, 2001

Hard work doing the US galleys. They were waiting for me when I got up Saturday morning, went off first thing this morning (Monday) and I didn't do anything else over the weekend, except go and eat some nice sushi.

Someone's done a lot of find and replaces—*never* a good idea in galleys. Dave Langford put something in *Ansible* recently about how on the galleys of my novel *Neverwhere* someone Found-and-Replaced all the flats to apartments. People said things apartmently, and believed the world was apartment.

None of these were quite that bad—they were subtler…

F'rinstance: All instances of the word round have become around. Fine for walking around the lake, less helpful for the around glasses, the around holes in the ice; blonde has uniformly become blond, and so blonder has become blondr; for ever has become, universally, forever, and for everything thus became foreverything, and we also got foreveryone, forevery time and so on. Each had to be found and caught.

Little things—the Icelandic þú became bú, which won't bother anyone who isn't Icelandic. Blowjob had inexplicably become blow job again. (I think a blowjob is a unit of sexual currency, whereas a blow job is something you can get—or indeed, give—instead of a wrist job, a sleeve job or a window job.) And once again every damn comma gets scrutinised. And I changed an advertise to an advertize which was nice of me.

I changed the copyedited "vast hall of death" back to "vasty hall of death" which was what I'd originally written; it's a quote from Matthew

Arnold, which was in its turn quoted by Roger Zelazny, and I think that people can get the idea that vasty's an archaic form of vast.

Not sure of the logic that has people talk about a "Motel 6" or "drive down Highway 14" but also talk about "Comparative Religion One-oh-one". But I just put a query next to it and left it.

I am, having read my book three times in three versions in the last three weeks, checking everything, finally feeling very done with it. Noticed some sloppy sentences this time through, ones that Fowler would have tutted at. If I could fix them with a word, I did; if they needed to be completely rewritten, I left them, figuring that perfection can wait. Maybe for the next book.

The first of the blurbs is in. It's from Peter Straub, who says, in an e-mail to my editor, Jennifer Hershey...

> Dear Jennifer –
> Many thanks to both you and Neil for sending me the early galley of *American Gods*. I think it is a terrific book, clearly Neil's best to date, and am very happy to offer the following quote:
> "From his first collection of short stories, Neil Gaiman has always been a remarkable, remarkably gifted writer, but *American Gods* is the first of his fictions to match, even surpass, the breathtaking imaginative sweep and suggestiveness of his classic *Sandman* series of graphic novels. Here we have poignancy, terror, nobility, magic, sacrifice, wisdom, mystery, heartbreak, and a hard-earned sense of resolution—a real emotional richness and grandeur that emerge from masterful storytelling."
> Will that do? It's a wonderful novel, and I congratulate both you and Neil for bringing it into being.
> Peter Straub

Which has me happy as a sandboy. (What is a sandboy? Why are they so happy?) I guess because I really wanted *American Gods* to be a book that had the power and scale and resonance that *Sandman* did (and which, by their nature, and not necessarily to their detriment, neither *Neverwhere* nor *Stardust* could have had—they were intrinsically smaller, lighter things). That it's done that for one reader—and that that one reader is a writer of whose work I have been a fan since I read *Shadowlands* at about 16— makes me feel like the last two years of hard writing really had a point.

The permission came in on the Tom Waits song "Tango Till They're Sore," and I got the first word from the "Please Don't Let Me Be Misunderstood" people, and I sent them the follow-up fax. Waiting on e.e. cummings still. But the permissions should be done *very* soon.

And an e-mail in from a correspondent who shall remain anonymous:

> I've looked at some of your journal and I'd never realised the actual effort and workload that goes into it *after* the book is "written". Nor why it took so long between concept and hardback appearance—until now that is. Is your brain "American Godded Out" or still on an enthusiasm roll?

Dear Anonymous of New Zealand. I'm still enthusiastic. But I'm very pleased I don't have to read it again this week.

And I'm pleased that some of the mechanics of taking a book to publication are coming out in the journal. People know that authors write books, and then books appear on the shelves. Some of them are bestsellers, and some aren't. But that's all most people know. One reason I liked the idea of doing this journal was being able to explain the stuff that happens between handing in the mss and publication. (That there are no authorial grumbles about either the UK or the US book covers is very unusual— I'm happy with them both and they both look like covers for the book I wrote.)

Someone on The Well asked, Why don't writers just edit their own books, kinda like musicians who produce themselves?

And the answer to that, Bill Clintonlike, is probably, it depends what you mean by "edit." Edit means so many things. Editors do so many things.

In the US they like to get more involved. This can be a good thing or a bad thing. Michael Korda once told me it all dated back to Jacqueline Susann, who wrote books that were readable, but all typed in upper case in something that didn't have a lot to do with English; so editors began getting their feet wet and getting involved in the writing process, making suggestions for things to cut, rewriting where they had to, and so on.

It's certainly true that UK editors tend much more to look at a manuscript, ask themselves "Is this publishable?" and if the answer's "Yes", they publish it.

(In my case, the best thing an editor can do while I'm writing something is to keep cheerful and encouraging, say nice things, and keep getting words out of me by hook or by crook. I'll sort out the problems for the second draft.)

Then there are copyeditors. Most editors now are too busy to actually spend 30-plus hours reading a manuscript with a blue pencil scrutinising each wayward comma. But, they figure, somebody has to do it.

In each case, the main thing an editor is meant to do when they do their jobs is to make you look good. I think the analogy is much less a musician producing her own records, and a lot more like an actor doing his own make-up and wigs, or an actor in a one man show doing her own lighting. Sure, you can do it yourself, but it's much easier, and you'll get a better look, if you get another pair of eyes and hands in to do it.

Editors make you look good. That's their job. Whether it's by pointing out that the relationship between the lead character and his father was never satisfyingly resolved, or by pointing out you've changed the spelling of the name of the landlady between her two appearances. Like the lighting guy, they are another pair of eyes.

And I always like another pair of eyes. If I'm writing a short story I'll send the first draft out to a bunch of friends for feedback; they may see things I've missed, or point out places I thought I'd got away with something that I hadn't. Or tell me the title is crap. Or whatever. I listen, because it's in my best interests to listen. I may listen and then decide that, no, I like my title, and the relationship between the protagonist and his father is just what I want it to be, or whatever, but I'll still listen.

(Something I learned ages ago. When people tell you there's something wrong with a story, they're almost always right. When they tell what it is that's wrong and how it can be fixed, they're almost always wrong.)

Of course, there are authors out there who are not edited. This is not necessarily a good thing. I read a bestselling book by a bestselling one of them. He had a flashback scene in which one of the neighborhood kids was wandering around, twelve years before he was born. An editor would have put a pencil mark beside it and said "Do you mean this?" and the embarrassed author would have admitted that, no, he wasn't thinking, he just mentally thought of the names of some of the kids and forgot that one of them would have been minus twelve in that scene, and fixed it. So I don't plan to become one of the great unedited.

I would say that when you find a good editor, you stick with them; and when you find a good copyeditor you stick with them as best you can.

(Often, in the US, they won't tell you who the copyeditor is. They are more anonymous than taxmen. Apparently, there have been too many occasions in the history of publishing of overstressed authors ringing up copyeditors at 2:00am and screaming "I'm going to kill you, you bastard—how dare you change my noble and beautiful *forgot* to an insipid and lustreless *forgotten?*" that you are actively discouraged from talking to them before, during or after the copyediting process. This makes it hard to know when you got a good one, and harder still to keep them when you did....)

We're very close to posting the details on the signing tour. Honest. And, whew.

posted by Neil Gaiman 2:38 PM

Wednesday, March 21, 2001

Nothing exciting to report on *American Gods* today. I'm back writing the *Death: The High Cost of Living* movie, which is

a) incredibly late—this is my fault, and the fault of *American Gods* being at least twice as long as I'd originally planned—and

b) hard writing. In some ways the hardest thing I've had to write in an age.

The biggest problem I'm having with it is, I already wrote it once, as a comic. That was in the Summer of 1992. One thing I knew that I'd do this time, was give the characters new dialogue—words you write to be read are not words you write to be spoken aloud. They do different things.

But the dialogue is really hard to write: I'll squint, and I'll squirm and I'll rack my brains, and I'll imagine, and then I'll carefully type a line. And then, later, I'll check, and find all too often I've just written the same line, often word for word, that I gave those characters in 1992.

So I'm worrying less about that, now, and more about just getting it onto the desks of the people who want to read it by the first of April.

Tonight, and until Sunday, I'll be attending the International Conference for the Fantastic in the Arts. Wearing the kind of beard that caused friction between Bertie and Jeeves in the beginning of a Wodehouse novel ("But Jeeves, dash it, it makes me look distinguished!" "So you say, sir," etc), and was always shaved off following the return of the prize pig or the marriage of Bingo Little at the end of the last chapter, to everyone's relief.

posted by Neil Gaiman 12:25 PM

Thursday, March 22, 2001

I wrote an incredibly tired post last night, told it to publish, it zapped off temperamentally into the ether, and I went to bed.

At IAFA currently. Thrilled that so many people—critics, authors and a couple of academics—have already read *American Gods*. More thrilled that the ones who have start by telling me that, yes, they liked my other books, but this is really good. No, really good. Had several conversations about the dedication (it's dedicated to Roger Zelazny and Kathy Acker) which was odd and sad.

Favorite comment on the beard, an astonished "You look like a grown up!" from an old friend. Hah! It still dies tonight.

Meanwhile, Joe Fulgham, over at The Dreaming, has done a lovely banner ad for *American Gods*. It has lightning on it and everything. (Go and take a look.) Please feel free to steal it and use it and link it to here, or to the countdown front page (www.americangods.com—probably best as we will be putting more stuff up here soon than just the journal), or to Amazon.com or your favorite local or online bookseller or whoever.

Or to create your own.

posted by Neil Gaiman 6:42 AM

Tuesday, March 27, 2001

Another long post was just written, telling you all that I was hiding out and doing nothing else but trying to finish the *Death* movie script; and what happened at IAFA; and that yes, the beard went half-way through, so I look like me again; and then I wrote all about the tour and how the US signings were almost finalised and will be announced here the moment they are.

Then I said that the US tour would be June 19th to July 2nd; the UK tour July 5th to 12th; the Canadian bit from July 20th to 25th.

And I mentioned that I wasn't doing any other *American Gods* signing this year (although I'm meant to be in Brazil at the end of May and in Spain in August). And I talked about how I'd just had a request from an academic journal in Brazil to reprint the bit of this journal that talks about what editors do (I said yes).

And all in all it was a lot like this post, only twice as long, and really interesting. But then I put down my foot and knocked the phone cord out of the wall, and that was that.

posted by Neil Gaiman 11:15 AM

So we're edging from the editing (and copy editing) process into the promotional process here. This is the third stage of getting a book published. (The first stage is writing it. The second is editing the manuscript. The third is promoting the book to the trade. The fourth is promoting the book to the public. The fifth is having a good sit down when it's all over and contemplating a nice restful career as a lion tamer or a steeplejack.) (Which reminds me, I've still not yet written about the day of being photographed for the author photos. One day soon.)

And I know this (that we're moving into promoting the book to the trade) because this weekend I shall be in Las Vegas, talking to Borders Books people—store managers and suchlike I guess—and telling them… actually I have no idea what I'm meant to be talking to them about— whether I'm "giving a talk" or making a speech, or just getting up there and affably winging it (something I quite enjoy doing from time to time). But I imagine that at the end of whatever it is we're going to be doing, they'll all know that *American Gods* exists.

They'll all have copies of the *American Gods* missing-the-last-chapter galleys as well, and I'll probably sign them. All I really hope is that they read them when they get home—or give them to the people who work in the stores who want to read them—rather than just stick them out on eBay, unread.

posted by Neil Gaiman 5:13 PM

Saturday, March 31, 2001

It's late at night in Las Vegas, a city I have come to to talk to a convocation of Borders Books managers. That's tomorrow night. Tonight I went to see Penn and Teller's show at the Rio (it was wonderful) and then went on a very brief excursion with them to a rave to see Ouchie the S&M clown (who was seen), and now back to my hotel room and bed.

Blogger, the thing that powers this journal, was down yesterday, so I didn't get to write about the good *American Gods* thing that happened. Which is, it's been picked up by the SF Book Club as the lead title for its month, and by the Book of the Month Club as an alternate pick, and they've paid real money for the rights, which is a good thing, on both counts.

Tomorrow's post will be all about the Borders talk and suchlike, I expect. And so (as that nice Mr Pepys used to write) to bed.

posted by Neil Gaiman 12:32 AM

Sunday, April 01, 2001

So this evening was the convocation of Borders Books general managers. Borders Books managers are very nice people who come up to you and say "I've never read anything you've written, but there's a girl in our accounts department who will kill me if I don't come back with your signature." I think tonight I must have saved several hundred Borders books managers from sudden employee-related death on their return home.

So, apart from the disaster, it was a great evening.

("What was the disaster?" I hear you cry.)

450 *American Gods* proofs were shipped to the Las Vegas hotel where the event is taking place. The Morrow rep picked me up, and drove me to the event. We walked in, and were met by two beautiful and radiant but troubled young ladies from Borders, who wanted to know if there were meant to be any books…

The boxes of books had arrived (according to an invoice) at the hotel some days ago, but nobody had actually seen them.

We hunted for them. People talked to other people on walkie talkies. Other people took to drink. I went and nibbled some salad at the buffet. Nope. No books.

Then I got up to make a speech. It was a fun speech. I apologised for the lack of books. Then I told them why I am currently breaking in a new leather jacket: Jonathan Carroll knew that I'd donated my old leather jacket to the Comic Book Legal Defense Fund (it raised over $6000 on eBay), and had, out of the blue, sent me a wonderful leather jacket he'd bought before deciding he was not a leather jacket person. I told them that, since he was in Vienna and wasn't going to be here talking to them, that they should all make an effort to handsell Jonathan Carroll books in their stores, and they should read him too. (And enough of them came up to me after the speech and asked for titles that I figure some of them were paying attention.)

And then I told them about *American Gods,* and answered a couple of questions, and then...

Lacking copies of *American Gods,* I signed pieces of paper. Also signed tote bags, tee shirts, and large fuzzy snakes. And many books brought along by people for themselves or other people.

Borders books people are very nice people, and I had a great time. Except for the disaster, of course.

(I've told them that if they find the books before I leave Las Vegas, I'll sign them for the managers.)

posted by Neil Gaiman 12:02 AM

Tuesday, April 03, 2001

Steve Erickson is one of my favorite authors, and he's one of those people whose opinions matter to me. We just got a blurb in from him. It's as beautifully written as anything by Steve...(Read *Days Between Stations.* Read *Tours of the Black Clock.* Read *Arc d'X.* Read the one about the 1996 election, the title of which I've forgotten.) [*American Nomad,* I think.] He says...

> Oh yeah, I know this place: the four-in-the-morning Hollywood where you wake in the dark from a dream of paradise, with the sinking feeling you've been had. Piercingly observed, jaggedly poetic, ruthlessly cutting a path through graveyards of dead stars and dead money and dead feelings, this novel is the map back to dawn.
>
> Steve Erickson

Which thrilled me, more than I can easily say.

The *Death* movie script has been handed in. Lots more movie stuff to do this month, before the Writers Strike starts. (Next stop, *Ramayana* treatment. Then *The Confessions of William Henry Ireland* treatment.)

But today is a sort of day off. At any rate, I went for a walk in the woods, and everything felt like Spring in a Disney nature movie, as the snow, which has been there since mid-November, has finally started to melt.

posted by Neil Gaiman 2:50 PM

Thursday, April 05, 2001

Sorry about the delay on these. HarperCollins were waiting for the last couple to be finalised. These are all the US signings from the June-July tour. They don't include the Canadian signings, or the UK signings.

(If your city, or state, or area of the country isn't on here, it's not my fault. I don't pick 'em. If you can get your local bookstore to wail piteously enough to HarperCollins, we might be able to get them on the *American Gods* in paperback/*Coraline* tour next May, if there is one.)

Neil Gaiman's Tour Dates

6/19/01 6:00 PM	New York, NY	Borders
6/20/01 8:00 PM	Huntington, NY	Book Revue
6/21/01 7:00 PM	Champaign/Savoy, IL	Pages For All Ages
6/22/01 1:00 PM	Evanston, IL	Stars Our Destination
6/22/01 8:00 PM	Skokie, IL	Barnes & Noble
6/23/01 1:00 PM	Lexington, KY	Joseph-Beth Booksellers
6/23/01 7:00 PM	Dayton, OH	Books & Co.
6/24/01 1:00 PM	Cleveland, OH	Joseph-Beth Booksellers
6/25/01 4:00 PM	Seattle, WA	Third Place Booksellers
6/25/01 7:00 PM	Seattle, WA	University Booksellers
6/26/01 7:30 PM	Menlo Park, CA	Kepler's Books
6/27/01 1:00 PM	San Francisco, CA	The Booksmith
6/27/01 7:30 PM	Berkeley, CA	Cody's Booksellers
6/28/01 12:30 PM	San Diego, CA	Mysterious Galaxy
6/28/01 7:00 PM	Los Angeles, CA	Vroman's Books
6/29/01 8:00 PM	Los Angeles, CA	Book Soup
7/1/01 2:00 PM	Minneapolis, MN	DreamHaven
7/2/01 7:00 PM	Rosedale, MN	Barnes & Noble

Feel very free to cut out the above and repost it anywhere you feel potentially interested people would like to see it. Tell the world. Go on...

posted by Neil Gaiman 10:38 AM

Friday, April 06, 2001

And the question comes in from places as far away and as far apart (except of course alphabetically) as France and Finland, "What is happening with foreign editions of *American Gods*? When will it come out in my country?" And the answer is...

It'll be a while. (Except in Australia, where they'll be importing the Headline edition from the UK.)

My literary agents, Writers House, are waiting for the bound galleys to come in from HarperCollins—they should be around any moment now. Then they will send out copies of those galleys to their sub-agents in various countries all around the world, who will show them to the publishers who will offer them money for the rights to publish the book.

(It's probably worth mentioning here that at last year's Frankfurt Book Fair, the foreign publishers were all told that *American Gods* was coming.

Really it was. So they are all prepared to read it. And, with luck, to like it and offer lots of yen, francs, marks, zloties and crumbulae.)

And then the foreign publishers will get translators in, who will try and figure out how to translate some things and still keep the spirit of the book, something that I do not envy them on. (A French example from Patrick Marcel, who translated *Neverwhere* and *Smoke and Mirrors* into French: Thursday in English translates as Thor's Day, in French it's Mardi—Mars's Day. This apparently trivial fact can be quite important in a book with gods in it.)

And then, probably sometime in the following 12-24 months, the book will come out. Sometimes I get sent copies. Often I find out about them only when I sign one for someone, or hear about them from people who grumble about the Serbian translations of my books, and I say "I didn't know I'd written any Serbian books".

Sometimes the publishers bring me in to do signings for them, and sometimes they don't (mostly they don't, but it's fun when they do). Sometimes the translations are good, and sometimes they aren't (I normally find out from people telling me how much better it is to read the book in English). (I'm still waiting for someone to come up and tell me how much improved the book was by being translated into Japanese or Greek; it's only a matter of time.)

posted by Neil Gaiman 1:32 PM

Saturday, April 07, 2001

Oops. Thursday's not Mardi. Mardi is Tue's Day. Tew (also known as Tyr) is an almost forgotten god of war and justice, and a much nicer guy than Odin. His hand was bitten off by Fenris Wolf.

I'm off for a few days, taking my son to see the various colleges that have accepted him, to see which one he wants to attend.

And a photocopy of the *American Gods* book cover arrived this morning. And it has the photo of me, large on the back, which was going to be my cue to tell you all the story of the photo day, but I'm running for a plane, so you are just going to have to be patient a little longer.

posted by Neil Gaiman 8:54 AM

Wednesday, April 11, 2001

I have been asked to give some do's and don'ts for people coming to signings. And although I've written dos and don'ts and suggestions for stores before (and may possibly reprint them here, for contrast), I don't think I've ever written any suggestions for the people who actually make the signings possible.

If you've never been to any kind of signing with me, the first thing you should know is, wherever possible it'll start with a reading and a question and answer session. Then you'll be herded into lines (or, the first 50 people will be called, just like at a deli counter) and I'll start signing stuff for people. And that will go on until everyone's done, and happy, and out the door.

So here you go… Some dos and don'ts in no particular order…

1. It can be a good idea to call the store first and find out if they have any specific ground rules. Some do, some don't. Will they be handing out numbers? Will you have to buy a copy of *American Gods* from them in hardback to get prime place in the line or will it be first come first served? What about books you bought somewhere else? Can you bring your ferret?

2. Get there reasonably early if you can. I'll always try and make sure that anyone in line during the posted signing times gets stuff signed. At evening signings I'll always stay and make sure everyone goes away happy, but on this tour there will be several places where I'll need to go from a signing to another signing, so don't cut it fine.

3. You may own everything I've ever written. I'm very grateful. I'm probably not going to sign it all, so you had better simply pick out your favourite thing and bring that along.

4. As a rule, I tend to tell stores I'll sign 3 things people bring with them—plus any copies of the new book you buy (if you have six brothers or sisters and buy one each, I'll sign them all). But stores may have their own policies—and we may wind up changing the rules as we go in order to make sure that everyone gets stuff signed.

5. Eat first. I'm not kidding. If it's a night-time signing of the kind that can go on for a long time, bring sandwiches or something to nibble (some signings with numbers handed out may make it possible for you to go out and eat and come back. Or you may be first in line. But plan for a worst case scenario of several hours of standing and shuffling your way slowly around a store). (If it's a daytime signing somewhere that a line may snake out of a store into the hot sun, bring something to drink. I always feel guilty when people pass out.)

6. You may be in that line for a while, so talk to the people around you. You never know, you could make a new friend. I've signed books for kids whose parents met in signing lines (although to the best of my knowledge none of them were actually conceived there). And while we're on the subject, bring something to read while waiting. Or buy something to read—you'll be in a book shop, after all.

7. Don't worry. You won't say anything stupid. It'll be fine. My heart tends to go out to people who've stood in line for hours trying to think of the single brilliant witty erudite thing that they can say when they get to

the front of the line, and when it finally happens they put their books in front of me and go blank, or make a complete mess of whatever they were trying to say. If you have anything you want to ask or say, just ask, or say it, and if you get a blank look from me it's probably because I'm slightly brain dead after signing several thousand things that day.

8. The only people who ever get short shrift from me are the people who turn up with tape recorders who try and tape interviews during signings. I won't do them—it's unfair on the other people in the line, and unfair on me (and I was as curt with the guy from the *L.A . Times* who tried it as I am to people who decide on the spur of the moment to try and tape something for their college paper). If you want to do an interview, ask the bookstore who you should talk to in order to set it up.

9. Take things out of plastic bags before you reach me. Firstly, it speeds things up. Secondly, I once ripped the back off a $200 comic taking it out of a plastic bag, when the back of the comic caught on the tape. The person who owned it was very sweet about it, but tears glistened in his eyes as I signed, and I could hear him wailing softly as he walked away.

10. Yes, I'll happily personalize the stuff I sign, to you, or to friends. If it's a birthday or wedding present, tell me.

11. Remember your name. Know how to spell it, even under pressure, such as being asked.
[If you have a nice simple name, like Bob or Dave or Jennifer, don't be surprised if I ask you how to spell it. I've encountered too many Bhob's, Daev's and even, once, a Jeniffer to take any spelling for granted.]

12. No, I probably won't do a drawing for you, because there are 300 people behind you, and if I had to draw for everyone we'd be finishing at 4.00am—on the other hand, if you're prepared to wait patiently until the end, I may do it then, if my hand still works.

13. If it means a lot to you, yes, I'll sign your lunchbox/skin/guitar/leather jacket/wings—but if it's something strange you may want to make sure you have a pen that writes on strange surfaces legibly. I'll have lots of pens, but they may not write on feathers.

14. At the start of the tour the answer to "Doesn't your hand hurt?" is "No." By the end of the tour, it's probably going to be "Yes."

15. Yes, you can take my picture, and yes, of course you can be in the photo, that's the point isn't it? There's always someone near the front of the line who will take your photo.

16. I do my best to read all the letters I'm given and not lose all the presents I'm given. Sometimes I'll read letters on the plane to the next place. But given the sheer volume of letters and gifts, you probably won't get a reply, unless you do. (On one previous tour I tried to write postcards to everyone who gave me something at the last stop on postcards at

the next hotel. Never again.) If you're after a reply or to have me read something, you're much better off not giving it to me on a tour. Post it to me care of DreamHaven books in Minneapolis.

(And although things people give me get posted back, on the last tour FedEx lost one box of notes and gifts, and on the tour before that hotel staff lost or stole another box. So smaller things I can put into a suitcase are going to be more popular than four-foot high paintings done on slabs of beechwood.)

17. No, I probably won't have dinner/a beer/sushi with you after the signing. If it's a daytime signing I'll be on my way to the next signing; and if it's an evening signing I'll be heading back to my hotel room because I'll be getting up at six a.m. to fly to the next city. If there actually is any spare time on the tour it'll've been given to journalists, and if there's any time on top of that old friends will have started e-mailing me two or three months before the tour started to say "You'll be in the Paphlagonian Barnes and Noble on the 23rd. That's just a short yak-hop from my yurt. We must get together," and would have got themselves put on the schedule. (Still, it never hurts to ask.)

18. If you can't read what I wrote, just ask me. After a couple of hours of signing my handwriting can get pretty weird.

19. If I sign it in silver or gold, give it a minute or so to dry before putting it back in its bag or closing the cover, otherwise you'll soon have a gold or silver smudge and nothing more.

If I think of anything else, I'll mention it as I go—or expand this one…

posted by Neil Gaiman 7:03 PM

Friday, April 13, 2001

"What's in that box you just opened?" asked my daughter.

"Pieces of paper," I said.

"It says *American Gods* on the box. I thought it was books."

"No. They're just title pages. 5000 of them."

"5000 in that box?"

"750 in that box. 4,250 still to come."

"Why are they sending them to you?"

"Because I have to write my name on them."

"On all of them?"

"Yes."

"Why?"

"Because America is a very big place, and not everyone can get to a book signing. This way stores who order them will be able to sell a signed, limited edition for the same price as the regular ones, and so people in Texas or Florida or Utah will be able to buy signed books. See down at the bottom where it says 'This is a signed first edition of a limited number of 5000 copies.'? I'll sign above there, like this."

"Does that say 'Neil Gaiman'? It looks more like 'Nel Gurgle.' "

"It's how I sign my name."

"Will they take a long time to sign?"

"I expect so."

"When will you do it?"

"When I'm on the telephone. Or watching TV. Or listening to music. Or travelling."

"Can I sign some for you, to help?"

"I'm afraid not."

"I could write Nel Gurgle as good as you can."

"It has to be me."

"Oh. Okay then. Have fun. I'm going to ride my bike."

First sunny, spring-like day of the year, and I'm writing Neil Gaiman on 750 pieces of paper. And I make a mental note to make sure that I don't sign more than 5000 and a few for spoilage—it's not at all unknown for people who ask you to sign 500 or 5000 sheets of paper to send you an extra thousand or so to sign, in case of spoilage, and they then destroy the remainder. Which is fair enough, except for my wrist and how fast the spring goes in this part of the world.

Lots more wonderful blurbs from authors I respect came in on the book, which made me very happy. (Including William Gibson, Jonathan Carroll, Chris Carter, Diana Gabaldon and Tim Powers.) I'll post them if I get a second. Meanwhile I'm going to carry on signing things.

posted by Neil Gaiman 11:29 AM

Monday, April 16, 2001

The whole process of getting and giving blurbs is an odd one.

(Minor side note. If memory serves, "blurb" as a word was created by American humorist Gelett Burgess (who also wrote the "Purple Cow" poem). It means, basically, the puff stuff on the back of a book that tells you you ought to read it. The other word Gelett Burgess tried to introduce was "huzzlecoo" meaning, I think, to schmooze. It failed to catch on.)

I've met people who assumed that the whole blurb-giving process was one that authors were paid to do. Not so.

Generally blurbs mean one of two things; either the person giving the blurb really liked the book, or that complex networks of favour and obligation have been called into play.

It's seldom simple logrolling—normally the reason why two authors say nice things about each other's stuff is that they like each other's stuff. But the process of getting something read, and of getting a quote can mean anything. It could mean that you have the same editor or agent or film producer as the book author, and they pressed you to read it. It could mean that the author is someone who did you a good turn once. And normally the favour is in getting the book read—anything after that depends mostly on whether or not the reader liked the book.

A very few blurbs make a difference. Clive Barker's career was given a huge leg up by Stephen King's "I have seen the future of horror and it is Clive Barker", and I think *Sandman* was given a huger boost than I ever realised from the Norman Mailer quote (although, oddly enough, DC has never run that on anything except *Season of Mists*). I doubt that they actually changed anything for either of us; they might have sped up processes that would have happened anyway, though.

Most of them probably don't do a thing. But in book publishing (as with movies) nobody knows anything. So they put them on the book jackets anyway and they hope.

Most successful authors could make a life's profession simply reading books and giving blurbs—in any given week I get two or three books arriving with nice pleas from editors to read their book and say nice things about it. Also I get a couple of things from authors.

As to what I blurb…It depends a lot on what gets read, what I have time to read, whether it's something portable and book-sized or a huge heap of paper, sometimes even if there's anything I have to say after reading something. It also depends a lot on whether or not I liked it once I have read it, if I did read it.

Sometimes I wind up reading something long after it's come out in paperback and just feeling faintly guilty, especially if I did like it a lot. But there is only so much time, and there's stuff I buy to read I never get time to settle down with…

It is good blurb etiquette, as an author, to say, if you cannot give a blurb, "I am sorry, I am too busy." This could mean that you are too busy to look at it, or that you looked at it and wish you hadn't.

It is not good blurb etiquette to do as an unnamed comics genius— oh, what the hell, it was R. Crumb—did when sent a reading copy of *Good Omens*, over a decade ago, which is to write a several page letter to the publisher telling them not only how much you hated it but also imploring them not to publish it. (Or so my editor said. She didn't send me the letter, which I thought a pity, nor did she run it on the back cover, which I thought might have been fun.)

It is good blurb etiquette if you're hoping someone will blurb your book to send it to them (or have your editor send it to them) and then not to bug them, unless you're heading for the deadline and you want to politely point out to them that unless you get a blurb from them soon it won't be used even if they did like it.

It's lousy blurb etiquette to bug an author. Saying things like "Well, why don't you read a chapter and if that's okay write something nice—one chapter, one lousy solitary chapter, is that asking so much?" and "Hey, no problem, if you're that busy I'll write the blurb, you can just put your name to it" are not usually ways to endear yourself to an author. (And yes, I've had both of them, and yes, I said no thank you.)

Because you're asking for two things—you're asking for time, and you're asking for some kind of endorsement. Mostly in an attempt to try and tell people what kind of book something is, in a kind of abbreviated word of mouth—"Gee. Maurice X. Boggs thinks this is an amazing book and Maurice X. Boggs is my favourite author, I should pick it up". This works best, I think, as a kind of positioning—Stephen King tends mostly to give blurbs to things that adjectives like "Gripping. Relentless," can be applied to. He might enjoy reading a heartwarming novel about a funny skunk named Zonko and how he melts the heart of a crusty old widower…but publishers are unlikely to send him that book with a begging letter asking him to read it and to say something nice about it.

Some authors stop giving blurbs. Every now and again, I stop doing blurbs, and every now and again I stop writing introductions. (And last year I was extremely unimpressed when a blurb I had written was actually printed by someone as an introduction.) The hiatus lasts for a year or two, and then I feel guilty or someone asks me at the right time, and I relent.

Some authors don't relent. Harlan Ellison stopped doing blurbs years ago. If publishers start dunning him for blurbs he lets them know how much he charges by the hour as a reader's fee to read the books, and makes sure they understand that there is no guarantee at the end of the reading he will feel moved to say anything at all, and in fact, he probably won't. I don't think any publishers have taken him up on this, which means that Harlan, as he takes great pleasure in telling people, doesn't give blurbs.

There are other problems with the whole blurb thing…

Once I was given a book by an editor I liked, by an author I liked. It was the editor's first major book. It was the author's first book in some years. It was a big deal for both of them. I didn't like the book. I wanted to, but I didn't. But I didn't want to let them down. So I wrote "When Thaddeus Q. Bliggins (not his real name) is writing at his best there's no-one in the field that can touch him" and felt that honour was satisfied.

My favourite how to blurb a book you don't like story was one my agent told me, about a writer she had at the start of her career, who was a good friend of A Famous Author, and was confident of his ability to get a blurb for his book—and certain that with a blurb from a famous author his manuscript would immediately be snapped up by a publisher after a frenzied auction. He handed over the manuscript to his friend, and the blurb came in. It was short, effective, enthusiastic…and entirely unusable, this being the early 80s, and the blurb being entirely composed of profanities, as enthusiastic as they were obscene. The book was never published. For *American Gods*, the books for blurbs went out to a fairly select band. Authors I thought would like it or respond to it who somehow seemed to map onto parts of the book.

For some of them I wrote personal notes to go with them. Partly because I know I respond well to notes from the author, and partly because it was fun to say some hellos. (In a couple of cases I even got to cheat and write a fan letter, or an "I've not seen you for ten years—howthefuckareyou?" letter). For some I didn't. For a few people I sent e-mails. The others went out from Jennifer Hershey, my editor, or Jack Womack, the book's publicist at HarperCollins (and a wonderful author in his own right).

And, as you've already seen if you're reading this journal, blurbs came in—most of them accompanied by letters saying that they really really liked the book (just in case I was worried that they were only saying nice things about it from a sense of duty).

As the deadline for the book jacket to be finalised approached, we made a few calls to remind people. (I phoned Terry Gilliam, mostly because I like talking to Terry Gilliam, to discover that he was on holiday for two weeks somewhere far away from a telephone. So no luck there.)

(A minor anecdotal interruption here: in 1989 Gollancz sent Terry Gilliam a copy of *Good Omens* for a blurb. Somewhere the letter and the book got separated and Terry read the book assuming it was something he'd been sent as a possible movie...and now, twelve years later, he's gone on holiday having just finished the second draft of the *Good Omens* movie script. Proving that the world is an odd place, but not unpleasant.)

The blurb deadline has pretty much, I think, come and gone on *American Gods*—if people say nice things about it now we can use it in the advertising, but they may have to wait for the paperback until people know that they liked it. However, one that I'll really try to get onto the hardback cover arrived out of the blue today, entirely unsolicited. Not just unsolicited but accompanied by a phone call reminding me that the party in question does not give blurbs.

> Gaiman's new novel walked in the door on Friday after-
> noon. By Saturday evening I had eaten it in one gulp.
> *American Gods:* alarming, charming, even winsome;
> Gaiman: serially inventive, surprising, purely remark-
> able. And, oh, is it well-written.
>
> Harlan Ellison 16 April 2001

I signed the sheets of paper for the limited edition from the box of 750 sheets. I signed and I signed. Eventually I asked my poor assistant if she wouldn't mind counting them, because I was sure I'd signed a lot more than 750 sheets. Turns out the box contained 2,500 of the things. Mostly I'm just signing them. Sometimes I'm drawing eyes, too. Very occasionally I've started doodling and drawing, mostly so far drawings of a very crusty Uncle Sam. And most of the time I'm using other colour inks than black, so that the people who pick them up don't go "Oh, they just print those signatures". They don't. It's me.

posted by Neil Gaiman 9:25 PM

Friday, April 20, 2001

Off to the UK for a few days to see some people and listen to some music. Am in an airport, and have just discovered that the modem was inadvertently removed from my computer, so I'll

a) be offline for a few days and

b) have to disappoint all the people I'd promised I'd finally tell the story of the day I got the jacket photo taken—I was planning to write it on the plane and post it this weekend. You may have to wait until next week.

(No, it's not a cruel joke by an evil author—and I'm mostly grumpy right now as I'm going to have to lug a notebook computer and bag around England for four days and it'll be about as useful as hauling a paving stone.) (Well, I also have a speech to write and a few other things, but really on the road it's an e-mail machine.)

posted by Neil Gaiman 3:31 PM

Friday, April 27, 2001

Went to England for four days. Heard some wonderful music. Came back. Spent a day at home (a whole day!) and then flew to LA where I am to be Master of Ceremonies at the Nebula Award banquet Saturday night.

I'll be doing a signing Saturday 28th of April (tomorrow, or later today, depending on when you read this) (unless you read this after Saturday, of course), at the LA book fair at UCLA at 1:00pm, at the Dangerous Visions/SFWA area. Come and say hullo if you're in the area.

Lots of interesting things happening—the permissions were all gathered in in a manic last-minute flurry which owed an awful lot to Kelly Notaras at HarperCollins US; the Canadian signings seem to have edged earlier and the UK signings have continued later and I'm not sure at this point I get a single day off (excluding transatlantic travel days) between June 18th and July 20th; I may be doing a reading in tandem with a Magnetic Fields concert in June in New York; various interesting media things happening—lots of magazines and periodicals doing reviews and features on the book.

And I am not writing about any of these things because, with the writers' strike looming, I am madly trying to finish writing some additional material for a very cool Polish/Japanese film called *Avalon*, so am spending all my time in my hotel room playing and replaying the video of the film and making notes and writing bits.

The best bit about the writers' strike is a bunch of contracts that have been being negotiated with various studios' business affairs departments for the last 18-months-to-a-year were messengered over to my hotel today, and I sat and signed, and signed, and signed. Obviously a strike, like a hanging, concentrates the mind wonderfully.

posted by Neil Gaiman 11:26 PM

Also today I read Henry Selick's first draft of the *Coraline* movie, which was really cool (and really faithful to the book, sometimes almost disconcertingly so).

And because I have this power (apparently there are currently about 19,000 of you reading this thing) I'll recommend a few things: while I was travelling I read and enjoyed Nalo Hopkinson's yummy *Midnight Robber,* M. John Harrison's magnificent short stories *Travel Arrangements,* and the *History of the Basque People* by the guy that wrote *Cod.* Also read Geoff Ryman's *Lust* on the plane home—a powerful and odd book, about, it seemed to me, everything except lust.

And am currently playing Hamell on Trial's lovely *Choochtown* a great deal, and because my assistant Lorraine left Lorraine Bowen's *Bossy Nova* CD in the car, I was getting very fond of the Bombay remix of the Crumble song before I came out to LA, bringing with me no music.

posted by Neil Gaiman 11:26 PM

Sunday, April 29, 2001

So here's the speech I made tonight, introducing the Nebula Awards. This was the text I went from, and I sort of smoothed it up as I went. "Black Pudding" was changed to "blood sausage" because few people knew what a black pudding was. [Note—the "HarperCollins Royalty Statements" is just a cheap laugh line, and not intended as a slur or commentary in any way on HarperCollins royalty statements; and anyway, I have been assured that Simon and Schuster's royalty statements are worse.]

And as soon as *Avalon* is done then I'll write about *American Gods* again. Maybe even… well, we'll see.

> It occurred to me recently that if I were now to meet myself at the age of 12—the age, as all of you here know well, that has been called the Golden Age of Science Fiction—I would, I have no doubt, be an extreme disappointment to my twelve year old self.
>
> He might be impressed by the fact that I'm a writer—but then, he knew he was going to be a writer. That I'm

that one of a relatively rare clan, a writer who makes his living writing, would make no difference to my 12 year old self. He is, after all, convinced that the simple action of writing a short story and getting it published is like winning the grand prize at the end of the Quiz Show: the roof opens up and goods and money tumble down. He also has a strong suspicion that supermarkets, bank managers, and car lots will, on production of a book with an author's name on the spine, allow the author the pick of the best of what they have, and never charge him a penny.

(My 12 year old self has not met any authors.)

As I said, he knows he wants to be a writer. And, with a 12 year old arrogance that is utter and absolute, he knows what kind of an author he wants to be. He wants to be the kind of author who wins Nebula Awards.

Which is to say he wants to grow up to be an SF writer, and an SF writer of a particular kind. He wants to grow up to write the kind of SF that changes how people see the world. He knows there's a difference between the Hugos and the Nebulas, and he likes the way that some books have won both of them. He wants to be a Delany, or a Zelazny or an Ellison. He wouldn't mind being a Heinlein or a Niven or a Le Guin. He wants to write SF.

And I would have disappointed him. I didn't grow up to be an SF writer, except possibly in the loosest most "SF doesn't stand for science fiction, it stands for anything we damn well please" sense of the word.

Understand, this came as an enormous surprise to me. My first book was a collection of SF quotes, after all. (I wrote it with Kim Newman, it was called *Ghastly Beyond Belief*, and it contained a raft of quotes from SF books and movies. My favourite was from Guy N. Smith's seminal giant crabs novel *Night of the Crabs* "He wasn't going to leave her alone that night, crabs or no crabs.")

I was sure I was going to be an SF writer, as sure as anyone can be of anything. I just didn't turn out that way.

Most writers of fiction are autodidacts, to some degree or another. We learn to teach ourselves what we need. We get in there fast and shallow and we suck the life and the juice from the subject in our own way. Then we manage to give the impression that we know everything about the subject in our writing.

I feel sorry for all the teachers who attempted to teach me the rudiments of subjects that I had no interest in. If I'd known that I'd need history and geography to write with, I would have studied much harder, just as I would have paid more attention in Maths if I'd known that one day I was going to have to make sense of HarperCollins royalty statements.

The subject I paid most attention to in school was SF. That they didn't teach it made no difference. It was what I was studying. I was reading all the SF that was published and available, and, having finished that, I was reading everything I could find that was out of print, dusty, forgotten.

I enjoyed the good books, and I enjoyed the bad books. I read everything.

But most of all I looked out for and hunted down and read things that had won the Nebula. Because I knew it was going to be good. Not just popular good, but well-written, and wise, and that it would stretch my head into places it had not been before.

I am almost 30 years older than that boy, and I have become both more blasé and more cynical about awards. I've won more than my share of awards. I've been an awards judge, and have learned that awards judges, like the makers of black pudding, do their business behind closed doors for a reason. I've learned that popular and democratic awards are too often fickle, and easily manipulated, and no guarantee of lasting worth.

Still, as individuals and as a group, the Nebulas are wonderful things. It's a fine thing to be nominated for an award. It's a finer thing to win an award—at least until the next morning, when you have to face a blank sheet of paper, and you find the writing no easier than it ever was—and, often, it's harder.

But the real importance of awards like the Nebula, I like to think, is in telling us, and, more importantly, telling the next generations of SF writers, where to look, where to go, where the best writing and the coolest ideas are to be found. And this, after all, is what we are here for tonight.

posted by Neil Gaiman 2:20 AM

Thursday, May 03, 2001

There. I'm home again from all the travelling, and now it's time to recharge my batteries, as I'm pretty much spent. Tonight I holed up in a small recording studio, reading short pieces (and a long one) for the next spoken word CD. More recording tomorrow night. More Avalon tomorrow. And I think I may start the second draft of *Death* as soon as that's done: it'll be more fun than waiting to see if there's a strike coming or not.

And meanwhile, let's talk about the triumvirate of *Kirkus, Publisher's Weekly* and *Booklist* reviews (and *Library Journal* makes up a quartet).

Overall, I'm not sure how much influence reviews have in the real world. I've seen a publisher (Workmans) get scared by a bad review in the *New York Times* and more or less dump a book, but the book itself—*Good Omens*—has gone on to become a perennial bestseller in paperback without them. (It's just about to be reissued in the US in a new cover.) And I don't know of any other publishers who have ever reacted to reviews at all, good or bad. (They send them to you, and I think they circulate them around in-house, and they are pleased by the good ones and try very hard to keep the bad ones from you. But they don't *do* anything different when faced by bad reviews, if you see what I mean.)

More to the point, I've seen books with amazing reviews, not to mention awards and enthusiastic plaudits from enormously famous writers sell the same number of books, or less, as the ones that don't get the reviews etc.

(Are sales important? Not as such, but they're the only way authors and publishers have of keeping score and comparing things: without sales you'd not know that, for example, *Neverwhere* in mass-market paperback was much more successful than *Stardust*, although *Stardust* did slightly better in hardcover. I suspect that *Stardust* will be much happier in the forthcoming "trade paperback", the larger format, with a cover that makes it look more like a fairy tale for adults—which it is—and less like a generic fantasy novel—which it certainly isn't.)

Most reviews come out when the book comes out. This is sensible, and strongly encouraged by publishers (who warn reviewers on the slips that go out with review copies not to review the book before publication date) because otherwise people cannot read a good review and then nip immediately down to the bookstore and buy a copy of two of the book.

There are exceptions to the embargo, though. *PW, Kirkus,* and *Booklist* all print their reviews a good way before the books come out, because they are reviewing for the trade: for bookstores and for libraries and for insiders. And their reviews become the Early Word on the book. (On several occasions I've had a good *Kirkus* review of one of my books followed up by movie and TV people calling to get hold of it, so I assume that they read it too, as a good place to go hunting for what they call "properties" and the rest of us call "stories".)

Kirkus, PW and *Booklist* each put a star beside books they especially like. People pay a lot of attention to the stars. (If ever you've seen the phrase "*Kirkus* starred review" after a quote on the back of a bookjacket, that's what it meant.)

Obviously, the reviewers don't always agree. *Neverwhere* got a great review in *Kirkus,* I remember, and a stinker in *PW* (which said that it just showed I was a comics writer and the book would have been okay if only it had had pictures). But since then I've been very lucky with my early reviews in all the periodicals (and/or lucky with my reviewers—*Booklist* names its reviewers but *Kirkus* and [I think] *PW* reviewers are anonymous, and so get to utter pronouncements like the voice of God).

So today my editor, Jennifer Hershey, phoned. She was just on her way to an international book fair in Jerusalem, but wanted to call and read me something before she left the office.

It was the *Kirkus* review of *American Gods.*

She read it to me, then she faxed me a copy.

I'll put the whole thing down here, because this is the first official review the book has got, and by this point, I hope, you're as curious as I was. Obviously, it's copyright *Kirkus Reviews* (although I don't think they'd mind me putting it up here). It's from the May 15ᵗʰ edition.

> An ex-convict is the wandering knight-errant who traverses the wasteland of middle America in this ambitious, gloriously funny, and oddly heartwarming latest from the popular fantasist. (*Stardust* 1999, etc.)
>
> Released from prison after serving a three-year term, Shadow is immediately rocked by the news that his beloved wife Laura has been killed in an automobile accident. While en route to Indiana for her funeral, Shadow meets an eccentric businessman who calls himself Wednesday (a dead giveaway if you're up to speed on your Norse mythology), and passively accepts the latter's offer of an imprecisely defined job. The story skillfully glides onto and off the plane of reality, as a series of mysterious encounters suggest to Shadow that he may not be in Indiana anymore—or indeed, anywhere on Earth he recognises. In dreams, he's visited by a grotesque figure with the head of a buffalo and the voice of a prophet—as well as by Laura's rather alarmingly corporeal ghost. Gaiman layers in a horde of other stories whose relationship to Shadow's adventures are only gradually made clear, while putting his sturdy protagonist through a succession of tests that echo those of Arthurian hero Sir Gawain bound by honor to surrender his life to the malevolent Green Knight, Orpheus braving the terrors of Hades to find and

rescue the woman he loves, and numerous other archetypal figures out of folklore and legend. Only an ogre would reveal much more about this big novel's agreeably intricate plot. Suffice it to say that this is the book that answers the question: When people emigrate to America, what happens to the gods they leave behind?

A magical mystery tour through the mythologies of all cultures, a unique and moving love story—and another winner for the phenomenally gifted, consummately reader-friendly Gaiman. (Author Tour.)

And it has a star beside it.

posted by Neil Gaiman 1:35 AM

Oh, and it looks like the 17th of June I'll be doing a reading, along with the Magnetic Fields (who will be making music, not reading) at the Bottom Line in New York. More details as they become available (including where you call for tickets).

I'm not sure how often authors and bands do gigs together out there, but it seems like something that should happen more often. I mean, I'd love to see Hubert Selby supporting Lou Reed…(And I did once see Nico supporting John Cooper Clarke.)

And the saga of the permissions is completely over: We wound up getting permissions on pretty much everything, even the Yeats and the Frost, except for the public domain stuff and a couple of things that were short enough that fair use seemed to cover them. Total cost for permissions: $890, and I have to buy Greg Brown a really nice sushi dinner next time he's in town.

posted by Neil Gaiman 1:59 AM

Friday, May 04, 2001

I just got sent some of the UK signing dates. THIS ISN'T A COMPLETE LIST (said in capitals)—and I'll post the complete list as soon as we have it—but I'm posting it anyway, to let any of you in the UK who want to come to a signing start making arrangements and plans…

Saturday, 7th July	1:00pm	Forbidden Planet	London
Monday, 9th July	1:00pm	Borders	Glasgow
	6:30pm	Waterstones	Edinburgh
Tuesday, 10th July	7:00pm	Borders	Leeds
Wednesday, 11th July	7:00pm	Waterstones	Manchester
Thursday, 12th July	1:00pm	Andromeda	Birmingham
	7:00pm	Ottakars	Walsall, W.Midlands

—Something I've encountered on my last few UK signings is stores selling tickets to readings/signings, with the cost of the ticket coming off the cost of the book (so you pay a pound for the reading and a pound less for the book), and others give away tickets to limit the numbers of people showing up. It's worth calling the shop if it's not one you know, or if it's not local, and finding out how they do things, and if there's anything you'll need to do to get to the signing.

posted by Neil Gaiman 3:31 PM

Sunday, May 06, 2001

I'm starting to feel faintly cursed.

Tonight I thought, well, I've signed about 4,000 of these title pages—decorating many of them with little drawings, doodles, staring eyes, portraits of Uncle Sam, and, following a slight accident this afternoon with a bottle of ink, fingerprints—I'll stop and do a blogger entry. I'll tell the story of my day being photographed for the back cover shot.

So I turned on the notebook computer, and listened as the charging cord made an interesting sputtering sound and an even more interesting burning-electrical-things smell, and then died.

It left a half-charged battery, which may just be enough to get the various files I'll need tomorrow off the computer and onto another. But it kind of put paid to my plans to write a leisurely sort of journal entry. So I signed another few hundred cover sheets instead.

This is the deal on the 5,000 signed books: bookstores can order dumpbins or risers or whatever they call them of *American Gods*. Ten copies of the book, a couple of the audio books, and a couple of signed ones. If you have a bookstore that has a stand of *American Gods*, and you know I'm not going to be signing in your area, then take a look and see if there are any signed books in there.

At my most cynical, I imagine a bunch of people driving from Barnes and Noble to Borders across America buying up the signed copies and immediately offering them on eBay (or hoarding them and then selling them on eBay).

The interviews have started. Telephone ones mostly at this point, and only one a day. Which is a good thing.

posted by Neil Gaiman 11:15 PM

Monday, May 07, 2001

The nice people at Mysterious Galaxy in San Diego e-mailed me to tell me what their phone number in fact is, and not whatever I posted here earlier.

Really what this web site needs is a page of tour dates. (I think the good people at Authors on the Web are probably toiling day and night to get neilgaiman.com up and running before publication date. But I'll see if I can get it to happen.)

5,500 limited signature pages have been signed (and many of them have been doodled on). This is an extra 10% to allow for spoilage, slippage, crashage, rippage and someone at the bindery spilling coffee on them. I don't know if they'll obsessively destroy the extra 500 if no coffee is spilled, or if they'll creep into the system. Possibly the latter—but seeing that no-one's actually paying anything extra for the signed copies, which will (as I said yesterday) go out with the unsigned ones, I'm not going to give it another thought.

I asked my publishers today if they had any spare copies of *American Gods* in proof as I had a few people I wanted to get copies to, and they laughed at me. Hollowly. So at least in proof stage, it's proving popular.

A couple of people who read this site asked at the Nebulas what the easiest way to get questions to me would be (if there were things I'd posted they wanted clarified or whatever). Either e-mail to the nice people who run the inkwell.vue area of the Well, or if you have Compuserve access come and find me in the Literary Forum—they've given me a whole little topic to myself there.

posted by Neil Gaiman 6:09 PM

Thursday, May 10, 2001

And here are the three Canadian dates, with information from HarperCollins Canada publicist Felicia Quon (isn't that a great name?):

Monday, July 23	7:00PM	Toronto, ON	Merrill Collection Toronto Public Library
Tuesday, July 24	7:00PM	Vancouver, BC	Virgin Record Megastore
Wednesday, July 25	7:30PM	Victoria, BC	Bolen's Books

My guess is that I'll be doing readings and Q&As in each place, as well as signing, but I may be wrong.

I don't quite know what'll be happening in Toronto, but for now I'd strongly suggest anyone who wants to come calls the Merril collection people and gets a ticket ASAP: I've spoken at the Merril Collection before, and I remember it as not seating more than about 400 people, and the inhabitants of Toronto tend to be among the most enthusiastic on the face of the planet (or at least, they turn up in astonishing numbers).

Picked up the latest *Locus* (April, I think—good interview with John Crowley and he's on the cover) and was amused to discover several photos of me with (and without) the Florida Beard alluded to in earlier posts in it.

Next one of these will be about tour planning I think.

Next week I'm getting my photo taken by *Entertainment Weekly,* so I promise I'll write my photo stuff before then. Honest.

posted by Neil Gaiman 12:56 AM

So next week I get my photograph taken for *Entertainment Weekly.* It looks a lot like it will happen at the House on the Rock, after hours, so I may, like my characters, get to ride The World's Largest Carousel.

Which, whatever happens or doesn't happen will probably be more fun, or at least, significantly less smoky, than the author photograph session for *American Gods,* last December.

Now, every now and again I do something really stupid.

For example, when I started writing *American Gods,* I swore a mighty oath that I'd not cut my hair or shave my beard until I finished it. By March 2000 I was starting to look like a Hassidic terrorist, and somewhere in there I said "Sod it," and shaved off the beard.

But the hair kept growing. I wasn't going to get a haircut until I'd finished writing *American Gods.*

When I tell people about this, they look at me as if I'm really weird, except for the Norwegians who tell me about one of their early kings who didn't shave or cut his hair until he'd united Norway. (And he didn't wash either. At least I still bathed.) So the Norwegians don't think I'm weird.

Anyway, my hair grew and grew (it does that, and whenever I'm tempted to grumble I remember all the people of my generation who would be only too pleased to have hair that grows too fast, or any kind of hair really), and finally it was last October and people who didn't know me were making Howard Stern jokes when they passed me in the street. And I was going to go on a Comic Book Legal Defense Fund Reading Tour...

So I finished the book. In first draft, anyway. And I went and visited Wendy at Hair Police in Minneapolis, and got my first haircut in 18 months; and then I went off on the CBLDF reading tour and raised many tens of thousands for freedom of speech, and this was a good thing. (Somewhere in there I talked Chris Oarr from the defense fund out of auctioning off my cut-off hair for charity.)

(You know, this would be much more fun if I could illustrate it with photos. Maybe when we put up the neilgaiman.com site I will.)

So I had short hair and nobody made Howard Stern jokes any more.

Now, author photos are weird things. For example, take the *Good Omens* photo session, in 1989, where Terry Pratchett and I were taken to a graveyard on the coldest day of the year. The expressions on our faces— variously described as brooding, intelligent, and mysterious, and by the *Times* of London no less, as sinister—are simply cold. (I was relatively okay. I had a leather jacket on. Terry wore an extremely lightweight jacket he'd borrowed from Malcolm Edwards, because of the notion that the authors dressed respectively in black and in white. I was black.)

The easiest author photos have been the various Kelli Bickman photos taken over the years, including my favourite, the *Smoke and Mirrors* back cover photo, with its infinite regression of authors on a TV screen. But Kelli's taking fewer photos these days, and is concentrating more on her artwork. (She's MTV Featured Artist currently...you can see some of her artwork at **www.kellibickman.net**)

The hardest was the one in the UK in 1996 for *Wired* Magazine. The photo you may have seen from that session is the one of me holding a glowing book. The one you've not seen was the one of me, naked and wearing angel wings surrounded by candles. The one that I still remember with loathing was the one that wound up on the cover of *Wired:* it was me covered in sand. (A visual pun: *Sandman.* Yes?) And I would like to give a tip for young photographers who may want to attempt this shot.

Do not use builder's sand. It may be cheap, but it burns the skin.

Trust me on this. I've been there. I know.

The *American Gods* photo session was nowhere near that painful.

I still think I may have messed everything up by having a haircut.

The photographer was a very nice lady named Sigrid Estrada.

(Kelly Notaras, my editor Jennifer Hershey's right-hand woman, took me down there. Jennifer herself, and my literary agent Merrilee Heifetz, wandered along during the course of the afternoon.)

Sigrid took one look at me and said "I thought you were going to have longer hair."

She looked very disappointed.

"No," I said, apologetically. "I don't."

She sighed. She shook her head. I never quite found out why this messed things up as much as it obviously had.

Sigrid had a plan for a photo. The plan involved a lot of smoke. Her assistant held the smoke machine. Kelly Notaras was drafted in to hold a piece of cardboard to waft the smoke. And I stood there while Sigrid shouted "Smoke!" at the assistant holding the smoke machine, and the machine would belch huge gusts of white fog at me, and then she'd call "Waft!" at Kelly and Kelly would wave the paper and try to get the smoke off my face.

And that's what we did for the next four or five hours. We did it with my leather jacket on. We did it with my leather jacket off. We did it with me standing up. We did it with me sitting down. We did it with me peering coyly from around the side of a huge sheet of paper. And all through this, the smoke was belched, and then the smoke was wafted. (Jennifer did some fine smoke wafting, too.)

Merrilee exerted an agent's traditional prerogative and ran up between smoke belches and tried to tame the hair on my forehead. It didn't tame, but she did her best.

And I began to understand what a kipper must feel like, at the precise moment it stops just being a herring, and realises that it has been smoked. For me that moment occurred at the point where Sigrid decided that it might be more...more whatever she was going for...if the smoke was splurted directly at my head, rather than just generally belched out around waist level.

I'd hold my breath and smile and be told that I shouldn't smile, not for the kind of photo that Sigrid had in mind. So I'd stop smiling, and the smoke would splurt and Kelly or Jennifer would waft it and Sigrid would click away.

Days would pass before the taste of the smoke machine finally left the back of my throat. Still, it could have been much worse. There was no builder's sand involved, nor was I being warned not to get too close to the candles or my wings would go up like tinder and burn my bare skin.

So a few weeks passed, and one day the contact sheets arrived. Lots and lots of photos of me. And smoke.

My son took one look at the contact sheet and said "Was your head on fire?"

"No," I said.

"It just looked like it was, that was all."

And he was right. All the smoke being let off at head level had managed to create a set of photos in which it was perfectly obvious that my head was indeed on fire.

Claudia Gonson (of the Magnetic Fields) was staying with us over Christmas. I showed her the contact sheet.

"They make you look like your head's on fire," she said.

"I know," I said. "It's a special effect."

"And all the ones of you not wearing the leather jacket make you look like David Copperfield."

"Yes. That's a special effect too."

"You don't want to look like David Copperfield, do you?"

"No, thank you. Let's stick with the ones with me with a jacket on."

We picked one black and white photo, and one colour picture. The best thing about the black and white photo was the smoke in the background, which, far from looking like my head (or indeed any part of me) was on fire, looked instead like a mysterious sort of background, which might be clouds or mountains or, well, anything really.

(You can see one at http://www.codysbooks.com/index.jsp, while the figure of me from that picture, much photoshopped, is up on the front page of this website.)

I think they're pretty good photos. I still feel vaguely guilty about getting the haircut, though. I just wonder what Ingrid could have done, if my hair had been longer. And whether whatever it was would have required quite so much smoke.

And I promised I'd post the info on the Neil Gaiman/Magnetic Fields gig: it's all here—http://www.bottomlinecabaret.com/—although I'll be reading from a lot more than *American Gods*.

posted by Neil Gaiman 10:33 PM

Friday, May 11, 2001

Got my hair cut by the wonderful Wendy from Hair Police (particularly wonderful as she didn't grumble that I was almost half an hour late), then stopped in to say hello to Greg Ketter at DreamHaven Books, to discuss the new series of spoken word CDs. (Regular readers of this journal will have noticed me recording the material for the first two CDs last week.) We were trying to figure out how long it would be before they could be released, and it's going to be a little while—probably not till the end of the year. Greg mentioned how frustrating it is that *Warning: Contains Language* now goes for $100 on eBay, and I said "Well, could we just print up a few to tide us over until we can get the new ones out...?"

Greg made a phone call. "We can have some in two weeks," he said, mildly astonished. So we're doing a small print run—about a thousand copies—of *Warning*. It's a double CD, and I hope it will be for sale at the various stops on the signing tour, and through DreamHaven. I don't know if Greg's doing enough that he'll be offering it through Amazon.com, or into the comic stores through Diamond. We'll see.

But you will be able to get copies, for a little while. And then after that the CDs on there will become part of the new Audio CD series.

So that's news.

And yesterday I got an e-mail from my agent saying that Harper have just bought the electronic book rights to *American Gods* (no advance. The e-retailer takes half, and Harper and I split the remaining half). And then they asked if they could do the rest of the books in the same way, and we said yes.

(That's not really news. But it's interesting.)

And I got home to find an e-mail telling me that it's been announced that David Goyer is adapting and directing a movie based on my short story "Murder Mysteries" for Dimension films—something that's been in the works for several years, and has just come to fruition.

I wish David much luck... (Thinks: I hope they do "Private Eye Angel" toys.)

And that's all the news for this afternoon.

posted by Neil Gaiman 3:54 PM

Saturday, May 12, 2001

I was doing a telephone interview about *American Gods* when I saw it on the screen. The interviewer was in Tokyo where it was gone 1:30 am.

For a weird moment I thought it was a joke, then I realised it wasn't. "Douglas Adams is dead," I said.

"Yes," said the interviewer. "I know. Did you ever meet him?"

I said yes. And I was obviously shaken enough that the interviewer offered to stop for half an hour, and I said no, it was fine, we should carry on.

After that the interview was pretty much a bust. Or at least, I don't remember anything else that was said. (Sorry, Justin.)

I'd known Douglas fairly well in the 80s—interviewed him originally for *Penthouse* then used the leftover material in a dozen other magazines, then in 1987 I wrote *Don't Panic—The Hitchhiker's Guide to the Galaxy Companion* for Titan Books, which involved lots more interviews with Douglas and his friends and colleagues, and lots more spending time in his flat going through his files and archives looking for cool stuff.

Saw him at David Gilmour's 50th birthday party, in 1996, and I told him how the *Neverwhere* TV series was going, and he said at least it wouldn't be the same experience he'd had with the *Hitchhiker* TV series, but it was.

Saw him in Minneapolis a couple of years ago for a signing for the *Starship Titanic* game. (Only a dozen people came to the signing. He started out by demonstrating the game, but it kept crashing and he couldn't get out of one of the opening sequences. It was kind of sad.) He'd previously asked me to work on a radio adaptation of the later Hitchhiker's Books, and I'd said no as I didn't have the time.

We'd e-mail from time to time.

He was a very brilliant man. (Not said lightly. I think he really was one of those astonishingly rare people who saw things differently and more clearly and from a different angle.) I don't think he liked the process of writing very much to begin with, and I think he liked it less and less as time went on. Probably, he wasn't meant to be a writer. I'm not sure that he ever figured out what it was that he did want to do; I suspect it's something they don't have a concept for yet, let alone a name—and if he'd been around when this thing was around (World Designer? Explainer?) he would have done it brilliantly.

(I hope that his death isn't followed by the publishing of all the stuff he hadn't wanted to see print.)

He was immensely kind and generous, with his time and his material, to a young journalist, over 15 years ago; and watching how he, and how Alan Moore (who I met around the same time), treated their fans and other people—graciously, kindly and generously—taught that young journalist an awful lot about how famous authors ought to behave. And how most of them don't.

& I'll miss him.

posted by Neil Gaiman 3:08 PM

Blogger is being very strange currently. I'm seeing all manner of interesting error messages, and am hoping that, sooner or later, I can get some of these posts to go up. (No luck yet, though I've graduated from the runtime 104 error messages to msxml3.dll error 80072f78 which seems like a step up.)

posted by Neil Gaiman 3:10 PM

Sunday, May 13, 2001

Now we're getting nothing but Error 210s. It's making posting anything astonishingly frustrating. Not to mention time consuming and practically impossible.

Spent a large chunk of yesterday replying to fanmail. (I always try to answer it. It goes into a box, and three or four times a year I clean out the box, scrawling postcards that answer questions & say thank you as best I can in the room on the back of a postcard.) I don't do it as often as I should, and get a wholly disproportionate sense of accomplishment when it's all replied to, and the box is filled with postcards.

And I pulled out my copy of *Don't Panic* (the original Titan edition of 1987, not the reissue that Dave Dickson wrote extra chapters for at the end, nor the US Pocket Books edition where page 42—which we'd left intentionally blank because the first time I'd printed out the book page 42 was [not on purpose, just a glitch from whatever computer program I was using to word process in those dim dark days] a blank piece of paper with "page 42" on it, and that seemed improbable enough to be some kind of a sign—was just part of the book…) and I read the book I'd written fourteen years ago, and heard Douglas's voice all the way through it, affable, baffled, warm and dry.

There are worse ways to say goodbye. And it may have been a strange one, but it worked, and we take our goodbyes where we can.

posted by Neil Gaiman 8:40 AM

Monday, May 14, 2001

Okay. It was a Blogger problem. Which is good to know. In my naivety I thought I'd broken it.

Today was nightmarishly busy, and strange. And I think the Douglas thing shook me up a lot more than I had realised.

Too many e-mails asking for "appreciations" on Douglas, or quotes on his death ("Why me?" "You wrote the book about him.") Most of the time I just sent them here, and told them to use what they wanted.

Wednesday, I drive down to the House on the Rock for the photo session for *Entertainment Weekly*.

Friday I go to Brazil—I'll be at a book fair in Rio on Saturday and Sunday (signings), then to Sao Paulo—Tuesday evening is a signing at FNAC. (What is FNAC? I do not know. See how exciting this is?)

Then to Buenos Aires (it's in Argentina. You knew that.) Details on what I'm doing there as they come. Then back to the US.

By the way, the UK tour dates (and the US dates) are on the May 4th blog entry—you'll need to go to archives to see them.

posted by Neil Gaiman 10:25 PM

Tuesday, May 15, 2001

Two messages from correspondents already informing me that FNAC is a French books and record chain. http://www.fnac.com/ is their website. So now we know.

posted by Neil Gaiman 1:40 AM

So, today brought an envelope, and in it, the finished book cover for *American Gods*. It's lovely. Big lightning bolt on the cover, gold letters, and the back cover is covered with wonderful blurbs, many of them melted down from ones already posted here. Also photo of me, with smoke in background and messy hair. Author delighted. Finished books should arrive on the 31st of May. Author excited.

Also e-mail today saying *American Gods* has been sold to Czechoslovakia and to France, which gives us the first two foreign sales.

The most interesting *American Gods* call was from the editor of the e-book edition of *American Gods,* which will be published at the same time as the novel, asking about what kind of things we can add to the e-book: I suggested that we add this journal…

And because none of that is very interesting, I thought I'd put up a link to some wonderful photos…here. For anyone who, like me, tends to think of the past in sepia tones…

posted by Neil Gaiman 8:29 PM

Wednesday, May 16, 2001

From *American Gods*, Chapter Five:

> Calliope music played: a Strauss waltz, stirring and occasionally discordant. The wall as they entered was hung with antique carousel horses, hundreds of them, some in need of a lick of paint, others in need of a good dusting; above them hung dozens of winged angels constructed rather obviously from female store-window mannequins; some of them bared their sexless breasts;

some had lost their wigs and stared baldly and blindly down from the darkness.

And then there was the carousel.

A sign proclaimed it was the largest in the world, said how much it weighed, how many thousand light bulbs were to be found in the chandeliers that hung from it in gothic profusion, and forbade anyone from climbing on it or from riding on the animals.

And such animals! Shadow stared, impressed in spite of himself, at the hundreds of full-sized creatures who circled on the platform of the carousel. Real creatures, imaginary creatures, and transformations of the two: each creature was different—he saw mermaid and merman, centaur and unicorn, elephants (one huge, one tiny), bulldog, frog and phoenix, zebra, tiger, manticore and basilisk, swans pulling a carriage, a white ox, a fox, twin walruses, even a sea serpent, all of them brightly coloured and more than real: each rode the platform as the waltz came to an end and a new waltz began. The carousel did not even slow down.

"What's it for?" asked Shadow. "I mean, okay, world's biggest, hundreds of animals, thousands of lightbulbs, and it goes around all the time, and no-one ever rides it."

"It's not there to be ridden, not by people," said Wednesday. "It's there to be admired. It's there to be."

There is nowhere in the whole world quite as strange or as special as The House on the Rock. Parts of Chapters 5 and 6 of the novel take place there—stuff happens, and some characters get to ride the World's Largest Carousel.

Nobody's allowed to ride the World's Largest Carousel in real life. It just goes round and round and round, like something from the Weisinger-era Fortress of Solitude.

I drove for 3 hours to get there. Jeff, the photographer, had a whole crew of people waiting. First, make-up. Then, the initial set up: a double-exposure picture of me and the strange nipple-revealing shop-window dummy mannequin angels that hang from the roof of the Carousel room. (One of the photos from today will illustrate the review in the *Entertainment Weekly* books section.)

Then down to floor level and over to the Carousel for shots of me with the strange animals moving round and round in the background. I spent most of the time trying not to look vaguely goofy. (This is my default mode in photographs. It's not intentional. Some people tell me I take good photographs, and I have to explain that that's only because they mostly don't print the goofy ones. The infamous CBLDF iguana photo is a good example of the kind of photo that people usually don't see. Goofy.)

The best part of spending four hours having your photo taken is often talking to the photographer. This was kind of out of the question here—the sheer volume of the music in the Carousel Room is initially almost unbearable; after about 20 minutes it becomes a sort of background noise and you kind of tune it out…but for the four hours of the shoot, Jeff and I communicated mostly by hand gestures of the "turn left," and "chin up" variety, because the music was so loud you couldn't hear anything, especially when all the kettledrums started banging.

(And for the breaks, Jeff was off setting up the next shot. I chatted to Dolores, his assistant, and signed her hardback of *Sandman: The Wake*. She hasn't read it yet, as she says if she does then the story will be over.)

The carousel room is the hottest room in the House on the Rock. It's the 20,000 light bulbs from the carousel that keep it so warm, said Bill, the man on carousel duty (he's been doing it for 16 years, making sure no-one vaults the fence and climbs onto any of the animals). I was cooking in the Jonathan Carroll leather jacket.

As the shoot wound down, Jeff and I got to chat a little. "How would you like me to make you look?" he asked. "Brooding, mysterious, scary, friendly—what kind of impression are you trying to give?"

I thought for a moment, and realised that I had no idea. "Could you make me look surprisingly fuckable for a writer, please?"

He laughed (and so did the rest of the crew) and said he'd do his best.

And we wrapped up the shoot, then I ate and drove another three hours back.

Actually, I'd settle for brooding.

Really, I'd settle for not very goofy.

posted by Neil Gaiman 11:11 PM

And an e-mail waiting for me on my return, from Rambling Jack Womack, the HarperCollins publicist…posting it as is for all the Los Angelenos out there…

Just talked to Jen Ramos at Book Soup in LA, and due to *overwhelming response* they're changing the event venue on the 29th to their larger space, and moving the time to an hour earlier (this works out fine within the rest of your schedule). Books will of course be sold on-site.

So, the new specifics:

Friday, June 29 7:00PM	Book Soup	Speaking/Q & A
	Beverly Hills Library	Signing

posted by Neil Gaiman 11:45 PM

Thursday, May 17, 2001

And this in from Lucy Ramsey at Hodder Headline—I think this is all the UK signings now. Could be wrong...

Saturday, 7th July	1:00pm	Forbidden Planet	London, WC1
Monday, 9th July	1:00pm	Borders	Glasgow
	6:30pm	Waterstones	Edinburgh
Tuesday, 10th July	1:00pm	Forbidden Planet	Newcastle
	7:00pm	Borders	Leeds
Wednesday, 11th July	7:00pm	Waterstones	Manchester
Thursday, 12th July	1:00pm	Andromeda	Birmingham
	7:00pm	Ottakars	Walsall, W.Midlands
Friday, 13th July	1:00pm	Waterstones	Bristol

posted by Neil Gaiman 7:38 AM

Tuesday, May 22, 2001

Actually there are two other UK signings on

Saturday 14th July	11:00AM	Ottakars	Norwich
	7:00PM	Waterstones	Canterbury

I'll post the details when I get a chance.

Sorry about the silence. I went to Brazil and have had a difficult time getting online. Right now I'm in an office in FNAC, a book and stationery store in the heart of São Paulo. There's a noise coming up the stairs like the low susurrus of a horde of vandals on their way to sack a city, or possibly just the crowd at a rock concert, which seems to be the people here to get their books signed. I'm meant to do a reading first, and may perversely do an *American Gods* reading, or less perversely a *Sandman: Dream Hunters* reading (in English, not in Portuguese, although the Brazilian edition is the one I'm here for).

Sore throat, mostly from shouting to be heard at the Rio book fair, where the background decibels were scary, and from continual interviews ever since.

Did an MTV interview today that was enormously fun.

And I have to go as the TV crew are here to interview me (45 minutes late. This is Brazilian Time, and it no longer causes me to turn a hair, although if this were the US I'd be having kittens.)

posted by Neil Gaiman 1:45 PM

Wednesday, May 23, 2001

So now it's the day after the signing. 1,200 people were in the signing line (an attempt to cap the line was abandoned after a riot was threatened,

I learned afterward) and records were broken for books sold at a signing (700 plus) and I was out of there by 11:30 at night, and that was all good.

The people were friendly. There were amazing gifts in quantity. My two phrases of Portuguese impressed everyone, and I managed to do 200 people an hour mostly because no-one really tried to stop and chat. But by the end of the signing I had utterly and completely lost my voice.

Now, a day later, I'm communicating in something between a whisper and a croak, and doing a lot of Harpo Marx style wordless stuff, and I'm hoping I can talk by the time the Argentinian signings and interviews start.

I suppose it's better that something like this happens now, rather than on the *American Gods* tour.

The people at Conrad have been the finest hosts I could have hoped for, and the Brazilian people are even more enthusiastic and delightful than I remembered. If it weren't for the traffic in São Paulo this place would be perfect…

posted by Neil Gaiman 11:52 AM

I'm in Argentina.

Spent today at Conrad, my publishers. I managed to do a press conference before lunch despite having no voice at all. I mean, none. Nothing. Nada. Zip. When I open my mouth this is what comes out: "… …"

The press conference only worked because Cassius, my editor at Conrad, spent the last four days with me as my translator and all-around help. He sat next to me at every signing I've done since I got to Brazil and listened to the answers I gave to the questions people asked. He learned that, mostly, if you ask me the same question, I'll give you the same answer, or similar. And he heard those answers over and over again.

So at the press conference, they'd ask a question, like "Are you working with Terry Gilliam on the *Good Omens* movie?" and I would simply lean over to Cassius and whisper in his ear, like the godfather (his simile), or like a particularly large and malevolent glove puppet (mine), and mouth "Can you take this one?" and he'd do three minutes of stuff he'd heard me say whenever I was asked the question before—and he'd say it in Portuguese, which was more than I ever could.

Then I signed lots of books for the people at Conrad, went off and ate lots of dead raw fish for lunch, and off with Cassius to the airport, where we sorted the stuff people had given me into CDs and letters (which I took with) and everything else (which he's boxing up and sending to me). He got me through obtaining my ticket, and got me checked in, while I stood and smiled and said "… …" from time to time. It was meant to be "Obrigado"—Portuguese for "thanks" but nothing ever came out.

The inability to speak was a bit of a liability when it came to trying to find out why a plane to Amsterdam was leaving from my gate, and why the Buenos Aires plane wasn't. (It was late arriving. But I got here eventually.)

So now I'm in Buenos Aires, where the french-fried potato is all the vegetables there are. (I ordered the macrobiotic salad from the menu in the late night eating place we went to. It looked wonderful from the menu description—all avocado and sprouts and stuff. The waiter explained, in Spanish, something which apparently conveyed the idea that this was simply something they put on the menu to lure in unwary tourists, and they didn't actually expect anyone ever to order it, let alone eat it. I asked what salads there were [silently and in English. Andres, who was minding me here, said it aloud and to the waiter and in Spanish]. The menu had a huge list of excitingly described salads. The waiter ran a thumb up and down the list, then pointed his thumb, hesitantly, to the "chopped up tomatoes and hearts of palm in salad cream" salad. "Is very good," he said, which someone must once have told him was the English for "This is all we have in the fridge in the kitchen." So I looked at the menu again, and decided I really didn't want to eat organs or steak, and settled in the end for some chicken, and french-fried potatoes.)

On Friday I'm told I'll be on a radio show with John Cale—who I've spoken to on the phone, but never met (you should read his autobiography, *What's Welsh For Zen?* It's wonderful and Dave McKean designed and drew and photographed it)—so tomorrow (Thursday) I plan to say nothing at all. Not even whisper. I want my voice back, dammit. Otherwise Friday's radio show will consist of Cale saying sonorous and interesting things in a transatlantic Welsh accent, while I occasionally add to the mix by saying, in my own transatlantic English accent: "... ..." and "...... ......" and even, on occasion, "...... ...".

posted by Neil Gaiman 10:58 PM

Thursday, May 24, 2001

Down day in Buenos Aires. Way down. Still no voice to speak of—lots of interviews scheduled for tomorrow. Keep your fingers crossed for me. The best thing that happened today was Dave McKean emailed me his cover art for *Coraline:* it's elegant, strange, beautiful and really, really creepy.

posted by Neil Gaiman 8:53 PM

Friday, May 25, 2001

The Rosedale signing listed on the tour schedule doesn't exist. It should read:

    7/2/01   7:00 PM   Roseville, MN   Barnes & Noble

And I'm sure they'll correct it on the tour page soon enough.

In another window, I'm doing a chat with a number of Argentinians and a Chilien who have just started to argue about the merits of anime. I hate it when things become surreal.

posted by Neil Gaiman 7:26 PM

Monday, May 28, 2001

I'm home. Hurrah... 22 hours on planes and in airports, and it's just nice to be in my own house, with kids all around, and I got to say things I haven't had a chance to say in two weeks, things like "What do you mean—you're going out? You've still got two English essays to finish, and a hundred-question physics test, and all that homework's due tomorrow. Of course you aren't going out."

I walked in the garden: the asparagus is high as an elephant's eye, and for that matter, so is the rhubarb. (Which is rather unnerving, actually.)

So waiting for me, when I got home, was a finished copy of *American Gods*.

This made me very happy.

The first thing I thought when I saw it was how much thicker it was than I'd expected. (465 pages plus about 15 pages of front matter. Or to put it another way, it's over an inch thick.) Also, how very much it looks like a real book.

The cover is lovely.

I opened it up very carefully. Black endpapers. Yum...

The first rule of new books is this: when your new book arrives, and you open it to a random page, and look at it, you will see a typo, and your heart will sink. It may be the only typo (er, typographical error) in the whole book, but you will see it immediately.

So I very carefully didn't open it to a random page. I opened it to the first page (*Caveat, and Warning for Travelers*) and read that instead. Half way down the page I noticed a comma that I could have sworn used to be a full stop...

But other than that, it looks lovely. Wonderful. Really cool. I checked the Icelandic, and that was now right, and all the weird copyediting things seem to be fine. The permissions are all there on the copyright page. Along with the weirdest little Library of Congress filing thing I've ever seen. This is what it says:

American Gods: a novel /by Neil Gaiman—1st ed p.cm ISBN 0-380-97365-0 1.National characteristics, American - Fiction. 2. Spiritual warfare - Fiction. 3 Ex-prisoners - Fiction. 4. Bodyguards - Fiction 5. Widowers - Fiction I. Title

And I wonder, who picks these categories? What do they base them on? I mean, it is undoubtedly true that Shadow, our more-or-less hero, is an ex-prisoner, and that his wife is killed in a car crash early in the book; but I feel deeply sorry for anyone who goes into it looking for fiction about widowers, ex-prisoners or bodyguards; while all the people looking for the things it has in abundance, like history and geography and mythology, like dreams and confidence tricks and sacrifice, Roadside Attractions and lakes and coin magic and funeral homes go by the wayside.

Still, I like "Spiritual warfare - Fiction." And "National characteristics, American". I like that, too, in a weird way.

Also waiting for me were the finished covers for the Harper Perennial (large format paperback) editions of *Smoke and Mirrors* (my short story collection) and *Stardust*. Which are wonderful...*Stardust* in particular, as it looks...well, grown-up, like a fairy tale for adults and not like a generic fantasy. (I wonder how many people bought the mass market paperback edition of *Stardust,* and were disappointed because it really wasn't what the cover promised—and how many were pleasantly surprised by what they read.)

Both published, interestingly, as "Fiction".

I think that both books are going to be out and in the stores for the signing tour. Fingers crossed...

If (like me) you've been waiting for the promised "first chapter" and the newsletter, I'm pretty sure that Harper are just gearing to send them out, because they just had me write something telling you how busy they've been getting neilgaiman.com into shape to go and meet the public, which will be going out to those of you who are signed up for the news option.

And, while I think of it, May 31st is when scifi.com's Seeing Ear Theatre launches "*Snow, Glass, Apples*"—the play for voices I wrote based on my short story (in *Smoke and Mirrors*), starring Bebe Neuwirth as the Queen. She is astonishing, and was a joy to work with, and I'm looking forward to the thing going live. Brian Smith, who produced and directed this (and my story "Murder Mysteries", which, starring Brian Dennehy, went up on the scifi.com site last year, and is still up in the archives section).

Every now and again journalists and people at signings ask me what my favourite medium is, and I tell them "Radio plays". They can do so much, inside your head...

posted by Neil Gaiman 1:11 PM

For those of you in Toronto –

I hear from Felicia Quon of the cool name that the tickets for the Merrill Collection reading/signing are half gone already. As far as I know, this is the only thing happening in Toronto (last time I was there I did a signing in Chapters that went on for quite a while) so if you want to be there, or know anyone who does, call: Merrill Collection of Science Fiction at the Lillian H. Smith Library Contact: Lorna Toolis 416.393.7748 is the info up at the Tour Dates page.

posted by Neil Gaiman 1:50 PM

Tuesday, May 29, 2001

So the reviews are now coming in: a trickle at first, then around publication date there should be a flood, and then that'll die back to a trickle again.

The last time I listened to a review (good or bad) was in 1987, and it was a review of *Violent Cases,* my first ever graphic novel (with Dave McKean drawing). The review said it was a good book, but it was too expensive. Dave and I took that to heart, and we went to the publisher, showed him the review, and asked him to lower the price.

So for the next two or three printings, the book was cheaper. We made a lower royalty. And no-one ever noticed or said anything, nor did anyone ever say anything when, with the next edition, the price went back up again. Which, I decided, was reason enough not to listen to reviews.

So this morning brought two reviews. One (positive) from the Summer 2001 *BookForum,* by Anthony Miller, who liked all the stuff on the road with gods in it but feels the book

> loses momentum when Shadow leaves the road and Gaiman turns his attention to small-town life

and one (mixed) from an anonymous *Publishers Weekly* reviewer which says

> Shadow's poignant personal moments and the tale's af-fectionate slices of smalltown life are much better devel-oped than the aimless plot.

Which is the other reason not to listen to reviews. You'd go mad.

(My favourite line from *PW:* "Mere mortals will enjoy the tale's wit, but puzzle over its strained mythopoeia". My favorite from *BookForum* "His at once comic and melancholic imagination, and his facility for navigating the nocturnal and supernatural realms, evoke some of the great writers of the fantastic, from James Branch Cabell to Jorge Luis Borges, along with flashes of Flann O'Brien and glimpses of G. K. Chesterton.")

posted by Neil Gaiman 2:03 PM

Wednesday, May 30, 2001

I just got backstage at the website for the first time, and have been fascinated by the statistics. For example, did you know that the most new people who've turned up here in a day is a hair over 1200? (Mostly it's about 500 new people a day.) I didn't. Did you know that 238 Finns, and 227 Brazilians read it, but only 47 Belgians? Me neither. Four people read this journal from the Cocos Islands. I didn't even know there *were* any Cocos Islands. See how cool statistics are?

Sean Abbott at HarperCollins ebooks tells me that they are going to be doing an eomnibus of my stuff, to promote the four ebooks that will be coming out in July. *Smoke & Mirrors* will get a couple of extra stories, as a bonus, while *American Gods* will get a bunch of these journal entries as its bonus.

posted by Neil Gaiman 10:35 AM

Thursday, May 31, 2001

I've spent the last few days doing occasional chunks of interview with a journalist named Janet Kornbluth from *USA Today,* about the Scifi.com Seeing Ear Theatre production of *Snow, Glass, Apples.* The article/interview's in *USA Today* today, which means it's at

http://www.usatoday.com/life/cyber/tech/ebrief.htm

(if you're reading this in a week or so, of course, it'll have crept off to some other place in the *USA Today* archives and you'll have to go and find it yourself.)

And if you don't know what *Snow, Glass, Apples* is, then you're better off going straight to the scifi.com website and listening to it. (To be honest, every site gives you more information than you need, going into it. I think when Harper do it as a CD, then all they will know is that it's a retelling of an old story…)

And—as an additional note—the play of *Snow, Glass, Apples* is in two parts, and they've only posted the first part this week… I can't see anywhere on the site where it says when the next bit goes up. Next week? In two weeks time?

The *USA Today* article also gives a link to americangods.com. (We actually spent more time talking about this journal, why I was doing it, what I got out of it, why I was doing it as a blog, all that, than we did about *Snow, Glass, Apples.* Janet may be doing an article on authors and online journals, so this place may pop up again.)

With *American Gods* coming out, I was hesitant to do the interview, to be honest, mostly because I remember what it was like to be a journalist. Most of the time, it felt like when I wanted to do an article or an interview, I would approach the editor and the editor would say "Mm. We've already done it/him/her." Particularly irritating when I'd wanted to write an article on Alan Moore or Art Spiegelman, to be told that the paper in question couldn't do it because they'd "already done comics this year"—and "already done comics" would normally mean they'd done an article on the 40th birthday celebrations of Desperate Dan or Korky the Kat, complete with a quote on the character's perennial popularity from a junior director at publisher D.C. Thompsons.

So let us hope that we can still get one of those nice *USA Today* articles on the book, when the book itself comes out.

posted by Neil Gaiman 7:36 AM

So I learned today that Chris Ewen, who is half of the *Future Bible Heroes* among many other things, has decided to make up for the fact that Boston is shamefully and scabbily mistreated on the upcoming signing tour (*viz.* by me not going there) by holding a shindig. Said shindig will be at the Man Ray club (http://www.manrayclub.com/)—click on Special Events: it's for Over 21s. "Come dressed as your favourite Neil Gaiman character or god and enter our costume contest to win fantastic prizes". "Fetish or Costume attire only"

They'll have books on sale there (and we'll try and make sure they have signed books for sale), and so all the Boston readers (who are over the age of 21 and willing to dress up) can get together and have a good time. (Probably have a better time than you'd have had in a long line waiting for me.)

I think it's a wonderful idea. If there's anyone else out there who wants to hold a "The bastard isn't coming to [Anchorage/KansasCity/Orlando/ NewOrleans etc]—but we're going to have a party anyway" event, drop a line to Jack Womack at jack.womack@harpercollins.com, and we'll try and help (and list it in this journal). Those of you in Helsinki, Hobart, Hong Kong and other such places who want to get together and party (or even just designate a pub for an *American Gods* get-together) should also contact Jack. If there's enough of you, we'll make a page for you here and at the forthcoming neilgaiman.com…

Often people come to me and say "As a best-selling author, with many published works to your name, and a basement full of awards, most of them in need of a good polish, you must have some words of advice for the world that you wish to share."

And I do.

It's this.

If you have a 25lb long-haired calico cat whose fur is all matted into evil dreadlocks, and who is too fat to properly clean herself, do not put fresh batteries into an ancient beard-trimmer and attempt to shave her. You will only cause distress to the cat, and create a mess. There are professionals who will happily do this kind of thing, for a small fee. Leave it to them.

(This has been a public service announcement on behalf of Furball the cat, currently believed to be hiding in the attic in a severely traumatised state.)

posted by Neil Gaiman 7:25 PM

Friday, June 01, 2001

Let's see. In no particular order…

1. Furball the cat is just fine. She turned out to have been asleep under my bed, and will be professionally shaved on Monday. Thank you for asking.
2. The second half of *Snow, Glass, Apples* will go up on scifi.com on the 7th of June.
3. Today's mail brought the new paperback edition of *Smoke and Mirrors*, my short story collection. Which means it will turn up in the shops any time now.
4. Today also brought the audio book of *American Gods*. I started listening to it, as a quality check, and was swept up into it. George Guidal, who is one of the top people, if not the top person, in the world of audio books, reads it. It's a wonderful little package of about 14 cassettes. (The CD version will be out for the end of the year.) Harper Audio should be pleased with themselves. I'm thrilled…it's unabridged, and it made me very happy. It's not cheap, but I think I'll send some out as Xmas prezzies this year.

Now playing: I Am Kloot's "Natural History". Good band, but I keep thinking of John Clute, the preeminent SF critic, and wondering whether they're fans…

posted by Neil Gaiman 6:53 PM

Sunday, June 03, 2001

Got up this morning in a fine mood and wrote a 2,000 word blogger entry in this here journal. It was long, informative, useful and funny. I even wrote an impromptu essay on how to pronounce "Gaiman". I recommended books. I philosophised. It was one of the great Blogger entries.

I set it to post and publish and walked into the kitchen to grab something to eat. Then, like a character in a bad French farce, my daughter Holly (16 in three weeks) walked in to the office, carefully closed the on-screen window with the journal in it (but none of the other windows)—before it had even posted, let alone published, the entry I'd just written—and got offline. Then she wandered off, probably vaguely happy to have done something useful.

I ate, cheerfully, crossed the hall to the office, sat down at the computer, saw what had happened, and started to express my feelings.

"You shouldn't say things like that," said Holly, wandering back. "It sets a bad example."

Sigh.

Then we went and watched Mike graduate from High School. Very proud, even if I find something really weird about the spectacle of 17 year olds in caps and gowns. ("Well, you're English," said My Wife. "It's one of those things they don't have there.")

I'm going to have to repost all the useful stuff. The rest of it is going to have to wait until I have some time...

So...

One of the essays I did for online places has gone up. It's at http://go.borders.com/features/neilgaiman.xcv. The most immediate note: From the Bottom Line Club website:

> SUN JUNE 17 MAGNETIC FIELDS Also Appearing: Author NEIL GAIMAN Reading From His New Book: *American Gods* **General admission tickets for both shows have been sold out. You can still purchase standing room only tickets for the shows right before showtime.** Doors Open 6PM for 7:30 Show/10PM for 10:30 Show All Seats $20.00

(Although I probably won't read much from *American Gods*—I'll do shorter things, I think.)

posted by Neil Gaiman 2:45 PM

Spoke to my friend Kelli Bickman about her book, *What I Thought I Saw*. Kelli is an artist and a photographer. Currently she's the MTV featured artist for Spring/Summer 2001—you can read about her and see her art here and her paintings here (click on the little light bulbs to move around)—and some of her editorial/illustration work for magazines at here.

What I thought I saw is a book of photos she took in London in 1996, on location of *Neverwhere,* the TV series, and of people behind the scenes, and in New York. Mostly people buy it because I wrote the introduction and it's got *Neverwhere* in it, then write to Kelli asking when her next book of art/photos is coming out, completely forgetting about me, as she's good.

She's moving out of New York soon. What I thought I saw is almost sold out. Kelli has several boxes filled with copies though, and is very keen to get rid of them (as all her life's possessions have to be loaded onto a truck soon and driven thousands of miles) and wanted to know if I had any brilliant ideas. I'll try and come up with something. In the meantime I thought I'd put something up here with some links telling people to order copies.

I should probably warn you that there's some nudity in there. (But, as DreamHaven gleefully pointed out when they solicited it, not of me.)

Kelli's mum, the redoubtable Connie Bickman, has a new book out. Connie's a photojournalist, and the book is called *Tribe of Women*. Gorgeous photos of women around the world, wonderful text.

And while I'm plugging stuff, let me point out that you should buy Eddie Campbell's *Alec: How to Be an Artist*. You need this book very badly. Go and look at Eddie's website...

posted by Neil Gaiman 5:10 PM

There's an e-mail interview about *American Gods* on the Barnes and Noble site here.

posted by Neil Gaiman 5:17 PM

Monday, June 04, 2001

This morning brought the new *Locus* magazine, which is not the same as the online *Locus,* and had two reviews of *American Gods*, one by Gary Wolfe, which I enjoyed—lot of very interesting points—and one by Jonathan Strahan, which was pretty solid. Both were very positive.

I'm still very tempted to review the reviews, though.

The Writers Write website also has a review up, at http://www.writerswrite.com/journal/jun01/fansf.htm

My comment on hoping that they didn't dig out and print all the stuff Douglas Adams didn't want published while he was alive seems to have been an unfortunate foreshadowing of events to come. See this slashdot article and its referent.

I went browsing through my hard disk and found the last will I wrote—which reminded me that I really need to write another will that reflects things like the country I currently live in and how many kids I have—and checked what I'd written a decade ago on the subject of unfinished stuff etc.

At some point I'll need to figure out exactly what I want done with fragments, juvenilia, unpublished stuff, and so forth (when I do I'll codicil or amend this will). In the meantime on my death all computer back up tapes, disks, and hard disks are to be placed in a bank vault, along with any personal papers, letters, poems, and so forth; they aren't to be released for at least 50 years following my death, by which time I trust I'll be decently forgotten anyway. Anything recently completed should be assessed by my literary executors on its merits.

Which is more or less how I feel ten years on. Although I do need to get my finger out on assembling the material for DreamHaven's *B-Sides and Rarities* book and the poetry collection. (Really, all I need is a week. Just a quiet week with nothing else to do. Maybe four days...?)

Still listening to *American Gods* the audio version. It's really good—George Guidal manages an awesome array of voices, and is a magnificent reader. (I wish I could say that I've been listening with unmixed pride, but in fact a couple of times now I've pulled out a copy of the book and checked that a sentence was in fact that badly written, and have marked it to be fixed for the next edition.)

posted by Neil Gaiman 11:36 PM

Tuesday, June 05, 2001

So I spent today, as I will spend tomorrow, working on writing a circus. Something I've always wanted to do, which is why I'm currently writing it. (The young lady who runs the circus in question spent a year or so not taking no for an answer from me, and her persistence seems to have paid off. I spent most of today saying things to her like "Can you do this…?" and "What about this…?" and at one point phoning an expert and getting a hasty lecture on the fluorescent qualities of laser beams for something I started wondering about.)

Seeing I plugged a lot of other people's stuff yesterday, I thought I'd point out that *The Day I Swapped My Dad For Two Goldfish* makes a really cool Fathers' Day present. (Yay! to Amazon.com for featuring it on their kids page.)

And yay! to Morrow for getting out the *American Gods* newsletter.

Incidentally, if you've received the newsletter with the extract from *American Gods* in it, I should point out that in that extract, in the phrase "the titter skin-crawling horror" the word "titter" should be "utter", and for that matter that the sentence "He practiced coin tricks from a book lie found in the wasteland of the prison library; and lie worked out;" reads better if you replace the word "lie" with the word "he".

(I hope when they put up the www.americangods.com/excerpt page that they'll put it up from a clean text.)

More reviews today—an enthusiastic one from the Barnes and Noble *Explorations* magazine, a nice mention from the *NY Post,* and one from *Booklist,* where the reviewer, who had loved *Neverwhere* and *Stardust,* hated it—the kind of complete and entire hate where the reviewer doesn't even stop to point out the things he liked about the book, if there were any. He just seemed to wish it was another book entirely, a kind of "this is spinach and I don't like spinach" review: I think *Coraline* (which comes out next May) will be to his taste.

Also brought home several boxes of books, notebooks and such from the office, to compile a sort of core of references I used writing *American Gods* for neilgaiman.com. It'll be incomplete, but a good place to start. (The single most useful reference work was probably *A Dictionary of Northern Mythology,* by Rudolf Simek.)

And I copy-edited a poster of my poem *Instructions* with art by Brian and Wendy Froud, which will be coming out this summer in a signed, limited edition, as a benefit for the Comic Book Legal Defense Fund. I think it's going to be popular, on the basis that my assistant and my daughter have both extracted a promise from me that they can get one when they come out, from the proof knocking around the office.

(If it's sucessful, we might do a poem I wrote for my goddaughter, as a benefit for RAINN...)

Ah, the Chapter One excerpt is up at www.americangods.com/excerpt.html (they left off the html on the newsletter). It's kind of odd—all the italics have fallen out as well. I'll see if we can get a cleaner copy up...

posted by Neil Gaiman 10:55 PM

Dropped out, with regret, from the Spanish convention in early August. I figure I'll have been on a pretty gruelling signing tour through three countries from June 17th to July 25th, with only a couple of days off, for a total of about 17 plane journeys including a transatlantic run to England and back; and that the last thing I needed immediately following that was a coach class flight to Spain, even for a con that sounds very relaxing and delightful.

So an apology to any Spanish people who were looking forward to getting things signed. Maybe next year.

posted by Neil Gaiman 11:26 PM

Wednesday, June 06, 2001

Let's see...First things first. The Beverly Hills Library just realised they'd double booked the evening of the 29th. So:

Due to scheduling conflicts at the Beverly Hills Library, the second of Neil Gaiman's two Los Angeles-area events will be taking place at the originally-announced venue: 7:00 PM, Book Soup, West Hollywood, CA. Also the Canadian signings at the bottom of the tour page are in Toronto, Vancouver and Victoria respectively.

And http://www.americangods.com/excerpt.html now has a real excerpt, with italics and everything.

The whole of *Snow, Glass, Apple*s is now up at scifi.com—http://www.scifi.com/set/playhouse/snowglassapples/ first and second parts...

Over at Barnes and Noble they've put up some very solid reviews, by Bill Sheehan and Sharon Bosley respectively.

> Like all such extravagant epics, *American Gods* is—as Gaiman clearly acknowledges—a vast, multi-colored metaphor that has much to say about our ongoing need

for meaning and belief and about the astonishing creative power of the human imagination. The result is an elegant, important novel that illuminates our world—and the various worlds that surround it—with wit, style, and sympathetic intelligence, and stands as one of the benchmark achievements in a distinguished, constantly evolving career.

That's what Bill says. (He wrote a wonderful book about the fiction of Peter Straub, by the way.)

posted by Neil Gaiman 9:57 PM

Friday, June 08, 2001

Dianna Graf (a very nice Tasmanian lady who used to have fuchsia hair and work as a fairy but currently doesn't) posted this on the Well today, apropos of me coming to Australia to sign books...

Are the bookshops supposed to wait for the publisher to contact them? Or are they supposed to contact the publisher first to express interest? I debated this with my local friendly bookstore owner yesterday and I hope I have convinced him to just take the plunge and make the call rather than wait

And this was what I wrote in reply...

Dianna—well, obviously any bookstore can sit back and wait for the publisher to contact them.

But if the publisher has the budget to send me to (say) five cities, and they've received enquiries from five cities, then a bookstore in the sixth city may sit by the phone for a long time.

And it may be that the publisher might phone a different store in that city. Or that another store in the same city has already phoned to ask.

Publishers like to send authors to places that they know are enthusiastic and interested. Unless your store owner is the only bookstore in a city you know I have to go to then it's much smarter for him to call the publisher...

I got some fanmail today grumbling about evil HarperCollins not sending me to the US southeast on my tour; but I'm pretty sure that if stores from the southeast—from Florida say—had made a noise about how much they wanted me, I'd be signing there.

I'm going to be signing in Seattle mostly because Duane at the University bookstore made sure that HarperCollins knew that he wanted me for this signing two years ago, kept after them, pointed out how many books he'd sold on my last signings there, and he'd book an auditorium for me to speak and sign in... And so HarperCollins said yes. I'm going to San Diego because the guys at Mysterious Galaxy were so keen on getting me there, that, at a point where I wasn't going to go there, they offered to fly me in to do a signing on their own dime, and the enthusiasm they showed meant that Harper rejigged the schedule to send me.

I'd add to that that there are only so many places you can go on a tour, and so many weeks on a tour, so you're never going to please everyone. And just asking and being enthusiastic doesn't mean that a store will definitely get a signing—but it certainly increases the chances of me turning up and sitting and defacing books...

I said here a while ago I'd post the advice to stores I wrote for Andy Heidel (who was the publicist at Harper before Jack Womack) to send out to stores for the *Stardust* tour in 1998. I cunningly wrote it in the third person so people would think Andy wrote it. I don't think I fooled a soul.

(Anyway, I went and found it on the hard disk. Incidentally, if you're planning to come to a signing, I already wrote a list of helpful things like this for people attending the signings. It's in the archives.)

So you're hosting a Neil Gaiman signing...

Here are our suggestions for the Neil Gaiman signing tour. Many of them are self-evident, but you never know...

Before the event: Neil will sign books for any members of the staff who need them signed, and any books that people have bought and left to be signed or phone-ordered, before the reading and the signing.

Neil will use his own pen for signing most articles, but even so, have some black felt tips, some silver and/or gold pens (thin felt-pen type), and a Sharpie or so on hand. You never know what he'll need to sign.

The Reading: Neil will do a 15-30 minute reading first, followed by a short Q & A session. (He'll do a longer reading in those stores which are organising events in auditoriums.) Please do your best to ensure that there is space enough that all attendees can hear the reading.

If your store needs to have a microphone for the reading, please have one.

The Signing: We strongly suggest that if you're expecting a signing of more than 150 people that you issue numbers to the attendees. Blocks of numbers can then be called to queue up as needed (i.e., "Now signing for 75 and below...").

In the past this has proved the most successful way to run large signings, as it allows those with higher numbers to browse the store (and, in the case of a really big signing, even to go and get something to eat) while waiting for their block of numbers to be called.

It helps prevent a stampede after the reading, keeps people good-tempered, and allows you to sell merchandise to the people in your store for the signing.

(Some stores would also use the numbers for a raffle, as well as for gathering names and addresses for mailings.)

Some common questions:

Can people take photos of Neil?
Sure.

Are there going to be limits on what can be signed?

Common sense is the watchword on this. Normally Neil will sign 3 items that people bring, along with anything of his they buy in your store for the signing. If 600 people show up however, that might well be cut to one item plus what they buy, or something like that. It depends on how many people show up, and how much time there is, and when your store closes.

He will also try to sign for everyone there for the signing.

If the line is short enough, people with extra things they want signed can go round again. If the line is long, then they can't.

Will he personalise books?

Gladly.

Does he want little post-it notes with people's names written on them, then?

No, he figures asking people their names is an automatic icebreaker. But he does want things out of plastic bags before he signs them.

How long will he sign for anyway?

As long as it takes. He'd like to take a break every 90 minutes or so, for the bathroom, to snack, to flex his hand, or just to spend 5 minutes not signing anything. Check if he needs a break, but don't push it if he says no.

Does he want someone with him at the signing table?

There should be someone around there to keep an eye on the line, to make sure it keeps moving, and that if someone seems to be trying to make Neil read their novel, look at their whole art portfolio, or discuss philosophy, to move in and say "Sorry, there are lots of people waiting…"

By the way, no interviews during signings. Every now and then a journalist or would-be journalist decides that the middle of a signing is the best place to turn up and try to do an interview. It's not.

Incidentally, Neil says that if the Mad Fan with the Gun shows up he would very much like it if a member of staff would take the bullet; but he appreciates that this is a lot to ask.

Is that likely?

Not at all. It was a joke. Actually, on the whole, Neil's fans are remarkably nice.

Would he like anything special to eat or drink?

Clearly Canadian (one of the berry flavours) to drink; no real preferences as to snack food, but Neil still says nice things about the stores on the last tour who had sushi rolls there to nibble on.

After the signing: Neil's fans often give him gifts. Whoever is looking after him will probably take care of posting them back to him; if not, he'll give you an address to send them to.

After the signing is over, is the time to get shop stock signed, if there's enough time, and he can still hold a pen. Reasonable quantities of stuff, anyway.

(I picked Clearly Canadian—a bottled, fizzy, sweet water—because I figured it was really easy to find, and it's not caffeinated, which can be useful if you really have to sleep as soon as you'll get back to the hotel at midnight, and have to be out of the hotel by 5:30am. I was wrong—there are lots of parts of the States where Clearly Canadian is impossible to find, and there were indomitable booksellers who worked miracles, or were broken hearted because they hadn't managed to work miracles, to get me some sugary fizzy water. I didn't have the heart to tell them that ginger ale would have been fine. I think on the current version of the thing that Jack Womack actually did rewrite himself, it just says something like fizzy water.)

And—pretty obviously—the above were guidelines for stores. They are free to—and can—set their own rules about how the signing runs, what gets signed and so on. If you have any queries, phone the store. If the person answering the phone doesn't have a clue, ask to talk to someone who does.

And talking about *Stardust,* I saw the Harper Perennial edition today, and it made me very happy. The mass market edition was kind of unfortunate—it tried very hard to look like a generic fantasy book, which it really isn't. The trade paperback edition looks like a fairy tale for adults—the cover is a photograph of a wood, with something strange and glittery happening on it. It looks cool. More to the point, it looks appropriate.

posted by Neil Gaiman 12:40 AM

When will I learn? Long blog about Annotations written. Pressed publish. It said it has done it...but instead it has sent it off into the space of dead words.

Lone and bereft I shall stop writing for a little and take small daughter for a walk instead.

Yes, I know. Copy it before posting or publishing. Or use a text editor. Don't just sit down and type. I know. I *do* know that. Yes.

signed

will write annotation thing again tonight probably

posted by Neil Gaiman 5:32 PM

Saturday, June 09, 2001

Strangely enough, I just realised that the last two posts haven't published, although Blogger obviously thinks they did. *(note added later. They have now.)*

Up early this morning to put comments on a zip disk filled with photos, going off to the neilgaiman.com site people. I don't yet have much of a sense of what they're doing or putting up, but we can modify it as we go. Yes, this journal will stay alive through the tour (for a start, it may be the easiest way to let people know what's happening in case of any sudden changes), and I expect it'll stay here and we'll link to it from neilgaiman.com...

Cheryl Morgan, who does a zine called *Emerald City*, e-mailed me her review of *American Gods*, which made me very happy, not because it was a good review (which it was, in both senses, favourable and well-written) but because Cheryl had clearly read the same book that I was trying to write. (As perhaps opposed to a recent interviewer, who kicked off with "Well, I've read your book. You must really hate America, huh?")

To summarise yesterday's lost annotation blog—I want to make a space on neilgaiman.com where there can be, if people have any interest in doing it, annotations of *American Gods*. Partly because I'm sure that people will enjoy sharing knowledge ("Actually, both the Burma Shave ads Gaiman quotes are invented, and the Largest Carousel in the World does not play the Blue Danube Waltz..."), partly to help the Casual Reader ("Czernobog, also spelled Chernobog or Tcharnobog, was a dualistic Slavic winter god now remembered chiefly for his appearance as the black winged thingie who appears in 'A Night on Bald Mountain' in the original Fantasia...") and partly as a help to translators around the world, who are good people with a thankless task, but who can sometimes get the wrong end of a stick, or just not know where to look for information.

(I saw a recent edition of *Stardust*—and I will not embarrass anyone by saying from which country—where "Redcap" was annotated as "Bow Street Runner, an early policeman" and "Unseelie Court" was demonstrated to be a nonsense word derived from the three English Words "Un" "See" and "Lie"; which showed me that the translator lacked a dictionary of fairies— for a redcap is a rather nasty goblinish fellow, with teeth, while the Unseelie Court is the Court of all creatures of Faerie who are actively antipathetic to people, all the ogres and suchlike.)

Don't know whether we'll do it with a message board, an e-mail list, or an e-mail to a central e-mail address yet. I'll probably keep half an eye on it—not to censor it (I have no problem with the "Gaiman clearly has no idea how the internal combustion engine actually works, as what he describes here is impossible..." type posts) but just to make sure it doesn't contain information that is simply wrong. (Such things have been known. See "unseelie" above.)

Now to post this...and to hope it publishes...

posted by Neil Gaiman 8:10 AM

Sunday, June 10, 2001

Spent a good part of yesterday trying to compile a bibliography of Books Consulted for *American Gods* for the not-yet-online neilgaiman.com—a sort of astonishingly incomplete bibliography, because otherwise I would have had to try and catalogue half a library, so I'm trying just to list the books in the boxes I'd put in the boot of the car (that's the trunk, for Americans) when I drove down to Florida to work on the novel, and the ones I tried to make sure were on the shelves in the cabin as I wrote the rest of the book... and the ones I filled my suitcase with when I went to spend two weeks writing in Las Vegas (an anecdote, it occurs to me, that I've not mentioned yet on this blogger. Oh well. Feel free to ask me about it if you are at one of the Q & A sessions between the reading and the signing.) I got down a lot of the myth and folklore books. Lots of mini-capsule reviews. Cannot for the life of me find the box of books on confidence tricks or coin magic.

http://www.writerswrite.com/journal/jun01/fansf.htm has a review of *American Gods* up... (the version up earlier was an early draft of the review posted in error).

Spent a couple of hours today in the basement, pulling out foreign editions of books for neilgaiman.com. I'm not sure whether I was more amazed by the stuff I didn't know I had—*Chivalry* and *Snow, Glass, Apples* in Japanese. A box of first editions of *Angels and Visitations*. A Large Print edition of *Stardust*. A folder of short stories and poems I wrote in my teens (didn't have the heart to burn them, but the idea of anyone ever actually reading them...ow!)—or the stuff I knew I had but couldn't find—The German hardback of *Good Omens*, for example—or the stuff I should have had but had never been sent—like the Swedish editions of *Neverwhere*, or the Spanish *Smoke and Mirrors* and *Stardust*.

posted by Neil Gaiman 8:25 PM

Monday, June 11, 2001

On the advice of Terry Pratchett, who is a wise road warrior and is the only person I know who has signed for more people, and in more countries, than me, and seeing it's going to be six weeks of living out of hand-luggage (for there may not be time to check luggage, and I can't risk losing all my socks and black tee shirts to the whims of Northwest Airlines), I decided to buy a Toshiba Libretto, for the road.

(That's a very small, full-featured notebook computer that weighs next to nothing, for the non-technically minded among us.)

I take Terry's advice on things like this. He's always right. I still have, and still (once in a blue moon) use, the Atari Portfolio he talked me into buying about 11 years ago. It runs on a cut-down DOS 2.1—I wrote "Murder Mysteries" on it and "The Goldfish Pool & Other Stories" and more episodes of *Sandman* than I can count—and I'd use it more except I feel faintly ashamed of being seen using such antediluvian technology when in the company of all the cool geek people I know. They have transparent plastic things that are violently green at you, and which take photographs, order take-out, check for the nearest good sushi restaurant, download basketball scores and double as mobile phones, all at the same time. My Portfolio is only good for writing stuff and storing addresses and phone numbers. Which is all I ever use it for, not having much interest in basketball, and being a writer. I think I once managed to prove it was possible to get e-mail on it some time in 1992, and never tried again...

Sorry. Got a bit nostalgic there for a second.

So. Flash new Toshiba Libretto. It's not a palmtop, it's a subcompact notebook, which seemed closer to what I wanted. I checked the web...

They don't retail them anywhere but Japan any more. But there's a company that imports them. And the new Libretto L1 has just been released. Like, a few days ago.

I sent an e-mail to the sales guy at the company yesterday and asked if they could get me one before I left on tour. His e-mail arrived today. Absolutely. Just call and order and they'd overnight it to me.

It seemed so simple. I was thrilled. I called immediately...

Someone answered the phone.

I started to order a Libretto L1, using a corporate credit card.

If you write for Hollywood, you become a corporation whose sole asset is you and whose function consists of lending you out. (Honest. You think I could make that up?) Mine is called The Blank Corporation, because I went blank when they asked me what name I wanted it to be when they were filling in the corporate paperwork. I think the company logo is a blank sheet of paper, roughly 8″ by 11″. So there is a Blank Corporation credit card that I never use, and I thought, finally, I can buy something that's an honest to goodness business expense with the card.

I gave the guy on the other end of the phone the credit card number. He said they could only send it to the Card billing address. I said ow, that wasn't going to work, as that address was in LA, and I'm not, and getting the people who run the corporation in LA to authorise things might take a couple of days—I wasn't even sure if I knew how to talk to the card issuers... Still, not to worry. Plan B seemed straightforward enough. I put the card away (still, I think, unused), and pulled out my normal everyday not-corporate-at-all credit card.

Gave him the number of the new card. He asked for the Billing address, and I began "P.O. Box..."

"I'm sorry," he interrupted. "We don't deliver to PO Boxes."

"Not a problem," I said. "I'll give you the house address for FedEx to deliver to..."

"But it's not the billing address?"

"No, the bills go to the PO Box, but FedEx doesn't deliver to PO Boxes, so we get FedEx to deliver to..."

"I'm sorry. We can't do that. We can only send it to the billing address."

"But you've just told me you can't send it to the billing address."

"We don't deliver to PO Boxes."

"So you're saying you can't send me the computer."

"Well, yeah."

"Um. If you don't mind me asking… Does anyone else in America import Toshiba Librettos?" I figured, if someone else did, I'd call them instead.

"Nope. Just us." He didn't seem perturbed by the question. I guessed he heard it a lot.

"So you're telling me that you won't deliver to PO Boxes, and you can't deliver to the house?"

"Well, how do we know it's your house? You could have stolen a credit card, and this could be a deserted house down the block you want us to deliver to."

"Er, yes, but it's not. It's my house."

"People do it all the time. That's why we only ship to billing addresses."

"Yes, but you won't ship to my billing address, will you? Anyway, you'll have the phone number and the PO Box number. For heaven's sake, I've ordered a thousand things and this is the first time.."

"Hey, this is $3000 of computer equipment you're trying to order! People scam for a lot less than that. You can get phone numbers easy as anything, rent PO Boxes. We don't know this isn't a stolen card."

I thought about pointing out that, for $3000 of computer equipment, I was kind of expecting someone helpful on the other end of the phone. I thought about pointing out that, if it was a brilliant credit card fraud, and the card company approved the transaction, then they won't be out any money. I thought about dusting off the Atari Portfolio and pretending it was a grand retro gesture…

Instead I said "Look, I can't be the first person ever to try and order something who had a PO Box and wanted it shipped to a house address…"

"We can only ship it to a billing address," he said. He had that one down cold. "Or you could do a wire transfer."

I said that that wasn't going to happen. I was getting testy. I've been in the US too long, I suppose—I'm sort of used to trying to buy goods and services from people who are actively trying to sell them to you. I said there had to be a way for him to sell me a computer and could we please resolve this…

There was a long pause. And then he said, doubtfully, "I guess we could send it by the postal service. They deliver to post office boxes, don't they?"

I assured him that they did.

And he said, yes, they could do that, he guessed. They couldn't overnight it, but I'd get it by Friday, with the US postal service. I said I hoped so. He took the details, said they'd fax me a bill for me to sign and send back to them.

The fax, when it arrived, included a charge for FedExing the package. I carefully wrote on it "If sending by FedEx please deliver to…" and the house address, before I faxed it back, not because I was trying to be clever, but because I had a sudden presentiment of the people at the company finding themselves suddenly and unexpectedly unable to get me a little computer, "because FedEx doesn't deliver to PO Boxes".

So I leave on tour in six days. Off to do the Magnetic Fields gigs and then to start signing my way across the States, the UK and Canada. With luck, I'll be keeping up this journal, typing on planes and in cars, and posting it from hotel room phone lines.

And with a lot of luck, I'll be typing it on a Toshiba Libretto L1, and not on an Atari Portfolio. Not even as a grand retro gesture.

posted by Neil Gaiman 10:30 PM

Wednesday, June 13, 2001

The Libretto L1 arrived today in my P.O. Box. (Express mail through the post office is astonishingly expensive, it turns out.) The Libretto L1 is an amazing, beautiful and magnificent piece of technology. It's like a children's toy: an almost full-size keyboard, a cinemascope screen, it weighs nothing and takes up almost no room.

Unfortunately, after half an hour, the screen light went off and didn't go back on again, just flickered sadly like an old-fashioned fluorescent tube trying to work. The manuals are all in Japanese, so they weren't much help, although they had drawings of smiley people plugging their Librettos into things. I called technical support. They said not to worry, they'd send me a new computer.

I said, "Look, if I promise you I'm honestly not an international Libretto thief, would you please just FedEx it to the house?"

"Are you…are you the Neil Gaiman who wrote *Sandman?*"

"Yes."

"Not a problem. You'll have it tomorrow morning."

So there. Big vote of thanks to Shane and Dave at Dynamism.com for all their help, and I'll let you all know what happens next.

(FedEx tomorrow will bring many cool things, including the new Tori Amos CD, for the booklet of which I have to find some words.)

Currently, behind the scenes on the signing tour, lots of logistical stuff is being worked out, last-minute problems are being solved, all that.

Today brought some good news about the *Death* movie—with luck I'll have news I can announce before the tour starts.

posted by Neil Gaiman 4:06 PM

I got a lovely e-mail today from a friend in the UK who'd read *American Gods* (actually, I got quite a few lovely e-mails today from people who'd read *American Gods*). This was a lovely letter from someone who'd just devoured it and really enjoyed it (to the point where she seemed almost embarrassed about it—she knew how long it had taken me to write, and how hard some of it had been to get to work, and she compared herself to someone who just finished off a huge meal that a chef had taken a long time and pains to compare). I assured her that the main thing for me is just that people enjoy it.

This is from my reply to her:

> Remember to tell people about it... I figure word of mouth is my biggest ally on this one... Try and work it into casual conversation:

> "Ooh, I'll have five of those Granny Smiths. And *American Gods* is a really good book." "Of course I'd love to write an article for you on 'What the Modern Woman Really Wants'. Read *American Gods*. When's the deadline?" "I'm saying that you shouldn't be charging me for a letter telling me that I have an overdraft when the account was actually well in the black. By the way, there's a brilliant book called *American Gods* you may want to check out."

Which, on a marginally more serious note, seeing the book will be out in five days, and some of you will actually get a chance to read it yourselves, is really my only request to any of you. If you like the book, tell people. Spread the word.

I am reminded of Geoff Ryman's lovely novel *253,* which includes a woman whose job is to ride the tube train under London reading a paperback book with delight, occasionally exclaiming aloud on the brilliance and wonderfulness of the book she's reading. Cheap advertising.

posted by Neil Gaiman 9:11 PM

My daughter Holly just came charging in. "Hey Dad!" she said. "You're at 82 on Amazon.com!" She had a huge smile on her face. "That's the highest it's been so far! And it's not even out yet!"

Then her face fell. "I'm away next week," she said. "I won't be here to check for you, while you're off on tour. You could get up really high on Amazon, and you'd never know."

Someone would tell me, I assured her.

"Have you put me in your journal thing again, yet?" she asked. "You know I read it. So far you've only told about the time I made your journal entry vanish. You should say something nice about me."

She is pretty wonderful, actually. Hi, Holly.

posted by Neil Gaiman 10:34 PM

Thursday, June 14, 2001

There's a cartoon by the incredibly brilliant Gahan Wilson, from his book of the same name, in which a man stares around him at the people worshipping the signs saying "Nothing" and the cathedrals erected with the word "Nothing" on them, in glowing bright lights.

"Is Nothing sacred?" he asks.

The cover of the Hodder-Headline UK edition made me think of that.

posted by Neil Gaiman 9:37 AM

Some days are instant Christmas. They put a smile on your face...

Today brought...

Tori's CD, *Strange Little Girls*. It's missing one track, but the other eleven are there. I knew what to expect this time, but my family are spellbound. It's just playing all the time in the background...as surprising and as wonderful the fifth time as it was the first...

The replacement Libretto. Working like a little dream—I'm just transferring over files from my notebook, then I'll load up Word Perfect and Final Draft, and it'll be all ready for the road.

and...just as I thought the day had brought all the presents it could...

I opened an envelope to see the UK editions of *American Gods*.

So, first of all, I got to learn that there is indeed a huge trade paperback edition of *American Gods* in the UK, and a hardback. The hardback is £17.99, the paperback is £10.00. Amazon.co.uk has been erroneously listing it as hardback for £10.00...so if anyone out there thought that was what they'd ordered, they may need to talk to Amazon, or to their local bookshop and make sure they are getting what they want.

(Incidentally, it's 500 pages long, not 352.)

The second thing I learned is that they're doing a very surprising promotion for the hardback, which caused me jaw to drop. I'm not sure I can say anything more about it until I've got an okay from Headline. It raised eyebrows and caused giggles in this house.

Normally the UK hardbacks wind up the most collectible of the editions, as they are printed in the smallest numbers. Looking at this edition, which is lovely, I suspect that may again be true, especially as people who think they've successfully ordered it may have problems getting it...

posted by Neil Gaiman 12:40 PM

There's a story on Inside.com about the Magnetic Fields gig on Sunday—I've put a pile of stuff onto the Libretto. Now I need to print out everything I might want to read on Sunday night—there are two different sets, and I'm very tempted to do two completely different readings.

I noticed today that I've suddenly and completely stopped worrying about the tour and the book and all that. It's too late: everything that is going to happen will happen, so I may as well get out there and have fun.

posted by Neil Gaiman 7:05 PM

Friday, June 15, 2001

So, just as everything gets *really* exciting, and I have a day to finish organising everything for the next 6 weeks, do several interviews including an NPR one and an online chat at excite.com tonight...

...comes the news that this blogger may have to be frozen for a couple of days, as the changeover to the still-nascent neilgaiman.com happens behind the scenes. Keep checking in here, as I'll post as soon as it goes live again (and this page will automatically take you over to its new location).

Also just discovered that the old Avon *Neverwhere* pages are completely lost, which is a pity, as they were lot of fun.

And powells.com have put up that journal entry that got out of hand—you'll find me talking about it in the archives, fairly early on. It was me trying to explain the book, and it just sort of grew. it's at http://www.powells.com/features/gaiman.html

posted by Neil Gaiman 11:24 AM

Saturday, June 16, 2001

So neilgaiman.com went live and ate most of americangods.com. I miss the old-style front page—I was rather hoping to see what happened to the *American Gods* WILL BE PUBLISHED IN... counter as soon as we got past midnight on Monday the 18th.

So, right now, if you're reading this, you probably have this page bookmarked, because you can't get to the working bloggerjournalthing from the main site.

As the cover note says on the home page, neilgaiman.com is, right now, very much a work in progress. Given another week, everything should actually work. Over the following few weeks it'll become much prettier and better organised, I'll try to get a few more things written for it, find fun archived stuff, we'll have more links to things, all that—but for right now what you see is more or less what you get.

The message boards look like they may be fun. Feel very free to chip in—and to use the *American Gods* TOUR section for everything from seeing if you can get a ride to a signing, to, um, meeting up at signings.

webmaster@authorsontheweb.com is the webmaster, and julia.onder@harpercollins.com is the publisher's webperson. If something seems to be broken...tell them. They will want to know. They've moved mountains to get everything up before the 19th of June...

Let's see, what else...? Oh yes. My assistant, the Fabulous Lorraine, has a new CD out. She and writer Emma Bull are a band called The Flash Girls, and they've made their first new album in about five years. (They were geographically challenged.) It's called *Play Each Morning, Wild Queen,* and it's very cool. (Their last album, *Maurice and I,* was also very cool, is still available, and has Alan Moore's song "Me and Dorothy Parker" on it.) It has a cover by Michael Zulli, and three songs by me on. Please buy it and make her independently wealthy. You can order it from DreamHaven books in Minneapolis.

posted by Neil Gaiman 12:02 AM

The Message board on neilgaiman.com should be working on Monday morning.

Today's mail brought a Dutch contract for *American Gods* (I'm always faintly pleased when the Dutch buy the rights to a book, as they all speak terrific English and import UK or US editions anyway).

Therese Littleton's review of *American Gods* is now up at Amazon.com... someone else who understood it.

I'm on tour from tomorrow morning, for six weeks...wish me luck.

posted by Neil Gaiman 10:44 AM

Monday, June 18, 2001

I did a wonderful gig—two sets—with the Magnetic Fields. I had a busy day meeting people about *The Day I Swapped My Dad for Two Goldfish* animated series, and then meeting HarperCollins people and getting to learn all sorts of cool stuff about e-books and soforth...

And in 50 minutes my book is officially published.

You probably won't get a long and sensible entry here for a few more days, until I stop moving and can think or at least type in peace.

Scott McCloud sent me his "Why I'm Not Neil Gaiman" cartoon, and it made me laugh very loudly. You get it for free if you donate to his website. And his website is a wonderful thing.

See you at Borders World Trade Center tomorrow, if you're in the NY area. The Libretto is working fine but if the bloody thing has a real apostrophe I can't find it. So I'm using these. ' ' '

posted by Neil Gaiman 8:14 PM

Thursday, June 21, 2001

Dateline *American Gods* plus one.

I'm in New York in a car on my way to the Huntingdon signing, with the Libretto on my lap. So…

This is what happens two days before publication: you fly in to New York, and do a gig with the Magnetic Fields. Two sets. I did two completely different readings—lots of short stuff, some new stuff, some weird stuff. Afterward it occurred to me that I did the readings completely for Neil Gaiman fans, and that the people who were solely Magentic Feilds fans (Stephen Merrit says that's how their name is most often misspelled) were probably very puzzled and perplexed. The readings I'd do for an audience entirely consisting of people who have no idea who I am or what I do would be very different from one I'd do for people who want to hear B-sides and rarities…

And I got to watch both sets of the Magnetic Fields—who also did two very different sets early evening and late. Which made me astonishingly happy. It's a very good thing to have your favourite band in the whole world be people you like to spend time with as well as people you like to watch. Highlights for me were Stephen's performance of "Papa Was a Rodeo" (first set version) and Claudia's "Acoustic Guitar" (second set version) and the second set duet of "Yeah, Oh Yeah".

Next morning—Monday—I slept in, for the last time for a long time, then went up to the HarperCollins office and Met People. Meeting People at your publishers is part of being an author they don't tell you much about. It's fun. People are in publishing because they love books. This is an important thing to remember. (A very few of them are in publishing because they once loved books. This is sad when it happens.) I met the e-book division. They love e-books, which is harder to do. Now, I have recently acquired an e-book and haven't had much a chance to play with it—so far I think the best thing about it will probably prove to be that you can read in the dark without waking up the person next to you. I will report back on the crop of e-books by me, which come out next week, and which I will look at on my new toy. After I met the e-book people I met the people who run HarperCollins.

(It's now half a day later, and I'm typing on the way to Newark.)

Let's see. Monday. Okay… so, I signed books for people at HarperCollins. I had dinner with people from HarperCollins. I went to bed. I went to sleep. After about half an hour I woke up completely and unexpectedly. As the e-book was by the bed, I read the instructions for the e-book in the dark, and practised the alphabet for making notes in the dark. If I had been someone in the bed next to me, I wouldn't have woken up, if you see what I mean.

Breakfast with the Harper Children's Publisher, my Harper Editor and my agent about *Coraline*. It'll be published in 2002—they want to move it from Spring to Fall, to get more attention for it. I say okay. (*American Gods* will still come out in paperback in May of 2002) Then we run, my agent and I, to her office, to meet my UK editor on *Coraline*, who is in

New York. She's from Bloomsbury, and I like her immediately, and look forward to working with her.

The day spins and whirls and somewhere in there I eat lunch (Onigashima on 55th St., really really good sushi) and somewhere a bit later I turn up at Borders in the World Trade Center for the reading and signing.

A host of friends turn up before the signing as I sit in a back room signing books for staff, and I say my hellos and check my pens...and by a little after 7:00pm I'm out there in front of the people.

It's been years since I felt nervous at a signing. This time I feel nervous: it's publication date. It's the first signing. I don't know.

Borders World Trade Center is a good store. I did a signing there for *Neverwhere* in 1997 and it was a tight squeeze then...and there are a lot more people there now. Over 500 of them, at a guess. Seating for about 80 people at the reading, which meant that three-quarters of the people couldn't see what was going on. (My apologies if you were one of them.) Surprised, as I said, to find I was genuinely nervous. Read the opening of the book as the nerves slowly dissipated, answered audience questions about an odd assortment of things (including, rather to my surprise, pumpkin-growing) and off we go signing...

Finished around 11:30 with over 450 *American Gods* signed. (Rule here—any copies of *American Gods* plus two other things.) Hurrah for Daryl and the staff...

Walk out of signing to find a few friends hanging around, including my friends writer Andy Heidel (former HarperCollins publicist, now Sci-Fi Channel man) and his fiancée Jen the Puppet Queen (Mama Lion on *Between The Lions*) and the wonderful Claudia Gonson (sings, plays keyboards for and manages the Magnetic Fields). They had been hanging around for hours to say hello and maybe even buy me a drink. I haven't eaten since lunchtime, and tell them so, and we wind up eating upstairs in a little Japanese place somewhere half a Manhattan away from Borders World Trade Center. Where we immediately bump into someone who had been at the signing but had, after three hours, given up and wandered off...

Get back late to hotel. Bath. Sleep. It's late. That was publication day.

Wake up rather in need of a shave to learn that I forgot to pack a razor. Right. I'll buy a razor. Run for breakfast with my agent, and from there to a meeting with a booking agency who want to represent me as a public speaker. Am kindly disposed to them because they represented Douglas Adams and had already approached me before he died—in fact I'd been ready to call him and find out whether he liked them... Not that I want a career as a public speaker I should add, but I need somewhere to send all the requests that are always coming in for me to go to universities and cultural festivals and such, and these guys are probably going to be better at saying "No" than I am.

On the way out I learn how many copies of *American Gods* were sold on the first day of publication at Borders, at Barnes and Noble, at Waldenbooks. ("Is that good?" I ask. I'm told that, yes, it's good. It's bestseller numbers. Now we just have to hope it keeps up for the rest of the week.)

Lunch at Yamaguchi on 45th St (their prices are twice what Onigashima was for worse food.) An afternoon of drop-in signings.

Drop-ins are just that. Hit and run attacks by an author, where you go in, sign the shop stock, go away again. This can be an unpleasant experience, or a pleasant one. Ever since a store in San Francisco had a line of 60 people waiting for me at one of these, I've forbidden publishers to tell bookstores any more about drop-in times than "He'll be in in the afternoon". But frankly, for as many places as you drop in and they're excited and have alerted their favourite customers to hang around the store all afternoon to meet you, there are as many stores that you get to be met by blank looks from store assistants and they explain that they aren't sure where Dave is, and Dave is the only person who knows where the single copy of your book that they are sure they have somewhere was put.

I sign a heap of *American Gods* at the Barnes and Nobles in Astor Place and Chelsea. (If you're in New York and you want a signed copy, that might be the best way to go.) Realize I'm not going to have time to buy a razor before the signing.

Out to Huntingdon, Long Island, to Book Revue. Sign staff stuff. Eat a hasty tuna salad (I'd learned my lesson on not eating at all the night before). It's a medium-sized signing in a thunderstorm, although lots more people can sit and see what's going on than at Borders. I read the *I Love Lucy* scene. It must have been a unique experience for the audience, hearing a bemused English author doing his Lucille Ball impression accompanied by ominous thundery rumbles. I'm not saying it was any good, mind you. Just that it's not an everyday occurrence.

(That last bit was typed in Newark airport. Now I'm writing sitting in Chicago O'Hare airport, waiting for Jennifer Hershey, my editor, who is doing this leg with me.)

Book Revue was a pleasant signing—nice staff, nice store—huge as a Barnes and Noble superstore, but it smelled like books, like paper and wood and old binding glue—and, as always, the people in the line were nice people. Finished a little after eleven. 170+ copies of *American Gods* were sold, many hundreds of people were made happy.

In the car on the way there and on the way back I got to talk to the book's publicity team, Jack and Dee Dee. It was good.

Got back to my hotel by around 1:30 am. Put in for the 6:30 wake-up call, ate a banana, did some packing. Noticed a message on my phone and called and discovered a package of images had arrived for me from England, so called down for them, and waited.

Package arrived. It made me happy. I slept.

And the wake-up call stumbled me out of the hotel and there was the driver. "Off to Newark," I said. "No, to La Guardia," he said. I panicked. We checked our papers, and I was right and he'd been given the wrong information. And I started typing this.

They may have served breakfast on the plane. I don't know. I was asleep. Now I'm in Chicago. A few minutes to post this and run. Then I really have to find a razor.

posted by Neil Gaiman 12:54 pm

Friday, June 22, 2001

In Chicago. Did a signing in Champaign this evening. Nice store, about 375 nice people, over 175 *American Gods* sold by the store, and they also had some sushi around for a tired author at the end. In the car on the way home I found myself unexpectedly doing a radio phone in with WGN's Steve and Johnnie. Then I slept in the car. Now I post this. Then I sleep some more.

Oddest interview was with a local paper today on the phone. "So," said the journalist. "I guess it must be a real rockstar life on the road. Do you travel with a full entourage? Like a chef and a hairdresser?"

Eagle-eyed readers of this journal may already have intuited that I was forced to disappoint him. For a moment I was tempted to start talking about Alyssa and Armando and Arnold (the butler)—but in the end I told the truth. It's me, a book escort, and—for a couple of days, for her first time on the road—my editor, Jennifer Hershey, getting a first-hand view of a signing tour.

I bet when she goes back to New York she'll recommend the whole chefs and hairdressers bit to HarperCollins. But until then, I'm my own entourage.

posted by Neil Gaiman 1:50 AM

This just in from Felicia Quon, HarperCollins Canada…

> "Hello Neil
>
> I know you are on tour (it sounds like it is going very well) , but I wanted to let you know that we have added a signing in Toronto. Here are the details:
> Sunday July 22 at 4 pm. Indigo Books & Music Toronto, ON. Signing only
> If this could be posted on americangods.com…

Her wish is our command. And Salon.com has a review up at http://www.salon.com/books/review/2001/06/22/gaiman/ which I really liked. It seemed to be writing about the book I'd written, and I was pretty conscious of the things she points to—Jesus actually did turn up in a scene which I cut, as it just didn't work, but I figured a book about American Religion was not the book I wanted to write, which was about American Belief, so I let some things go…

In Chicago. Did The Stars Our Destination at lunch time, (about 200 people, about 140 *American Gods* sold). And I have been assured by Jennifer Hershey that we have become the fastest ever selling American title in Oslo. Hurrah for Norway.

posted by Neil Gaiman 3:42 PM

Saturday, June 23, 2001

Ahoy shipmates. Belay there. Avast, and other nautical things.

So I'm in a car with Jennifer Hershey, on the way from Lexington to Dayton, being driven by the lovely and competent Gwenda Bond. Gwenda in her real life does something in the governor of Kentucky's office, and she is an angel in human form. Well, more or less.

Last night I signed in the Barnes and Noble in Skokie—a huge store. I read some of Chapter Four, with Czernobog and the Zorya, answered questions and signed, signed, signed. About 150 books sold, for a total of 300-odd for the day in Chicago. My favourite present was a double CD of a 1996 Elvis Costello Chicago gig.

Somewhere a little before midnight Jennifer Hershey and I got into a car driven by Bill Young, the Author Escort, and we drove through the night to Lexington. Got to our hotel at 6:30 am to find that Gwenda had already checked us all in and set everything up, I went and found my room and went to sleep in a real bed. Woke up, showered, did a little e-mail (not much—I'm way behind right now, and probably will be for another month). It was around midday, and Gwenda turned up bearing sushi for us all for breakfast. (Really good, by the way. I never thought of Lexington as one of the great Sushi places in the world. Whodathunkit?) And then we drove to the signing.

Some time ago Gwenda used her mysterious influence to have me made a Kentucky Colonel. Now, to celebrate me actually turning up to sign books in the Commonwealth, she presented me with a certificate and a card proclaiming me an Admiral. I shall hope that Kentucky does not declare war on any other states during my lifetime or my lack of nautical knowledge will come out.

I read some of Chapters 7 and 8, up to the autopsy-in-Cairo scene, did a Q & A, then signed for a few hundred people—a real Head Down and Get On With It signing in order to be out on time. Strange and wonderful gifts. ("It's wonderful. What is it?" "I'm not sure. But it's small. You said on your journal you liked small.") Nice people—I say that every signing, but I'm always pleased and surprised by how very nice everyone is.

After the signing, I signed the pre-orders (books for people who had phoned the store and ordered copies but couldn't be there) and a small amount of shop stock.

There's an urban legend among authors that simply the act of signing a book that the store has in the back sells it. "A signed book is a sold book," they say. Actually this is tosh. Bookstores return books for credit, and signed hardbacks enter the system all the time; while the covers are ripped off signed paperbacks and the insides are thrown away (or walked off with). A signed book is just a book.

On this tour there's not much stock being signed, mostly because there's not been time, but if you're hunting a signed book it's always a good idea to call a bookstore after an author's been there.

And now we're driving to Dayton—it looks like we'll be on time, which is a relief, as I'd not been certain it would be possible. (This was because someone had told us it was a certain 3-hour drive if we were lucky. Not the way Gwenda drives it wasn't.)

Much later. We're in a hotel room, waiting for room service. It's 1:10am and we put in the order a bit before midnight. We're hungry and we're getting kind of sad. The hotel is filled with drunk Jaycees. A couple making love in one of the elevators asked me if I had a room free that they could use. On the good side, there's a minibar in the room. On the downside, it's completely empty. At 1:00 am we phoned down to the front desk and we told them that we didn't have any food , and they said they'd tried to bring it and knocked on the door and we didn't answer, and I said they hadn't and they went off to investigate.

There. They investigated. They're bringing it up to us. Really they are.

The food came at 1:30 am. It was cold where it should have been warm and warm where it should have been cold and tasted like they really had made it when we called down for it, ninety minutes before. We ate it anyway. We didn't care. Then Jennifer and Gwenda said goodnight and went off to their room, and I sat here and typed this final entry.

Books and Co. in Dayton does wonderful signings, and this one was no exception. But I have to be up in a little under 4 hours time and on the plane to Cleveland, so details will have to wait for another time.

posted by Neil Gaiman 11:01 PM

Monday, June 25, 2001

Cleveland was hard—left the hotel at 5:30 am, flew out from Dayton, slept for 90 minutes on the store manager's sofa, and then interviewed over breakfast by Julie Washington from the *Cleveland Plain Dealer*, who remains one of my favourite American journalists, mostly because I can make her laugh, then signed for about 400 people at Joseph Beth in Shaker

Square (over 200 copies of *AG* signed) (great store, great people), ran for the airport made the plane, slept like a dead thing... saw my family for maybe ten minutes in Minneapolis airport, traded laundry (dirty for clean) (I got the clean) hugged them and got onto the next plane...

Michael Dirda reviewed *American Gods* in the Washington *Post* at http://www.washingtonpost.com/wp-dyn/articles/A31265-2001Jun21.html

posted by Neil Gaiman 11:25 AM

Cheryl Morgan e-mailed me to tell me that her review in EmeraldCity is up. This is a link to the review: http://www.emcit.com/emcit070.shtml#Spirits, but read the rest of it as well...

posted by Neil Gaiman 11:58 AM

Several hundred FAQ type e-mails waiting for me to look at, but I shall answer the most frequently asked and burning one right now and right here...

It's pronounced Gaym'n...not Guy-man, or any of the other ways people pronounce it at each other. Honest.

On the run...

posted by Neil Gaiman 2:04 PM

Tuesday, June 26, 2001

M. J. Rose has done an article in *Wired* online about this very blogger http://www.wired.com/news/culture/0,1284,44751,00.html. And seeing that she has only a limited amount of space, and only quotes one sentence from the e-mail I sent her, I thought I'd post the whole thing here. The questions I was responding to were about marketing and the part an author plays in it...

> Dear MJ
>
> To be honest, I haven't really thought of any of this as marketing. I'm not saying it's not, and I'm not trying to be willfully naive or disingenuous here, but I wouldn't have done the journal if it was a marketing thing. I did it because I was really interested in the process of taking people behind the scenes in making a book. I'm the kind of person who never manages to keep a diary, but I enjoyed having a topic on Genie, when there was a Genie, where I could post what was happening. For the last year I've had a topic on the Well, again as a kind of diary and info and news source.
>
> The Blogger seemed like a good way to take readers and the curious backstage. Part journal, part diary, part

stream of consciousness. I really enjoyed the feeling of having someone to talk to.

I talked to Jennifer Hershey, my editor, about what I had in mind—that I wanted americangods.com to be the most basic of sites, with nothing on it but the journal, tour info when we got it, a way to order the book, and that was all. And I didn't want it to be publicized—I liked the idea that anyone interested would hear about it and go and see it; it meant that I could start writing without any feeling that the world was looking over my shoulder. I think the first few posts may have been marketing posts, in that I was trying to announce and explain the book, but very quickly it turned into a way of explaining the process of taking a book from handing in the finished manuscript to the end of the author tour—there's even a kind of plot there, as the readers of the blog and I get to learn whether *American Gods* goes onto the bestseller lists or the remainder table.

I thought it astonishing how many unique hits we were getting and how "sticky" such a simple site was, and felt faintly justified in my theory that content is more important than delivery mechanisms.

I don't think it takes time away from writing—at least, not more than one normally winds up giving to the process of getting a book out there: it took a lot more time to write my name on 5000 pages (to be bound into the books) than it did to write a couple of blogger entries about signing 5000 pages. It was a good way to explain, to record what I thought, to let off steam.

As for surprises—I think the biggest one was how many people were reading it. And how many of the people who were reading it weren't necessarily Neil Gaiman fans or readers but were people who read and enjoyed the blogger—they read a little of it and got hooked. I liked that. I still do.

With neilgaiman.com I was a lot more nervous— I've shied away from an official website for many years, feeling that fans did it much better than I ever could, and that they had a level of interest and curiosity in the author of *Neverwhere* and *Sandman* and his work that I could never aspire to. But HarperCollins wanted to do it, and I went and found a few things for them to put on there, and suggested some initial topics, areas and directions, and now it's gone live I'm getting interested in it—trying to make it cooler, better looking, containing more—I'm already starting to think about a few things I've written that that no-one's ever seen that are sitting on a hard disk somewhere and might quite enjoy being read. And I'm trying to think of some ways of allowing the fans to contribute more—given the volume of traffic on the message boards I think that may be a lot of fun.

Hope this is of use—

written in the car on the way to a signing in Champaign...

Neil Gaiman

Am now kind of tired after Seattle... off to San Francisco in half an hour. Must...get...dressed...must...pack...must...eat nice breakfast room service person brought...must...do something about hair...anything...

posted by Neil Gaiman 7:30 AM

Ahem.
This Journal would officially like to extend a Happy Sixteenth Birthday to Holly Gaiman. Who also passed her driving test today. Just wish I was there to give her a hug. (But she's coming in to LA as a birthday present so I'll see her there...)

posted by Neil Gaiman 3:03 PM

Wednesday, June 27, 2001

Lovely article about, well, mostly this blogger actually, along with the very wonderful Lisa Gallagher of HarperCollins, at http://www.cnn.com/ 2001/CAREER/readingup/06/26/american.gods/index.html. And I'd say more about it, but at that point you start walking through a hall of infinite mirrors...

I'm pooped right now in San Francisco. Will try to grab some time in the car on the way to Screen Savers later today to write about the last few days...

posted by Neil Gaiman 10:22 AM

Thursday, June 28, 2001

There's nothing quite so unlikely as typing a blogger entry on a sofa in a TV studio, but that's just what I seem to be doing right now.

And for that matter, I want to make a point of saying that I am now, as of twenty minutes ago, no longer an author. Nope. Now I am officially a *New York Times* Bestselling Author. And I've learned where the apostrophe is on the Libretto. (It's just above the 7 key.) Two good things in one day.

…there. TV over and done with, and Amacker Bullwinkle is driving me from the Tech TV studios to a dinner with Charles Brown, editor and publisher of *Locus* http://www.locusmag.com/ , and I'm typing a little as I go.

Amacker drives a little like a Brazilian taxi driver who took me and my editor from the Rio book fair to the airport last month. The traffic speed was maybe 40. He never drove at less than 70, nipping into tiny spaces, lurching manically from lane to lane. As soon as I was sure I wasn't going to die, it was kind of fun. Amacker would like that taxi driver. I think they went to the same driving school.

So today I signed in The Booksmith on the Haight—like the lunchtime signing at The Stars Our Destination in Chicago last week, this one was also a drop-in signing that became a real one, but without a reading, which is a pity as Shadow and Wednesday walk that street in *American Gods*. I'll read that section—the Easter bit—tonight, I think.

It was a good signing—my third at The Booksmith. The best thing about signing at The Booksmith is this: they do a trading card of the author. I think they have a web site where all the trading cards are listed. http://www.booksmith.com/cards/cards.html.

After the signing we drove to the Tech TV offices. My cellphone rang as I was greeting Roger, the show's producer. I've not been answering it much on this tour—it usually rings when I'm talking to people or signing or reading or something, and I just let it ring, but this time I answered it. It was Kathy Hemming of HarperCollins.

"I've got a fax in front of me," she said. "You're at number 10 on the *New York Times* list!"

And I phumphed and goshed and grinned like a lunatic and said thank you a lot and she said no, thank you and all things considered it was a Very Good Thing.

Then I went on Screen Savers, walking two inches above the floor. Leo, the host, had been reading this blogger and he wanted to see the Libretto, so I pulled it out, and everyone gathered around and they all wanted to know the same thing.

"$2,200," I'd say. "600 MHz. No it doesn't weigh anything." and I wound up taking it onto the show. And starting this entry there…

The first time I was ever interviewed on TV was in 1987. John Lloyd (eminent UK TV producer and writer and stuff) was presenting a show called *South of Watford* and he interviewed Dave McKean and me about *Violent Cases*, in a pub called the Café Munchen (now The Conservatory, unless it's something else).

We chatted before the interview, friendly and relaxed. And then it was time to turn on the TV cameras. They were turned on, and John turned to me and asked the first question.

I froze.

I froze utterly and in every way. My mouth slowly opened and nothing came out. I forgot how to speak.

John said, "Stop rolling," to the camera people, and told me everything would be fine, and reminded me it wasn't live, and then he told them to turn on the cameras and asked me the question again.

I've never been nervous or tongue-tied on TV since, but I can't forget that time. It lurks in the back of my mind, a little adrenaline-kicker before every TV appearance.

(Sorry about that. I just fell asleep for twenty minutes. We must be nearly there…)

…and for the first time ever we're in Continued on Next Rock territory, as I'm going to have to post this so far and go to sleep. It's 1:30 am and I've just spent an hour signing stuff back at the hotel room, after the Cody's signing… and I have to be out of here at 7:00 am and I am so tired you would not believe it, and I'm not sure I do. So I'll finish talking about Screen Savers (it's on until mid-afternoon on Thursday) and everything else, later.

posted by Neil Gaiman 1:35 am.

Friday, June 29, 2001

You're probably thinking to yourself, I wonder where he is now? That one's easy. He's typing this in a train on the way from San Diego to Los Angeles. Which means that by the time he posts this, he'll be in his room in his hotel in LA.

And you may be wondering, I wonder how he's holding up? And the answer is, Okay, all things considered. Tired on a short of sleep sort of level, tired on a cellular level, much crankier than is my—his—sod it, we're back into the first person—my usual wont.

The hotel in San Francisco didn't help.

If they can, when travel agencies book authors into hotels, they put them into good, solid, businessy hotels, or sometimes into really good hotels. There are a couple of hotels (there's one in Portland for example) that are particularly keen on touring authors, and greet you with copies of your book to sign for their library.

And if you've got the kind of author who may not be eating until back in his hotel room very late, you make sure that the hotel has overnight room service.

For reasons no-one understands, I wound up in a little tourist hotel in the Japanese district of San Francisco. It wasn't the kind of place that had overnight room service. It wasn't the kind of place where the concierge would let you know that you had had six boxes of books to sign delivered to your room. For that matter, it wasn't the kind of place where, once they'd agreed that the books existed and would be delivered to your room, they actually bother to deliver them to your room.

Also, it was an additional 15-25 minutes away from everywhere we needed to go, and when your day is running to the minute, the hour you can lose getting to and from the hotel comes out of sleep time.

This was particularly frustrating to Ellen Fishman, who was my author escort.

I know I meant to write about Author Escorts before, and have indeed mentioned them in passing. But I should probably explain them a bit more before continuing.

In the UK, if a publisher sends an author on tour, they often send a publicity person with them. Most of the publicity people are attractive young women, and there's not one of them that won't tell you horror stories of the time that author X or celebrity Y, who they were accompanying around the country at the time, decided that the real reason the publisher had sent an attractive young lady on tour with them was for purposes of sexual relief. After a glass or two of wine at the end of a long day's signing and interviewing, they'll even name names.

In the US, when a publisher sends an author on tour, they contract out their care to an Author Escort. Every city has one agency, some have more than one. Author escorts pick you up at the airport holding a copy of your book in their hands. (It's a good thing if you look like your author photo as that's how they recognise you.) They get you to your hotel, to the radio station or the TV studios. Every doorman and parking lot attendant in the city is their crony. They know the back ways. They will make things work and deliver you to wherever you are meant to be on time, guard you at the signing, get you back to your hotel.

Ellen has looked after me each time I've gone to San Francisco. Stephen King once said if he was having a heart attack and needed someone to get him into a hospital and treated he'd want Harlan Ellison by his side. I'd want Harlan too, but only if Ellen Fishman wasn't available.

Some of them are that good. Some of them aren't. I've only had maybe two who were useless in all the time I've done signing tours.

On my last tour I asked all the author escorts who the worst people they'd ever had were. (It wasn't for me. Jonathan Carroll asked.) They all declined to answer, and then I'd tell them who the others had said (luckily my first escort had a number of opinions, and one bookstore was particularly voluble about the worst person they'd ever had sign there) and they'd say "Oh let me tell you about her," or "I had him, he was a sweetie" and then they'd give me their lists.

At the time Brett Butler made number one, but only because Jeffrey Archer hadn't toured for a while. The ones who remembered him still looked nervous when his name was mentioned.

And sooner or later I'll finish talking about author escorts, Screen Savers, and survival tips for on the road.

There. Now we're three signings behind on the blogger. Cody's, Mysterious Galaxy and Vromans...maybe I'll get a chance to write about them tomorrow. Right now I just want to post this and sleep.

Oh, for all the people who have come up to me and asked why I call this journal a blogger—"Is it a British thing?"—you should go to http://www.blogger.com/ and find out...

Still. I'm now in a nice hotel in LA, and Holly's here, which made me a lot less cranky than I was. She was thrilled when we opened the door to the hotel room to find lots of people had sent flowers, champagne and faxes telling us that the *New York Times* List thing was a good thing, and she was astonished that journal-reading people came up to her at Vromans wishing her happy birthday and congratulating her on passing her driving test. (Her license has a photo of her with an ear to ear grin on it. It's astoundingly cute.)

I've put in a request to the powers that be to make this journal (a) easier to read. (I want larger type dammit.) And (b) to make the links visible without having to pass the mouse over them to reveal them (which seems to defeat the purpose of them being links). I hope we can make it happen soon...

posted by Neil Gaiman 2:08 AM

And the FAQs aren't working because I haven't had a second to start work on them. The questions are coming in just fine...

Still, until we get an FAQ working, let me point you to http://www.raintaxi.com/gaiman.html, an interview in *Rain Taxi*, which may answer some *American Gods* questions. Or may not.

posted by Neil Gaiman 2:12 AM

Saturday, June 30, 2001

Just posting this because there are still 6 boxes of books to be signed and removed from my bed before I can go to sleep.

http://cbldf.safeshopper.com/13/cat13.htm?279 It's got a bunch of stuff you won't get anywhere else, and is, I think, the only place you can simply order one of the signed 5000 books online. And that's not all. It's all for a good cause. Check it out.

And here's a review: http://www.likesbooks.com/heidi23.html.

And this http://www.cc.gatech.edu/people/home/idris/Essays/Shakes_in_Bush.htm is for any of you who think that stories are universal. Read it and ponder.

I go home in a few hours. This makes me very happy. I like the idea of sleeping in my own bed. Maybe walking around the garden and saying hello to the pumpkins. Reading Maddy's bedtime story. Not travelling, for just a few days.

"How are you doing?" asked most of the last fifty people in the line at tonight's signing as they came up.

"I'm tired," I said. "But I'm pretty good."

"Get some rest," they said, one by one, concerned.

I have nice readers.

posted by Neil Gaiman 1:38 AM

I'm home, and I almost got through today without signing any books. But there were some copies of Biting Dog Press's beautiful limited edition *Murder Mysteries* to be signed waiting for me at DreamHaven, so I went there from the airport. (Link at http://www3.sympatico.ca/ george.walker/gaimanbkad.html although it displayed rather oddly in Explorer for me.)

There were also two copies of *Angels and Visitations* to be signed, some *Warning: Contains Language* sleeves. And, um, about 500 presold mail-order copies of *American Gods*. So my day of not signing anything rather failed to happen. Still, it's a genuine down day. And it was good to play with Maddy. The garden has erupted, there was an awful lot of waiting mail, and pretty soon I'll have a bath and go to bed and sleep like a dead person.

Starting to suspect that the Ebook *REB 1100* is going to prove useless and frustrating unless Gemstar decides to allow it access to more content, and cheaper. I keep batting my head against the whole thing of price and convenience, and with access to Public Domain stuff cut off, no way of sending my own content to the thing (which would be genuinely useful), and no easily discernable way to access the kind of stuff I'd need—most of which is out on Project Gutenberg (nice people, who lost a page with some in-copyright stuff on it when I pointed it out to them.) Which is a pity, because as a delivery mechanism, it' s rather wonderful. But it's a bit like having a TV that will only play a handful of proprietary shows. Unless the content is easily available, and in quantity, and it's the content you want, then the delivery mechanism is almost beside the point.

I signed all those books last night, by the way. They were for Golden Apple and Dangerous Visions respectively, for any LA bookbuyers looking for a signed book. And I was at one point tired enough that I wrote the name of the person on the post-it note instead of my name on a copy I was just meant to sign. So I sighed and blinked and did a drawing of Mr Wednesday, hoping the person would forgive me.

The weirdest thing about the whole *NY Times* Bestseller thing, is that the rest of the world doesn't know, and won't till next Sunday—when I shall be in the UK...

posted by Neil Gaiman 9:46 PM

Sunday, July 01, 2001

Someone at one of the stops put a piece of paper down on the desk in front of me. Secret advice for blogger users it said. When I opened it up, it said, write your blogger entry in notepad first. But unless I'm writing from the road, I never do. I just head over to blogger.com, enter the blogger and start typing.

I just typed an entry, hit...some key...and everything I'd typed to that point vanished completely. So I'm doing it again.

Let's see...first of all, ignore previous comment on the *NY Times* bestseller list not being out till next Sunday. That was written because I'd lost a day and thought it was Sunday—this was caused by:

(a) a two week long marathon tour across America (except for the South) without much sleep at a city a day and

(b) buying the Sunday papers on the way home. Mock me if you wish—you try doing a tour like that, and be happy if all you lose is a Saturday.

And the list is up at: http://www.nytimes.com/books/01/07/08/bsp/besthardfiction.html — and thanks to Jade Walker for letting me know, over in the Well. Jade does a really good online e-zine for writers called *Inscriptions*—if you write, want to write, or you just like writers, you should go and look at it...

Talking about Except for the South, there were some people who came a really long way to get their books signed on this tour. Most of them were from Texas, and many of them drove... I felt guilty and was pleased at the same time. My assistant tells me I'll be a guest at Aggiecon next year, so people won't have so far to drive...

(Which reminds me: we probably need a page of my future appearances, conventions etc somewhere at neilgaiman.com...)

Okay. Now to shave and then—onward to DreamHaven!

posted by Neil Gaiman 9:46 AM

The problem with trying to keep some kind of record of a tour like this, is you need to have the time to write entries about the tour...

Today was DreamHaven Books in Minneapolis. I've known Greg Ketter, the owner of DreamHaven, since 1984 (we met on a train to Brighton), I've been signing in his store as long as I've been doing American signings, from a tiny store to a medium sized store to the giant purple building he currently occupies.

The staff of DreamHaven are good people. The customers are triffic. The DreamHaven web site at **dreamhavenbooks.com** is without doubt the best place on the web for going and finding stuff by me you might not find elsewhere. Some of it, like the book *Angels And Visitations*, or the CD, *Warning: Contains Language*, Greg has even published.

I try and do too many signings there—one a year or thereabouts—just to make sure that the numbers don't get too huge. Even so, today's signing started at 2:00 pm and I left the store, hand hurting, everything signed, a couple of minutes before 9:00 pm.

Barnes and Noble tomorrow marks the last of the US signings. I wish I'd got to write more about the various US stops as they went by—I never talked about Keplers (700 people, but only about 300 of them braved the signing line) and Vromans (they gave me two bottles of ink. Burgundy—although it's pretty much purple—and brown) and Book Soup (my favourite bookstore for browsing and buying whenever I'm in LA, although much too small a space for the signing—I wish the Library they were meant to be holding it in hadn't fallen through) and many of the rest of them I only touched on, or may not even have mentioned at all.

The UK tour will kick off with a Forbidden Planet signing next Saturday at 1:00pm, although there will be a lot of other stuff to do with launching the book that I'll try and report back on here, much of which is very different to the way it was done in the US.

For a start, there will be a launch party.

Launch parties are fun, on the whole, for everyone except the author (who has been out of the country for several years) and the publicist organising the party. This is because the invitations are split squarely between the author's friends (who all have several years of catching up to do) and People The Author Should Meet—who can be buyers from book chains, people from publishing, journalists, or just people who somehow got to the party. And the trick is for the publicist to get the author around the room in order to talk to everyone there without the author's friends ever feeling slighted as he gets yanked away from them after a measly three minutes.

I have very understanding friends, but I still worry about getting all the way around the room.

(Normally, an hour into the launch party, everyone's downed as much of the publisher's wine as they can and the publicist is having a fit as two journalists are found trying to make love under an antique table, and an ancient feud about a long-ago book review surfaces and there's a screaming match between five old friends and someone else starts crying in a corner and the last thing anybody cares about is the author anyway, nor will they remember much in the morning. But still, as long as publishers persist in holding the launch parties, and as long as the wine keeps flowing, people will keep coming.)

I'm looking forward to the UK tour. I have no idea how long the lines at the signings will be over there, or how the book will do. I know that Hodder are behind it all the way—they're doing the hardback at a discount with a money back guarantee, which I learned when I saw it a couple of weeks ago—as good as Stephen King or your money back. I'm not sure that's what I'd have said about it, and I keep getting the urge to write to Steve and explain that it really wasn't my idea. But if it gets people to pick up the book, I'm happy. I just hope they aren't looking for chills and real horror because, while there's a lot of stuff in *American Gods,* that's not really the territory it covers.

How long have I been typing this? I should go to bed. Good night.

posted by Neil Gaiman 11:19 PM

Monday, July 02, 2001

http://www.nationalpost.com/artslife/arts/books/story.html?f=/stories/20010630/607032.html is our first review from Canada...

And tonight is my last signing for *American Gods,* on this tour, on US soil.

So I thought I ought to say thank you. After all, I didn't go out and buy the books. I didn't stump up $26 for a hardcover, or drive hundreds (or in a couple of Texan cases, thousands) of miles to go to a signing. I wasn't the one telling my friends and family and just people I met on the bus to go and buy *American Gods.* I didn't host the signings, or pluck up my courage and order a book for the very first time on the internet, or talk my editor into letting him or her review the book or any of those things. I wasn't the guy in the bookstore handselling *American Gods* to everyone who came past me. That was you lot did that.

And yes, I worked hard on this book for several years. And I wasn't the only one—the people at HarperCollins—the ones you know about because I've mentioned them here, and the ones you don't, because I haven't, like the local reps who are actually out there selling the books in to the bookstores, the marketing staff and so on—they've worked hard, too.

But without you lot supporting the book it wouldn't have meant anything. We're currently at #5 on the Independents list, and at #8 on the chains list from the *NY Times.*

So, my thanks.

(No, this isn't goodbye. This blogger has at least another month to live, I'd say. But I wanted to say thanks anyway. I'm tremendously grateful to all of you.)

posted by Neil Gaiman 1:59 PM

So...last US signing done. Braindead. Handhurts.

Nice review at SFsite—http://www.sfsite.com/07a/ag107.htm and go and browse the rest of SFsite while you're at it.

And a reminder that The Dreaming, at http://www.holycow.com/ dreaming is still the best and fastest place to find news and reviews, mainly due to the diligence of the astonishing Lucy Anne (dunno how she finds that stuff so fast) and of webmaster Joe Fulgham. There's a link there to a fascinating article by Michael Dirda on fantasy which says everything I've been saying for a long time now and says it quicker and better. Go and read it. Print it out and make people read it.

Honest.

posted by Neil Gaiman 11:48 PM

Wednesday, July 04, 2001

So, later today—it's now the 4th of July, which seems very appropriate, given the book—I fly to the UK.

In the meantime, advance word is we'll be on the *NY Times* list for a second week, and the book is now in its fourth printing. (Yay!) With luck, the 5th printing will have my wayward apostrophe back.

I see the Vancouver signing in the Virgin Megastore is apparently limited to 200 people. Not sure how I feel about that, but it's not my call, so if you want to be there get your ticket or whatever it is early.

If you're reading this and I owe you an e-mail, take comfort in the fact that you are not alone. There's a host of you. Cohorts. Legions, even.

posted by Neil Gaiman 12:34 AM

A very happy 4th of July to all our readers.

And while my family bustles about setting up the barbecue etc, I'm just about to fly to the UK for round two.

Warren James from the Hour 25 radio show e-mailed to tell me the interview he did with me is online at www.hour25online.com.

See you in England…

posted by Neil Gaiman 11:19 AM

Thursday, July 05, 2001

So I am here in my hotel.

Very very tired—got off plane at Gatwick 8:30 am, met by Lucy Ramsey (Headline publicist), train to London, taxi to hotel, lunch with publisher, interview with *Daily Telegraph*, interview and photosession with *SFX* magazine (both interviewers forgiving of long pauses. Hope photographer equally as forgiving of dissolute and unkempt and unshaven and (because room not ready) unshowered sort of look.)

Then in taxi to British Fantasy Society open night. I signed some books and gave a short talk on the book and talked to more people and then Lucy rounded me up, took me back to the hotel (around 9:40pm),

I went to conveyor belt sushi bar in hotel and ate sushi, then came down to hotel library and sent this, and now I'm on my way to bed…

Tomorrow I'll tell you about the interview I sat and listened to here in the hotel library waiting for the room to be ready. Tomorrow starts very soon…

Julie Washington's piece in the *Cleveland Plain Dealer* is now online…

Also getting a number of complaints from people about neilgaiman.com crashing their browsers. Suggest you e-mail the details to the Authors on the Web people (their details are on the bottom right of the front page). Of course, if it's crashing your browsers you won't be able to read that or, I imagine, read this.

And on that note I shall go to bed. Goodnight.

posted by Neil Gaiman 3:11 PM

Friday, July 06, 2001

For some reason the last one didn't publish, so let's try again…

Just did the oddest radio show; suddenly found myself having to have opinions about Pyramid Selling, Legalizing Heroin, Foxhunting, Bullfighting and Right vs Left wing Libertarianism. Occasional nods to me being an author were made, by the host, after checking his press release—"Neil, it says here you wrote *Good Omens,* with Terry Pratchett, a novel about the end of the world. Now if the world really were ending do we think that we'd start looting, or just be peaceful" etc. V. odd…

Ate more conveyor belt sushi for lunch, but I think that's it for me and conveyor belt sushi. (But surely, you must be sick of sushi by now? chorus the multitudes who have been reading this blogger. Er, no, not yet, says author.)

posted by Neil Gaiman 5:57 AM

Interviews are funny things. Yesterday morning, in the hotel library, waiting for my room to be ready, I listened to the singer from the Cardigans, Nina, being interviewed at the chair next to mine. She was a nice Swedish lady. Some people wanted to talk about the music, and she did okay on those interviews.

Some were less prepared.

Like the Australian celebrity journalist with his appalling list of questions.

"So—what *don't* your fans know about you?"

"Well, my private life. But it is private."

"Come on love. Give us something. A secret. Something nobody knows. Come on."

"…Er… I have a wart between my toes…?"

"Can't you get it frozen off?"

"Well, nobody can see it. It's between my toes."

"Do you have to wear larger shoes then?"

"No." (Embarrassed pause.) "I wear pointy shoes."

"That wasn't much of a secret really, was it." The lady from the Cardigans shrugged apologetically. The reporter looked down at his list of questions... "So what's the craziest thing a fan's ever done?"

"They are very nice."

"Crazy. Come on, one of your fans must be a little bit crazy..."

And so on, and on, and on.

At least most of my interviewers know who I am. (Except for the radio interviewer today. But then, it's always a pleasant surprise when radio interviewers have read anything. I knew one who admitted to putting slips of paper into a book when the author was coming to the interview—three slips, one near the beginning, one in the middle, one near the end. It made it look as if he'd not only read the book, but he'd found important things he wanted to talk about. I doubt a single author was fooled.)

Today was interviews, launch party, dinner, and back to hotel by 12:30 am...tomorrow, a signing at Forbidden Planet in Oxford Street. Starts at 1:00pm...

The interviews (and the interviewers) were good. Not a warty-toe question in the lot of them. Very different. My favourite was Nick Hasted who interviewed me for *UNCUT,* in something that felt a lot less like an interview and more like part of a conversation Nick and I have been having, an hour or so at a time every 2 years, for 6 or 7 years.

posted by Neil Gaiman 5:08 PM

Finally understood the whole UK hardback-paperback thing.
1. There's a UK hardback. It costs £17.99, but is currently discounted to £10.00 with a money back guarantee.
2. There's a trade paperback. it costs £10.00 but is only for Australia and New Zealand.
There.

posted by Neil Gaiman 5:21 PM

And incidentally, there's a fun interview up at
http://www.writerswrite.com/journal/jul01/gaiman2.htm

posted by Neil Gaiman 5:29 PM

Saturday, July 07, 2001

Entertainment Weekly's review's out! And I hear the House on the Rock photo is good.

Not impressed by the review though—shallow reading, and the reviewer seemed to have missed a number of things (e g., Messrs Stone, Wood, Town et al. aren't gods of any kind—that's made about as clear in the text as anything can be) and he manages not only to give away the end but to demonstrate that he hasn't understood it either. Lots of nice quotes of the kind one can stick on a dust-jacket, and the ranking on Amazon's soared since it came out, which means it's done its job of telling people the book's out there.

GRADE: C–

posted by Neil Gaiman 4:27 AM

So, I was definitely wrong about the whole hardback/trade paperback thing on *American Gods,* as people turned up at the signing at Forbidden Planet today with copies of *American Gods* in trade paperback they'd bought at Borders. Lucy Ramsey couldn't explain it and went off to investigate (on a Saturday afternoon, bless her).

Not sure why Borders would be selling £10.00 paperbacks when everyone else is selling £10.00 hardbacks—and slightly concerned that, as the ISBN is different, any copies sold through Borders won't show up on any bestseller lists, which would be a pity.

Several people came—for the signing at Forbidden Planet—from France, Spain, Sweden and Finland (there were many Brazilians and New Zealanders there too, and many other French, Dutch, Spanish etc people there, but none of them had come specially). I felt faintly guilty for not doing something more exciting than just signing books, since they'd come such a long way...

(A strange sweet moment that sat in the middle of a 4 hour signing like a haiku, as a young lady tentatively put out one hand to touch my hand while I signed, I think just to reassure herself that I was real.)

The *Daily Telegraph* had a photographer at the signing. People kept asking him to take photos of them with their cameras, so he'd put down his massive telephoto thing and use people's little disposables to snap us together. It made me smile.

posted by Neil Gaiman 12:59 PM

Sunday, July 08, 2001

Wrote a blogger post today in the library of this hotel, but the computer crashed utterly and terminally just as I finished. And all the sensible things I said at the time have been entirely forgotten.

(Jetlagged author tries to remember things he said, but he can only remember mentioning that the lyric version of "New Age" on Tori's *Strange Little Girls* CD is not as reported the one from the Velvet Underground's

Loaded but actually the version from the Live 1969 LP, and I can only remember that because it's playing in the background as I type this.)

I think I warned people that on some of these stops the bookshop is selling tickets to the reading—you get the cost of the ticket back from the price of the book if you buy one, although you shouldn't need a book to get into the line. Some stores do the tickets for the reading but let anyone into the signing line, whether you have a ticket or not. And most of them won't do any of that stuff either way and you'll just get to the bookshop, be read to or not depending mostly on whether it's a lunch or evening signing, and shuffle along a line that will move much too slowly until everyone's done.

posted by Neil Gaiman 1:23 PM

Tuesday, July 10, 2001

So the UK tour is now well underway and right now I'm happy as a sandboy (what is a sandboy? Why are they happy?) as it's proving to be almost a holiday after the US tour.

The US tour was 90% signing, with a very few interviews.

These UK signings are—so far—proving easy: enough people at each signing to justify the signing—60 or so at lunchtime, 150 in the evening (Manchester will be bigger). And the rest of the time is being spent doing interviews: over breakfast, over tea, in railway stations and hotel lobbies.

The difference between the US and the UK? Hmm…well, more of the copies of *Good Omens* have been pre-signed by Terry Pratchett, so I get to do more punch lines than set up lines. More men than women—in the US it was a solid 50/50. And the lines are—I am happy to say—shorter.

This morning's breakfast interview was with a journalist from the *Scotsman*—who first interviewed me when he was a young fan and I was a young comics writer over a decade ago. I got to grumble to him about the *Scotsman*'s attempts over the years to put together an article showing I thought that J. K. Rowling nicked Harry Potter from Tim Hunter. According to Joe from Waterstones they've run such an article on more than one occasion—"I think you were on the front page on a slow news day" he said. (The local *Metro* newspaper had an article about it when I arrived—although this was more presented as a tragedy I had survived—plucky young writer's prize creation could have been huge but then J. K. Rowling stole his thunder sort of thing. It sort of ignored that Tim is owned lock stock and barrel by Warner Bros, and that if anything I think Harry Potter has actually encouraged them to make the *Books of Magic* movie. But then, nobody asked me.)

Odd hotel last night—the Point Hotel in Edinburgh. It looks and feels like an elegant modernist five star sort of hotel—vast white rooms, double Jacuzzi style baths and so on—but then you start noticing that the lifts only work sporadically, the only soap in the bathroom is an empty wall-unit in the shower, that the lobby staff sent away a taxi sent by the BBC to take Lucy Ramsey and me to Radio Scotland (the Brian Morton show. Good radio by someone literate.) because we weren't waiting for it in the lobby, rather than calling the rooms or leaning into the bar where I was being interviewed by *Scottish Book Collector* ("Are you for people who collect Scottish books, or for Scots who collect books of any kind?" "Er, both really.") and telling me the taxi was there. (The mad dash to make it to the radio station in time for the interview was the kind of thing of which heroic ballads are made.)

Which reminds me—upcoming radio appearances for people who live locally, or who like seeing whether you can find various stations on the internet:

Weds 11th July	4:30ish GMT	Andy Peebles, BBC Radio North
	11:00 PM	Andy Peebles, BBC Radio North
Thurs 12 July	9:30 PM	The Late Show, BBC Radio midlands
Friday 13 July	10:00 PM	Gideon Coe, BBC London Live
Sunday 15th	4:00 PM	Giles Brandreth, LBC

Saw the *Entertainment Weekly* photo. Not a bad picture at all, but the hair-and-make-up guy had managed to transform my normal tangle of barely kempt hair into something I don't think I've ever seen on top of my head.

Now in Leeds in a really lovely hotel.

As far as I can establish, the UK hardback selling at £10.00 (£6.00 right now through Amazon.co.uk) is only for a limited time. So if you're planning on waiting to get one, as a gift or whatever, you may want to get it now and put it away, as they'll be climbing back to £17.99 soon enough. (This information, like all other information posted here about the UK edition, is liable to be utterly wrong. On the other hand, it turned out there were only a handful of trade paperbacks on sale in the UK, all through Borders in London—they think—and only for a couple of days.)

Right—the phone rang, interviewer in the lobby. Got to go.

posted by Neil Gaiman 9:29 AM

Wednesday, July 11, 2001

There seemed to be a certain amount of confusion about what was actually happening at the Vancouver signing/reading so I investigated. Felicia Quon (this column's Canadian correspondent) reports:

This is from the organizer at the Virgin event in Vancouver...

The wristband guarantees that you get into the reading/Q&A and that you get to have your book signed. Wristbanded folk get in first as well. There will be a separate lineup for those without wristbands.

So it looks like a book guarantees you a place at the reading, but that you can still get into the signing with or without one.

posted by Neil Gaiman 5:13 AM

Sorry about the FAQ thing not happening yet…it should be up soon, and once it is I'll start answering questions. Honest.

In the meantime, I'm also answering questions (or, sometimes, failing to, which I was always assured was an author's prerogative) about *American Gods* over at Readerville and at The Well.

posted by Neil Gaiman 5:23 AM

Oh, and a little websearching produced:

> Sandboy: As happy as a sandboy is an expression which implies blissful contentment. I believe that the saying is truly Bristolian in origin. On Bathurst basin, in the City centre is the long established Ostrich Inn. The Inn is immediately adjacent to the Redcliff caves which, in their day, were a prime source of sand. Past landlords of the Inn used to send little boys, i. e., Sandboys into the caves to collect sand to spread on the floor of the Inn to soak up the beer and ale droppings (much like butchers used to put sawdust on the floor of their shops). The Sandboys were paid for their efforts in beer. They were indeed happy.

Lovely signing in Leeds last night, marred only by the sad death of the sound system, so I did it unmiked (thanks to James and Juliet for all their help). Then to dinner with lots of really nice Leeds booksellers.

I lost weight on the US tour. This one, however, has such luxuries as breakfast, lunch and dinner built in, so I'm sure I'll gain it all back, and more. (sigh.)

posted by Neil Gaiman 5:44 AM

Thursday, July 12, 2001

Let's see, where were we? More to the point, where am I? (Stops. Thinks. Birmingham. Right. Knew it was Birmingham.) Just on my way to do a lunchtime signing at Andromeda Books—mainly because Andromeda was the place I signed first. It was with Kim Newman, in 1985, for a book called *Ghastly Beyond Belief.*

Tonight is Ottakar's bookshop in Walsall—not a place I'd've picked to do a signing, on a tour that doesn't take in Oxford, Cambridge or Reading,—but we'll see how it goes.

The last couple of evening signings have been fun—Leeds two nights ago, and last night in Manchester, at Waterstones. They sold tickets (£3.00 each) and people kept coming, several hundred of them, so the event moved from Waterstones to the church next door, which meant, I was told, No Swearing. It also meant that people didn't get any free wine, 'cos it was a church.

So I read the Essie Tregowan story. Toward the end people got quieter and quieter and you could hear every squeak and echo. People laughed less, though.

The people and the organisation were both terrific. I saw Ramsey and Jenny Campbell and several other friends and old acquaintances, all-too briefly in every case. Thrown out of the church at 10:00pm as that was when the burglar alarm went on by, but a final dash of speed signing did it, then to the radio.

I had a few seconds before the interview to talk to the interviewer, so I checked to see if he'd read the book, and he hadn't, which was good to know, as I explained more than I might have otherwise. But what was meant to be a five-minute interview turned into a half hour chat on the air, and was very enjoyable.

Then back to the hotel, where there was no food to be had, for it was gone midnight, and all I'd had to eat since breakfast was some Tesco's sushi that someone had brought to the signing ("my girlfriend says I'm mad but…") so Lucy and I went to an Indian restaurant next door, and when the food wasn't what I'd ordered I shut up and ate it, because I just wanted food and sleep. And then we walked back to the hotel, went off to our rooms, and slept the sleep of the dead. Well, I did. At 7:30 Lucy rang to say that she was still stuffed from eating a huge Indian meal at 1:00am and thought she'd skip breakfast, and I decided to do the same, so lay in the bath and read several pages of Harry Stephen Keeler's *The Chameleon* (the second half of the sequence that begins with *The Mysterious Mr. I*). An astonishingly brilliant and postmodern sort of device and structure underlies both books, marred only by the fact that the mystery of the narrator's identity is starting to become wearisome. But as unreliable narrators go, this one is certainly up there.

On the train to Birmingham I planned to work, and instead I slept.

We're edging up the UK charts—number 19 last week, number 16 this week.

posted by Neil Gaiman 4:28 AM

http://www.usatoday.com/life/enter/books/2001-07-12-american-gods.htm is a fun review of *American Gods*...

Today was nice—small lunchtime signing (50 people or thereabouts altogether) and so was the evening one. In between I grabbed some food and did several interviews, and after the Ottakars in Walsall signing we made a mad dash to get to Pebble Mill in time for a live interview, not enormously helped by having the only taxi driver in the midlands to whom one can say "BBC Pebble Mill, please" and whose reply is "Where's that, mate?" Lucy Ramsey talked a lot on her mobile, and I sat in the taxi and didn't worry. We were talked in (via Lucy and her mobile) by a security guard at Pebble Mill.

I am, on some things, a world class worrier, but when it comes to getting places on time, if I'm actually travelling towards them in a car or a train or a plane, I just shrug and go, I'll get there on time or I won't. Nothing I can do about it either way. And I don't worry.

So I didn't, and we made it by the skin of our teeth, and the interview was fun. And now I'm back in the hotel before midnight, which is more or less a first.

posted by Neil Gaiman 3:43 PM

Friday, July 13, 2001

http://authorpages.hoddersystems.com/NeilGaiman/ is the Hodder Headline website for me and the book and is an awful lot of fun at first glance.

I'm typing this in the offices of AOL.com UK where I'm just about to do an online chat—the first online chat of this tour that I've actually got to type my own answers for, rather than talk to someone down the phone.

posted by Neil Gaiman 11:18 AM

More from the Strange Stuff People E-Mail Me Department:
http://www.bookreporter.com/authors/au-gaiman-neil.asp is an interview with me (you have to page down past the biography stuff).
http://www.kiplinger.com/spending/ is—right now anyway—something that lists the best prices of "this week's bestselling book, CD, DVD and software." *American Gods* is the book (and Fatbrain is currently the best price, it says).

Did a signing in Bristol at lunchtime which was lovely. It should have been an evening signing with a reading and stuff, really. Saw Diana Wynne Jones and several other friends, albeit too briefly in every case. But I got to tell Diana of Maddy's addiction to *Warlock at the Wheel*, finally... Then got the train back and did an AOL chat, then London Live radio, now back in the hotel.

Up at the crack of dawn tomorrow to go to Norwich for a lunchtime signing, then on to Canterbury where I shall see Dave McKean and his family, which I am looking forward to.

Sunday is the Giles Brandreth radio show on LBC, and a desperate attempt to see as many people as possible. Monday is editorial meetings, sign 300+ books in the Headline offices, and, in the evening, do some filming and reading and such with Tori for some album stuff. Tuesday morning I fly home.

Wish I had some trenchant and brilliant comments to make on the media or something, but mostly I'm just pooped. People have stopped assuming I'm American though, and my daughter Holly, when I phoned home last night, said "Dad! You sound so English!" which I shall take as a compliment, although I'm not entirely sure that was how she meant it. Really, my accent is just a universal sort of case of "you aren't from round here, are you?"

posted by Neil Gaiman 3:45 PM

Saturday, July 14, 2001

Got up this morning at 6:50 to head off to Norwich (an acronym, Alan Bennett once wrote in a comedic sketch, for "Knickers off ready when I come home") for an 11:00am signing. If this seems a bit of an early start to you, remember that Norwich is the only city that Lucy Ramsey ever got Terry Pratchett to a signing too late, and that she wasn't ever going to let it happen again.

It's 10:00 am now, and so we're cruising through Norwich looking for breakfast...

...there, and by the magic of the new paragraph break, we had breakfast and then I did a signing in Ottakar's of Norwich—nice people (I always say that, don't I? Well, it's always been true of the people at the signings, and on this tour it's been true of all the people who run the shops. It's not always like that—every author will tell you horror stories of irritable store staff who view the author's presence in the store as an unaccountable intrusion. Normally in these cases they also didn't ever bother to do anything to tell anyone you were coming to their store so you're not just a bother, but a demoralised bother because nobody came. My last one of those—I'd managed to forget it until I was reminded by Lucy—was at W. H. Smith's in Brighton in 1999.)

Was hoping for review coverage of *American Gods* today, and didn't see any (most of the review coverage I saw was for children's books, inspired by yesterday's Carnegie Award). On the other hand, we're in at #9 in the

Independent book list; while the *Times* has a list of the fastest selling books, and we came in at #4 as the second fastest-selling hardback fiction book in the UK (after Tony Parsons' new novel) which has to be a good thing, as it means we're selling through the people in bookshops and through word of mouth.

So, now in car en route to Canterbury...

...Canterbury signing was lovely. A great one to end the UK signing tour with. Saw Dave McKean and family, and just got back to the hotel (at 2:00am).

And that was today, except that I also answered a nice e-mail from an *Entertainment Weekly* journalist about this journal, and failed to answer an e-mail from a *New York Times* journalist about this journal (tomorrow, I suppose).

Oh, and during the Q&A someone asked if I really was existing on nothing but sushi, and I had to admit that my peregrinations around the UK had been practically sushi free. F'r example, tonight I ate—before the signing—at the Café Des Amis in Canterbury, which is Dave McKean's favourite Mexican restaurant. Sometimes he just goes there with his notebook and sketches or thinks, and he wound up designing and doing all the art on their menu and notecards and stuff, because he wanted it to look nice.

posted by Neil Gaiman 6:30 PM

Monday, July 16, 2001

This is what I did today. I got up. I checked out of the hotel and went to the offices of Headline, where I met my editor and discussed which of about seven books was probably going to be the next one I'd write. Then I signed a little over 300 books, some for retailers, some for the reps to be able to use to make people happy.

Left London on the Gatwick Express. Saw my family, or bits of it. Went back to London on the Gatwick Express. Did a strange but kind of fun thing with Tori, where we sat and were filmed talking in a hotel with galaxies in the lifts (er, elevators) and see-through glass bathrooms. Read the short stories for *Strange Little Girls* and then we talked about each story and each song and what it meant. I think they'll edit it into something and put it out on the web in some form.

Then went to see They Might Be Giants with my friends Jonathan & Jane. Wonderful, marvelous, funny gig. Amazing musicianship, too. Hung out in the backstage bar with friends, and was introduced to the Johns of TMBG and told them how good they were. Then hopped the Gatwick Express for the last time today and off into the wilderness. Fly home early tomorrow.

I have to write on the plane, unless I fall asleep. Which I may do. You never know.

posted by Neil Gaiman 7:14 PM

Wednesday, July 18, 2001

And yesterday went in a kind of a blur. I got on a plane and, eventually, I got home. There were plane delays, and on the way home we had to stop for a bit as there was a fawn with a broken leg to be helped, and a hysterical lady who had hit the fawn with her car to be calmed down, both of which we did, and then home and seeing kids and, finally, sleep.

And then wide awake at 4:30am—it's now 6:30-ish and I'm still awake, with no prospect of going back to sleep. There are teetering stacks of things that have arrived in my absence to be dealt with, to be read, listened to, filed. There are things that were meant to have been written before the tour started a month ago that need to be written.

But today, I think I may just potter around. I think I'll have a bath, go for a bike ride, and pick things from the garden and cook them, and just take it easy. Or as easy as I can.

posted by Neil Gaiman 4:47 AM

http://enjoyment.independent.co.uk/books/reviews/story.jsp?story=83991 is the *Independent* newspaper review of *American Gods*, and the word from the UK Booktrack charts is that we continue to creep up steadily: from 19 (pre-publication) to 16 (last week) to 12. Now that the reviews have started to appear, I hope we continue to rise.

The UK Booktrack system is interesting as, like Soundscan for CDs in the US, it tallies sales through every outlet. There's no US equivalent. Publishers pay it more mind than the public do, though.

posted by Neil Gaiman 5:33 AM

Just as a reminder—the Canadian leg of the tour is next. There's one stop that isn't listed yet on the "On the Road" section of the website—I posted it before, but, just in case anyone's missed it... It's Toronto this coming Sunday. (Just a signing—the reading's the following day at the Merril Collection) (and not, as it's listed on the tour dates, the Merril collection. Named after Judith Merril, whose collection *SF12* did more to the inside of my head at the age of 11 than any single book I've read before or since):

Sunday July 22 4 pm.   Indigo Books & Music Toronto, ON

posted by Neil Gaiman 7:33 PM

Friday, July 20, 2001

Not dead, only resting. Wrote an introduction for a reprint of Pat Cadigan's novel *Synners,* and poem for an Arne Svenson (he's a photographer) book of photos of sock monkeys, but that's been it for work. Now a huge backlog of stuff, filmic and comics, awaits me…and then off to Canada on Sunday. The schedule I've been sent runs pretty much by the minute, but there seems to be a fair amount of sushi on it, which is nice.

Last night I took part telephonically in a meeting of the Board of Directors of the Comic Book Legal Defense Fund. This is a not for profit organisation that looks out for comics writers, artists, publishers and retailers who need defending on a First Amendment basis (that's Freedom of Speech, for those of you not immediately *au fait* with the US Constitution)—every little legal case, and big ones, and ones that never turn into legal cases at all. They all cost money. And the cases the CBLDF has defended range from the Californian Tax authorities trying to reclassify comics from "literature" to "sign painting", to Mike Diana's imprisonment for drawing his mini comic "Boiled Angel" (we lost that case. His sentence included three years' suspended imprisonment, a $1000 fine, 1000 hours of community service, and he was forbidden to draw anything that anyone might consider obscene—and the local police were empowered to do 24 hour raids on his rooms to make sure he wasn't committing art. On appeal we got him able to leave Florida…) to the normal run of the mill cases where retailers are accused of selling comics from the over 18 section of the store, marked for over 18s, to undercover cops over the age of 18.

It was a long meeting—most of the people were in San Diego, where the meeting started at 8:00pm. Here in the Midwest it started at 10:00pm, and round about 1:30am this jetlagged author started noticing that the world on the other end of the phone was a very very long way away.

The CBLDF is always after people for money. This is because the price of liberty in the US is not just eternal vigilance, but it's also cash on the nail to lawyers, to fly in expert witnesses, to all that stuff.

Go buy their merchandise. Check out their website (www.cbldf.org). Become a member—they send you a membership card and several goodies, but mostly you just get the satisfaction of knowing you're doing something good to preserve the First Amendment and freedom of speech (which people know applies to prose, but are a lot more uncertain about when it comes to comics).

They've got the *Live at the Aladdin* video for sale—it's come out, and it's the film of (and a mini-documentary about) the Portland leg of the *Last Angel* reading tour I did last October. If you've never been to any of the *Guardian Angel* tour readings, you should get the video to see what you missed. And if you went to any of them you should get the video to remind yourself of the fun you had.

The questions in Portland weren't quite as strange as the ones from New York ("Can I be your sex slave?" was one from New York I remember taking me slightly by surprise, and my answer "Um, no" was possibly not the epitome of a graceful comeback) and the lighting makes me look like an early Bernie Wrightson drawing, but you need this video. (And I don't get a penny of it. It all goes to the CBLDF.)

The *Last Angel* Tour in 2000 was the last tour I was ever going to do for the CBLDF—I'd been doing them since 1993, and thought it was time that other people got out there and did stuff. It hasn't really happened, although Harlan Ellison and I are going to do readings for the CBLDF on alternate evenings at Madcon this October in Madison. It's http://www.madcon.org/.

(Yes, I know, we need an updated APPEARANCES section of this website to list things like this.)

As I was saying, no one's really leapt into the breach yet, so if any of you have any favourite comics people you want to see live on stage, tell them you'd pay to come and see them. I keep telling Jill Thompson that she could fill a theatre with *Scary Godmother* readings—maybe with slides—but I don't think she believes me.

Anyway, I've mentioned the CBLDF store on this journal in the past, but it's worth pointing you all there again. It's the only online place I know of that you can just go and buy one of the 5000 signed limited copies of *American Gods* (except eBay, I suppose. hang on, I'll look.)

(Nothing at all.)

(Hmm... try looking for **signed** *American Gods* instead of **singed** *American Gods*...)

Yup. They've got 'em at eBay, where they've been selling for as much at $60, but if you order them from the CBLDF they are a lowly $35 and all your money goes to a good cause AND they have other cool stuff too, so go and click on http://cbldf.safeshopper.com/13/cat13.htm?626 to go straight to their Neil Gaiman store section, or on http://cbldf.safeshopper.com/ to see what else is on offer, or just head straight over to http://cbldf.org/.

And tell people to go and do likewise. Spread the word. Tell them Neil sent you. Look, if enough of you start doing it, I'll get the FAQ blogger up and running. I'll do a review of *Strange Little Girls*. I'll go and find some goofy stuff sitting on the dustier bits of the hard disk and set up a "Goofy Stuff From the Dustier Bits of the Hard Disk" section of the website. Honest.

And in the meantime, if you run into Jill Thompson, mention to her casually you'd pay good money to see her up on stage doing *Scary Godmother* for the CBLDF...

posted by Neil Gaiman 1:29 PM

Reading *Locus* online, I saw a link to *January* magazine's review. http://www.januarymagazine.com/SFF/americangods.html is the kind of book review I like as an author—not because it liked the book (although it did) but because the book I read about in the review was the same one I thought I was writing. And so many of the reviews and comments that come over the transom, some of them enthusiastic and some of them damning, are reviews of books that I don't remember writing at all.

...which reminds me. Who was it defined a novel as "a long piece of prose with something wrong with it"?

A friend said to me recently, shocked, "You don't read your reviews do you?" and I had to admit that, sure I do. I don't pay much attention to them—I always liked Kingsley Amis's comment on bad reviews that "they might spoil my breakfast, but they don't spoil my lunch"—other than to do a sort of tally of how many good to bad we're getting, and to see which ones actually seem to sell books.

posted by Neil Gaiman 3:57 PM

Saturday, July 21, 2001

There's a terrifically fun article at the *Daily Telegraph* website at http://www.telegraph.co.uk:80/et?ac=005591874619727&rtmo=Qe pxkHzR&atmo=rrrrrrrq&pg=/et/01/7/21/bfsf21.html and the photograph of me signing at Forbidden Planet actually looks like me. And I like that it's about more than just me plugging my book, and is actually about something. The quotes are in context and accurate, too (although Zadie Smith didn't write me a fan letter; we had an e-mail exchange in which she mentioned she was a big Sandman fan. Different thing).

posted by Neil Gaiman 11:12 AM

Sunday, July 22, 2001

In Toronto—did a signing at Indigo for around 350 incredibly nice people, then signed the last 100 copies of *Murder Mysteries: A Play for Voices* for George and Dave, the Biting Dog Press gang. Dinner was sushi with Felicia Quon, who eagle-eyed readers of this blog will remember has the coolest name in the world, and who I met for the first time today, and Steve-from-Harper-Collins, and Mark Askwith. Mark Askwith is the Man Behind the Curtain. He is the Eminence Gris. He Knows All, Sees All, and Says Nothing.

Actually, that last bit isn't true. Mark says a lot, amusingly and to the point, and is a dab hand with an anecdote. We met on the streets of Gotham City—quite literally. It was in Pinewood Studios, in England, in 1988. Tomorrow I will be interviewed by lots of people, and several of those will be Mark Askwith.

And I'm very tired, so will leave it there for tonight.

Oh, one thing. Several people at the signing asked about the stories I wrote for Tori's *Strange Little Girls* album. To clarify, they won't be on the CD—I think the plan is to take a sentence from each one and put it by the relevant photo for the CD, then to run the whole story in the Tour Booklet. (One person asked me if the new album was really any good, as if I'd probably just been trying to get people's hopes up to help sell a dog of an album, which rather puzzled me. So, for the record, yes I really like the album. I think it's the best thing Tori's done in a while, and it's, in my opinion, her most personal album for years. I would be astonished if there wasn't at least one track on there that every dyed in the wool Tori fan loved immediately, and equally as surprised if there wasn't at least one track that they disliked equally as strongly—it's that sort of record.)

And one more thing...Happy Birthday Mike for yesterday. Mike—my son—was 18 yesterday, and can now go off and die for his country. But I rather hope he doesn't.

posted by Neil Gaiman 9:40 PM

Tuesday, July 24, 2001

An FAQ question in from Brazil points out the inconsistencies of yours truly. After all, I have cheerfully maintained recently that Felicia Quon has the world's coolest name. But in the back of *American Gods* I say Owl Goingback has the world's coolest name. So which is it?

I asked Felicia about this as she bundled me away from the Merril Centre last night, and she said, rather pointedly, "Yeah, I was wondering about that myself." And when I last raised the subject of World's Coolest Names with Owl Goingback, he wistfully told me about a man on the tribal rolls of the last century called Big Meat, and said he's always wanted to be called Big Meat. So they weren't much help, really, all things considered.

So, for purposes of simplicity, I think currently that Owl Goingback has the world's coolest boys' name and Felicia Quon has the world's coolest girls' name.

And FAQ thingie in from Germany wants to know if I will ever answer any of the FAQ questions. I expect so—probably when the current incarnation of the journal is done, a new one will arise, based on answering the FAQs (very few of which are actually frequently asked, and several of the ones that are seemed to be asked by the same person several time in the hopes of making them Frequently Asked).

And Rabbi Michael Unterberg asks if there's any reason the Golem in *American Gods* has the word Life on his forehead, instead of the word Truth (Hebrew Truth—Emet; If you erase the first letter it becomes Met, death, which is how you kill a golem.) And the answer is, yes, relying on rotten authorial memory. I'll fix it in the paperback.

Someone at the Indigo signing asked, for a friend, about three continuity queries. One she'd misread (the whisky bottle Shadow takes from Mad Sweeney's hands is not the same bottle as the one the police took from his hands the previous day), one was intentional (a barefoot Shadow acquiring shoes in chapter 16), and one was a fossil.

Fossils plague authors. Ammonites and trilobites left in the text from previous drafts that you've somehow missed—that everyone's missed. You think you've caught them all, but there's always one that slips through...

I'll scribble on the copy of *American Gods* back at home that I've been scribbling on since I got it, revisions and fixes for the paperback.

Meanwhile, we're now in seventh printing for the US hardback of *American Gods*. (And, hearteningly, the trade paperbacks of *Smoke and Mirrors* and *Stardust* have now gone back to press several times in paperback.)

Let's see. Toronto, yesterday. Woken up by room-service breakfast (which is the only reliable alarm call for me at this point in the tour. Someone knocks on the door. I have to get up and open it and then, somehow, sign my name to a slip and do some simple addition. All of these things are more likely to wake me up than picking up a phone and hearing a pre-recorded voice say "This is your wake up call...) and I had just finished cleaning my teeth when the phone rang for the first interview. This was Chris from Parsec, who had interviewed me a few years ago. Then downstairs for the second interview (canoe.ca) then off to the Beguiling for a drop-in-signing and then to *Space* for an interview with Mark Askwith.

Mark has been interviewing me for about 13 years now, initially for the much lamented *Prisoners of Gravity* TV show, and more recently for *Space* and its related stations. He always plans a number of shows, so in interviews he darts, conversationally, from topic to topic like a madman on a bus, leaving me trying vaguely to keep up and just trusting that he won't cut stuff to make me look like an idiot.

Yesterday we lurched from the book to the nature of Fantasy to The Web, and at one point he handed me an Elvis Presley Hawaiian doll and asked me to talk about it. (Why, Mark, why?)

Then over to U8TV—a real life "Reality TV" show set in a loft. The behind-the-scenes people, Michael and Jodie, were fans, and I was interviewed on a couch by a strikingly pretty inmate of the loft named Jennifer who had read the book and, because she was a real person and not a TV interviewer, had made notes of sensible questions she wanted to ask. And it was a really good interview, although the most interesting bit for me was chatting to her before the interview started about what it's like to live your life—or a small fraction of it—in the public eye. "I'll be walking down the street and people I don't know will tell me I should dump my boyfriend, or that I looked better as a redhead..."

Back to the hotel lobby where Christopher from Reel to Reel was waiting to interview me, and from there to *TALK! TV* (or possibly *TALK TV!*) and not only was I interviewed by a nice guy with amazing spectacles named Roberto but at the end, when he asked me to sign his book, he handed me a gorgeous fountain pen filled with sepia ink, and we neeped about ink and pens for a few moments.

Half an hour for a sushi dinner at 6:00pm, and Felicia "The Organised" Quon had already handed me a menu at some point that afternoon in the car, to make things faster. Joined by Nalo Hopkinson and her partner, David. She's reading *American Gods* right now, and thanked me for not attempting to give Mr Nancy an inauthentic West Indian patois. (Her lovely novel, *Midnight Robber*, is written almost entirely in a strange and beautiful hybrid Trinidadian/Jamaican patois. She knows from patois.) (Later, when Mark Askwith wasn't around, we made Nalo go up and introduce me at the reading, in a transparent and blatant attempt to get the people to go out and buy her books.)

Sold out hall, and I read them the whole of Chapter One and Sam's speech. Then a Q and A (during which I wound up at one point talking about Harry Stephen Keeler, but cannot for the life of me remember why), then a signing. Had a strange epiphany three quarters of the way through the signing, as my hand hurt and my elbow hurt, and I was tired and my handwriting had become something barely legible, and for a moment I felt weirdly grumpy and sorry for myself, and then I thought Yeah, but I'm still enjoying it. It's fun. These are nice people. I have the coolest job in the world.

So I grinned and asked for a pot of tea, and I kept on signing.

I think the greatest distance travelled was the young lady who came up from New York by train for it, although probably someone came in from Newfoundland and didn't mention it.

Signing over with at around 11:00ish and back to hotel.

Author up at 6:30am-ish (room service wake up, see above), shower, pack and downstairs where Victor was waiting to take me to the airport.

The whole Toronto experience was hugely improved by having a driver named Victor who moved us from place to place effortlessly, and I was pleased that Felicia had given him a copy of *American Gods*. I scribbled an appreciative message on it for him, and he was happy.

And then onto the plane. I suspect there's some kind of irony in the longest single internal flight of the tour (well over 5 hours) being the one that was, I discovered as I got to the airport, in coach, and to be on a completely crammed plane, armed with a full complement of squalling babies. And the less said about the flight the better. I have a magic "This man flies too damned much" card that makes upgrades happen on some airlines, but Canada 3000 is not one of them. Canada 3000 is the kind of airline that makes you check small roll-aboard luggage because they have limited space.

I'm typing this on the plane right now. The babies are all crying, and it's been a long 5 hours. Luckily, I only have two interviews, two drive-by signings, and a Virgin Megastore signing and reading to do in what remains of today.

And I hear very good things about Vancouver sushi.

The plane landed 45 mins late, and I was met by Gwendolynn the Vancouver publicist (www.prdiva.com) who is a Powerhouse. Which is a good thing. And off to Sushi with an interviewer named Matthew. Good Sushi. Good questions. Exhausted author. And then back to hotel to post this and then, for 45 minutes I hope, nap.

posted by Neil Gaiman 3:11 PM

The sushi in Vancouver is as good as I've been told.

The signing at Virgin in Vancouver was very interesting. Possibly not the most tightly organised of the tour, and the reading was, of necessity, done unmiked, but the people attending were very kind.

Victoria tomorrow.

Message in from Ms. Tree of Melbourne, Australia, asking why it hasn't been mentioned on this blogger that she came all the way from Melbourne, Australia to get to the LA signing. And here am I mentioning the people who came up to Vancouver from Portland or down to Bristol from Preston and I never mentioned her. And I didn't mention the people who flew in from Singapore either. Bad Neil. Wicked Neil.

posted by Neil Gaiman 11:34 PM

Wednesday, July 25, 2001

The Onion has a review of *American Gods.*

And I am in Victoria, BC, and will soon be doing the very last signing of the tour. Doug, the HarperCollins rep, started explaining to me that this was rural Canada and that a hundred people showing up at a signing would be a lot. I told him I wouldn't mind if it was only a couple of dozen, and I wouldn't, although I'm not sure I convinced him.

Did several interviews and TV this morning, and finally managed to see Joe Fulgham (who does The Dreaming website, over at www.holycow. com/ dreaming) having managed to miss meeting him for dinner last night, and miss seeing him for donuts in the green room at the TV station. We ate lunch together for ten minutes and then I ran to get the seaplane to Victoria.

posted by Neil Gaiman 5:05 PM

Ever since the cover for *American Gods* came out people have been showing me pictures and sending me images, saying "Hey, doesn't this look like the *American Gods* cover?" and it never does.

But I saw this one in a bookstore the other day… I'd be willing to swear that it's the same image, only with a ghost car instead of a lightning bolt.

posted by Neil Gaiman 5:14 PM

Thursday, July 26, 2001

There.

It's over.

I'm done.

Victoria, British Columbia. Beautiful city, lovely place, wonderful people. Really well organised event in its own space with a reading and Q and A for about 250 people. It made me happy. I even had a working microphone. Everyone was incredibly nice, and it left me with a really nice taste in my mouth, to end the tour on.

I'd love to come back some time and actually get a chance to look around. (Flew in on the seaplane from Vancouver, with a view of island after island.)

Home tomorrow…

Now back in the hotel room, and unbelievably tired. G'night.

posted by Neil Gaiman 12:37 AM

In the harbour outside my window tugboats are chugging. The water is blue, the sky is bluer, and I ought to be thinking about breakfast and not typing this.

Apparently Doug-the-HarperCollins-rep's "rural Canadians" line seems to have touched a nerve, or several.

He's kind of from Victoria (although he's now in Vancouver), and drove me around yesterday showing it off more proud of a place than anyone I remember in ages, while pointing out that, really, I should come back here and sign some more. Or just come back here. And bring my family.

I think he was just trying to prepare me for the worst should the room be half-empty and not (as it was) filled to capacity. I suspect he was also rather nervous, having heard from a number of sources about the problems with Virgin Vancouver signing.

But he need not have worried. It was enormously pleasant. The only moment that hurt was the guy who wanted to give me a disk with his stories on, and I had to tell him I wouldn't read them and send back a critique. ("But they're very short." "That's not really the point. There's about a thousand pages of stuff that people have given me to read waiting at home. Even that won't all get read now, let alone replied to, because I physically don't have time.")

Things I am not going to miss about touring:

1. Having rushed lunches at 2:00pm (having done something through lunchtime) followed by dinners at 5:30pm because once I've finished eating I have a reading and signing to do.
2. Getting neither the lunch or the dinner described in (1) and trying to survive on what you can actually get from room service at midnight.
3. Flying. Airports. Planes. (Except I liked the seaplane trip from Vancouver to Victoria and back.) Cars. Trains.
4. Trying to hear people's names correctly and spell them right in noisy rooms. Trying to sign through the blue after-image of a flash photo.
5. The slow deterioration of my handwriting. At the start of the tour people didn't have to look at whatever message I had inscribed in their books and ask "what does this say?" or occasionally "what language is that in?"
6. Being tired.
7. My signing hand hurting. My signing wrist hurting. My signing arm hurting.
8. Hotels.

And to keep it even, things I'll miss:

1. The people.
2. Good sushi. (Last night's pre-signing sushi was lovely. Another reason to come back to Victoria.)
3. Seeing friends.
4. Having a real excuse for not having written you an e-mail, script, movie, novel etc.
5. Knowing exactly what I was doing for six weeks, pretty much minute by minute. Now it's back into the unknown…

posted by Neil Gaiman 9:16 AM

Friday, July 27, 2001

And I'm home.

It doesn't look like yesterday's entry posted, so I'm not going to go on about how big the sunflowers are or how good it is to see the kids again or anything until I find out whether things are working or not.

posted by Neil Gaiman 6:36 AM

A down day. Not sure that I could have done anything had I tried, but I didn't try. Just watched the showreel from the first director to want to make *American Gods*; she might be an interesting choice.

Current plans for the blogger-journal-thing that you are reading… I've a few wrapping up entries to write over the next few days, and then, yes, it will be done. But NESFA Press, who do cool books for Boskones, will be doing it as a book—expanded in places, probably edited occasionally, and undoubtedly annotated. So it will be available in a solid form that can be used to prop up a wobbly table, early next year.

However, we currently have 445 FAQ messages in the in-box, and as soon as I can get to talk to someone who can actually make things happen at this web site, we'll do some redesigning, and move a few things around, and I'll start something that's half FAQ (or just interesting Q) and half journal. Or at least, that's the plan.

Meanwhile, I can assure the person whose copy of *American Gods* is missing chapter 9 and 10 that it is indeed defective, and if you take it to your bookstore they will indeed replace it. *American Gods* is a book that has both chapters 9 and 10 in. Demand the full complement of chapters. Accept no substitutes.

And talking about Boskone reminds me, I really need to make a conventions section of Neilgaiman.com—this year I'll be going to New Orleans (to see Steve Brust), Madison (to finish a story with Harlan Ellison—who has his name in big letters on the web site), and to the Chicago Humanities Festival. Next year is Boston, and Chicago (again) for the World Horror Convention (because Gene Wolfe's the other guest of honour, and Gahan Wilson's the toastmaster, and I've known Jo Fletcher for 18 years, by gum), and also Aggiecon in Austin (because they've been sending my assistant mangos for years in a vain attempt to get me down there).

There's also a con and some signings in Italy in September 2001 I think (because my wife loves Italy more than anywhere else in the world).

And unless they're in Australia or Japan or somewhere cool I don't get to go too often, I think that'll be it for cons and appearances and suchlike for quite a while.

posted by Neil Gaiman 7:10 PM

Saturday, July 28, 2001

Hurrah for *Wizard* magazine. A few months ago they published that some film that I had had in my basement for some years was irretrievably lost. (The people who sent the film to me told them this, for their own reasons.) This month I was told that *Wizard* had published an update— that there was film in my basement, but it was in unusable condition— which was an amazing thing for them to know, since, as far as I can tell, the boxes haven't been opened since they were owned by Eclipse, pre-bankruptcy.

So I thought I'd go down to the basement and look.

Not only was it not at all damaged, old or unusable (because my basement is the other half of my library, and shares drainage tiles and moisture control and sensible things like that) but there was an awful lot more of it than I had thought there would be from the labels on the boxes, including some things I'd thought gone for good—which will, I think, soon be seeing print from a delightfully unexpected source.

Which is enormously fun, and I owe it all to the responsible journalism of *Wizard* magazine.

Also, while I was looking for the film, I found, inside an enormous envelope, an *amazing* piece of artwork by Michael Zulli that I don't ever remember seeing before: it's called *The October Man,* and it's a *Sandman* portrait that he did in 1994, in what looks like chalks and coloured pencils—good enough to be a poster or a book cover: a brooding, moody Morpheus on a jut of ruined masonry against a thundery sunset. Autumn-yellow birch-leaves tremble from a branch, while golden oak-leaves are blown past in the chill wind that whips strips of crimson cloth at the top and bottom of the picture, like rags of a theatrical curtain.

And, as far as I know, I've never seen it before in my life.

I don't know when Michael gave it to me, and dammit, I remember that stuff. And furthermore, if it had been a gift and I'd known about it, it wouldn't have been in an envelope in the basement, it would be in a frame on the wall. How did it get here? How did it get down there? A mystery that needs to be investigated. I shall report back.

posted by Neil Gaiman 4:28 PM

There's a review of *American Gods* in the *New York Times Book Review,* at http://www.nytimes.com/2001/07/29/books/review/RV112648.html. It seems a fairly positive review—and is the first time I've been reviewed in the *Times* since 1990 (for *Good Omens*). (They never mentioned *Sandman* in the years it was being published, although we learn here it is respected.) It's obvious that the reviewer didn't have a great deal of room, so she basically just does a plot summary. But I am now officially "A fine, droll storyteller" (The *New York Times*). (Which makes me sound a little like an after-dinner speaker—"So an English God, a Norse God, and Buddha walk into a bar...")

Tidying up some videos I ran into an old clip of Tori performing "Silent All These Years" on the Jonathan Ross show, circa 1991; Clive Barker and Anne Bobby were on the same tape. Everybody—Tori, Jonathan, Clive and Anne, looked so young.

(There was a nice man at the Victoria signing, who said "I saw you on *Prisoners of Gravity* on TV ten years ago. And you don't look any older now. I guess you have a portrait in your attic, huh?"

"I do," I told him. "And the weird thing is, it looks this age too."

But the truth is, I pretty much look my age, I think.)

Anyway, I promised I'd donate something to one of the RAINN auctions—I might donate that tape, although probably it's something that the Tori fans all have copies of and would yawn at. (How does one find out these things?)

Changing the subject, this in from *Publishers Weekly*.

> "Gods' Odds"... by Daisy Maryles—7/9/2001 News Behind the Bestsellers
>
> ...are looking especially rosy at this point, as Neil Gaiman's *American Gods* has been garnering excellent reviews and is being supported by publisher Morrow's aggressive and innovative marketing campaign. Thanks to the carefully conceived February launch of a dedicated Web site (www.americangods.com), suspense built rapidly for the book and, according to assistant publicity director Dee Dee De Bartlo, it "was one of Amazon's Top 100 weeks before it was available." (On-sale date was June 19; copies in print total 83,000 after three trips back to press.) "It's flying out of the stores at record speed," De Bartlo adds—a pace that will certainly pick up, given Gaiman's just-concluded 10-city coast-to-coast tour. (No rest after that, however, as his 10-city U.K. tour started last Saturday, and will be followed by a three-city Canadian tour.) The author is perhaps best known as the creator/writer of the monthly cult DC Comics horror-weird series *Sandman,* which won him the Will Eisner Comic Industry Award for best writer every year from 1991 through 1994. Harlan Ellison, who knows a thing or two about dark fantasy novels, calls Gaiman's latest "alarming, charming, even winsome," and its author "serially inventive, surprising, purely remarkable."

posted by Neil Gaiman 9:45 PM

Tuesday, July 31, 2001

http://www.cnn.com/2001/COMMUNITY/07/30/gaiman/index.html is yesterday's online conference. It links to the CNN interview of last week. (I said Venn Diagrams, but love the idea of Zen Diagrams. One circle labelled One Hand Clapping, the other labelled Sound: now, grasshopper, where do they intersect?)

Today I'm doing an interview with Audiofile about audio books—then a little rest from interviews before the Australian Interviews begin.

(Oops. Nope. Lorraine-my-assistant just said that the interview's not till next week. It just migrated onto the wrong to-do list.)

Trying hard to get caught up with everything waiting for me, which was too much to do anyway; and then I had a rather unexpected meeting with A Director in a secret room round the back of Minneapolis Airport on Sunday morning which means that my plate suddenly got a whole lot fuller. Heigh ho.

Yesterday I caught up on the final script for Harlequin Valentine which means Diana Schutz at Dark Horse can sleep a little more easily. Today it's *Ramayana* and looking over the stuff that came in from NY on Avalon. And the *Sandman* Calendar—a piece of interesting merchandise I'd long since given up on asking DC to do (I first proposed one in about 1993— it would have had the dates of famous dreams on it, and all sorts of great things. They said no, as people didn't buy calendars…but that was then…) which has suddenly turned up.

Wizard sent me an e-mail apologising for printing stuff they knew wasn't true when they printed it. It was, it seems, a mistake. They've promised to check such material with me in the future.

I am on record (in an long-gone interview in I think *Skeleton Crew,* called "The Luggage In The Crypt") as not liking *The Sound of Music.* I was taken to the film many times as a small boy, not yet in a position to fight back, and disliked it more every time (why, I asked myself, why would that cool Mary Poppins have traded in her umbrella and carpet-bag for this?) (Many years later I wound up standing next to Julie Andrews on a stage, listening to her swear like a trouper—not that surprising, with a moment's reflection, as a trouper is exactly what she was—and I decided that she was definitely a lot more Mary Poppins than Maria.) Anyway, I now have a daughter who is barely older than I was when *The Sound of Music* was first inflicted upon me, who has decided that *The Sound of Music* is the single best thing in the world, and must be sung at all times and played at all others. I think that's what they call karma. Or poetic justice. Or something.

They have announced that the heat index is in the Please Do Not Go Outside zone. I think I'll be working in the basement library today, rather than out by the lake. (It's a wonderful cabin-office, and has No Telephone, but it also has No Air Conditioning.)

And I got sent the cover of the new edition of *The Books of Magic* with the very cool new John Bolton cover, this morning. A lovely piece of work…

And on with the motley.

posted by Neil Gaiman 10:21 AM

Wednesday, August 01, 2001

I mostly wind up posting what I did in the way of media, so here's one posted before I did it: tomorrow (Thursday the second of August) I'll be on NPR's *Midmorning Edition,* broadcasting from KNOW in Minneapolis/St Paul. Talking about *American Gods,* I guess. I'll be there on the 10:00am segment.

And now I have to go and finish reading *The Werewolf Club and the Lunchroom of Doom* by Daniel Pinkwater to a young lady whose current vocabulary seems to consist of "We Come In Peace" "Greetings! Earthlings!" and, occasionally, for variety, "No! Says Alien Maddy!" Still, it makes a change from highlights from *The Sound of Music,* so I suppose we must be thankful for small blessings.

posted by Neil Gaiman 6:09 PM

Spent a small chunk of today working with Shelly Bond on the *Sandman* Calendar—we assembled a bunch of useful birthdays for people who seemed somehow, to our fevered minds, *Sandman*-important, and some *Sandman*-related dates; and we found some pieces of artwork nicer and more relevant than some of the ones that they had already picked out, and I think overall we made something fun. I found a date for *Alice's Adventures in Wonderland,* and established that the date of the composition of "Kubla Khan" was both unknown and contentious.

I am sending the Mysterious Piece of Artwork to DC, with suggestions that it become a poster or something. And I spoke to Mr Zulli about it. "Oh yes," he said. "I remember it well. I did that in 1994. Sent it to you then, or maybe in 1995."

"But what did you think when I never mentioned it?"

"Oh, I thought you were busy or something. I guess I thought you didn't like it."

If it was me, I suspect I would have been on the phone every day, going "Hey, did you see it yet?"

Yesterday was so hot it was dangerous. Today was wetter than you would believe. I attribute both of these things to the overnight stay here of Ms. Claudia Gonson (and friend); the last time Claudia was here it was Xmas Day, and we had the coldest day on record for several years. Claudia says she's coming back to the Minneapolis area for the renaissance festival (see *Sandman* # 73 for details) in September. I expect to see Shakopee washed away by floods, or carried off to Oz by a cyclone when she turns up there, or possibly witness to the first Minneapolitan volcanic eruption since the Silurian Age…

posted by Neil Gaiman 7:28 PM

Friday, August 03, 2001

Still home. Still writing. Still trying to catch up.

This *Guardian* story made me astonishingly happy today, and I would be hard put to explain why.

I also promised the Usual Gang of Reprobates in the Compuserve SFMEDIA forum that I'd mention them sooner or later here on the journal. They're going to be discussing *American Gods* in Section 12 of SFMEDIA in a week or so. So I'm letting any Compuserve people know that that's the place to go and start to chat about it…

posted by Neil Gaiman 10:23 PM

Saturday, August 04, 2001

So I'm reading *Entertainment Weekly* this morning, after breakfast, in a lazy sort of way, trying to decide whether I'm going to spend my Saturday writing the first notes on a strange sort of collaborative tale I'll be doing with Gene Wolfe, to be published at World Horror Con next year, or whether I'm going to read *Black House,* the new King/Straub collaboration (as opposed to *The Talisman,* the old King/Straub collaboration), and I'm turning the pages the way one does at the back of *EW,* especially when one hits the music section (their tastes and mine usually failing to intersect) and I turn a page and notice a photo of Andy Dick and look up to the top left of the page and see a photo of Snoop Dogg, and stop to read the article, which is, it turns out, about blogging: keeping journals like this one.

And I'm in there, and they say some very nice things about this one (if you're coming in late, we're really at the tip of the tail here. Read the archives…). And finally, after reading the whole article, I notice there's also a photo on the page, immediately under the picture of Andy Dick, that I had singularly and utterly failed to notice the first time, and it's a photo of me.

Which left me really puzzled. I mean, I thought I'd be—at least to me, if not to the rest of the world—more recognisable than Andy Dick. Apparently not.

How odd.

posted by Neil Gaiman 11:38 AM

Sunday, August 05, 2001

The weather continues much the same i.e. nightmarishly hot, and the garden continues much the same too, i.e. weird: things are either growing with nightmarish fecundity or not growing at all with neither rhyme nor reason splitting the two camps, and strange green plants get bigger and stranger, and several exotic pumpkins are ripening which seems rather early in the season if you ask me. The corn is high, the sunflowers are higher, and down in the garden things sway and shift and slip and shuffle even when the wind's not blowing. If you were to tell me that some of those plants ate small animals I'm not sure I'd entirely disbelieve you…

Reading *Black House* today. It's odd finding oneself, whether one wants to or not, playing the game of "spot the author"—and knowing that, the way things work, whenever I'm sure who wrote what I'll be guessing wrong, like the people who "know" just who wrote what in *Good Omens* (a book I wrote with Terry Pratchett) always seem to have guessed wrong. Which means if I ever hit a passage in *Black House* that *has* to be written by King, I bet it's by Peter, and if ever I get to a section about obscure Jazz greats, I bet it's been written by Steve, just to confuse me.

Strange, though. It's set about 60 miles away from where I live, at just this time of year, in the heat, with the orange tiger-lilies blooming and blowing by the side of every road, just as they are right now. And it's as much as sequel to *Low Men in Yellow Coats* as it is to *The Talisman*. The whole book is written in the present tense, and I felt proud of myself for noticing that the mood and opening were in a weird way reminiscent of the similarly titled *Bleak House* but then they actually had someone read aloud and quote from the opening of *Bleak House*…

I mentioned in the last entry that I don't usually use *Entertainment Weekly* as a guide to music. I do tend to use *UNCUT* though—they have these wonderful CD compilations on the cover and I keep finding new favourites through them. Thea Gilmore, Hamell on Trial and Black Box Recorder were all first encountered on *UNCUT* compilations. (So thank you Michael Bonner, who put me on their mailing list.)

posted by Neil Gaiman 5:23 PM

Monday, August 06, 2001

Surprised this morning to discover that what looks like more or less random paragraphs extracted from the first couple of the stories I'd written for Tori's *Strange Little Girls* have started floating around the net, and suddenly got a real insight into how artists must feel, having worked themselves into an exhausted frenzy, gone without sleep and racked up a bill of hundreds of thousands of dollars recording a new album, mixing it, getting it into a form they are proud of, only to have everyone's first exposure to it be a badly compressed 56K MP3 of a premixed version released to a couple of journalists…

If that's how the artist wants it released, fine. But if not, I dunno—it's like a strange sort of race between curiosity and respect, and, knowing human nature, curiosity will always win, and always be disappointed.

Not, I should add, that I spent thousands of dollars or went without sleep to write the *SLG* stories. But I had always thought that people's first exposure to them would be as a sequence of 12, in the correct order, to be read or heard in combination with the photos they refer to, and in context of the songs.

posted by Neil Gaiman 10:37 AM

Tuesday, August 07, 2001

Last year, at a reading in Chicago, I read a poem called "Blueberry Girl", as a favour to a very nice couple who had paid a ridiculous amount of money to the Comic Book Legal Defense Fund in order to have dinner with me.

I was surprised the following morning to find that helpful people had forwarded to me lots of web correspondence from other people who were very disgruntled that this hadn't been taped for their benefit and wasn't available on the Web.

Now, for my own reasons, I didn't want the poem out on the web: I wrote it for a friend at her request, it was hers, and I liked the idea that if I read it at a reading it would be, in some way, special.

So, since then, before I've read it, on those occasions I have, I've made a request: would people bootlegging the reading please mind turning off their tape recorders for this bit. And each time I've heard the satisfying chunk-chunk-chunk across the hall of tape recorders being switched off. And then I've read the poem.

Which may be either trusting or foolish of me, or both. But so far no-one's e-mailed me to tell me that copies of "Blueberry Girl" are wandering around. And my personal belief that, on the whole, if you treat people like grown-ups they will, on the whole, act like grown-ups, and nice grown-ups at that, has been upheld.

Something I was reminded of this morning, as I learned that the person responsible for posting the stuff I was grousing about yesterday sent in an incredibly grown-up apology about it, and promised not to do it again. So thanks for that, Luciano. Apology accepted. (And taking a hint from my own posting on curiosity I have decided not to try and find out who he is or how he got the stories, and to let it all lie.)

With luck the FAQ thing should be working by the end of the week. Or so I am assured.

When I get a moment, I'll try and post a sort of wrap-up retrospective of the tour. I realised that most of the strangest, oddest, most fun or most interesting moments went unrecorded on the blogger because I was writing the entries on the run. Like the strange moment in Vancouver Airport where I looked at shelf after shelf of recently published bestsellers in mass market paperback, and realised they were all, without exception, black, red and gold, and, in an effort to stand out, they all looked identical.

One answer, by the way to a number of Frequently Asked Questions, which all begin with "Where can I get a copy of..." is DreamHaven Books in Minneapolis. On the web at www.dreamhavenbooks.com—they are very good people who always try to have more or less everything of mine in stock, if it's in print, and often if it's not.

(On the other hand, currently, the only answer to where to get a legitimate copy of the BBC *Neverwhere* seems to order it from Amazon.co.uk—it's at http://www.amazon.co.uk/exec/obidos/ASIN/ B00004CSV2 and then, if you're in the US, get a PAL to NTSC transfer made so you can watch it.)

Spoke to my editor at HarperCollins. (Interested to hear that *American Gods* has started creeping back up the *New York Times* list again...) We spoke about the mass market paperback of *American Gods*—one of those easy short conversations that worlds probably hinge upon.

Me: So what are we doing for the cover of the mass market paperback of *American Gods?*

Jennifer: Well, we like the hardcover, so it'll be the same image, just reconfigured a bit for paperback.

Me: Should we make the lightning stand out a bit more?

Jennifer: Maybe. I'll see what the design people say.

Me: Okay.

So there you go. You now know as much as I do. As long as it's not black, red and gold, I'll be happy.

posted by Neil Gaiman 7:19 PM

Wednesday, August 08, 2001

Today brought a strange review: http://news.mysanantonio.com/ story.cfm?xla=saen&xlb=640&xlc=271163&xld=100

If I hadn't known better I'd've probably thought it was a parody. You don't expect real reviews to complain that the book was too difficult for the reviewer.

I think my favourite paragraph is:

> For the casual reader, *American Gods* comes under the heading of sensory overload. Perhaps there is such a thing as too much detail; this novel has that. Some of the sequences are almost Kubrickian in their complexity; and knowledge of other religions is required.

All this, I think we are meant to infer, is a very bad thing. (Wonders briefly if we should put a sticker on all copies sold in San Antonio: *San Antonio Express-News* WARNING—Knowledge of Other Religions is Required.)

Have agreed to do a book review for the *Washington Post,* mainly because I've been on the receiving end of so many reviews recently it'll be fun to exercise those muscles myself.

Signed some posters today for RAINN auctions... And my assistant, the Fabulous Lorraine, has pointed out to me it's time to start thinking about this year's Christmas Card. She's also pointed out to me it's probably time to stop doing *American Gods* interviews and to concentrate on writing...and she is, of course, right.

posted by Neil Gaiman 3:25 PM

Friday, August 10, 2001

Mark Askwith e-mails me to tell me that any Canadians who get *SPACE —THE IMAGINATION STATION!* can watch the SHELFSPACE on *American Gods* on...Sat. Aug. 11 at 12:54am and Aug 13 at 10:57am and 2:08am...

And I have to stop typing now to be interviewed by *Smeg Radio* in Sydney, Australia. Honest.

posted by Neil Gaiman 4:09 PM

Saturday, August 11, 2001

Finished the second draft of the whatever-it-is-I'm-doing-with-Avalon. Not quite ready to write the review of *Strange Little Girls* I thought I'd write, having just got the whole thing, all 12 tracks in a final mixed version. Fascinating how the whole shape of the album changes with "Happiness is a Warm Gun" on there; it's an eleven minute monster I want to hear a lot more times before I say anything sensible. But "Raining Blood" works much better now, following it. (It was never happy following "I Don't Like Mondays.")

Meanwhile, something I should have said something about here in this journal weeks ago—http://www.harpercollins.com/hc/perfectbound/ is the website of HarperCollins e-books. All formats of e-book are supported here (although, confusingly, the "chapter to go" facility, which turns up with any format you click on, is only for Palm Pilots), and it's where you'll find out all about the e-book versions of *Stardust, Neverwhere, Smoke and Mirrors* and *American Gods.* Although I couldn't find anything on the site about the various nifty add-ons and things they've done for each of the books. (*American Gods,* for example, has edited highlights of this journal pre-June on it, *Neverwhere* has a few interviews, while *Smoke and Mirrors* has a few extra stories in, just to drive bibliographers mad. I have no memory of what cool electronic extra *Stardust* has.)

Talking about electronic futures, there is a wonderful article on *Salon* at http://www.salon.com/tech/feature/2001/08/09/comics/index.html in which we learn that Scott McCloud's polemic about comics and the internet, *Reinventing Comics* is, according to Gary Groth (publisher of *Fantagraphics*) not just wrong, but dangerous agitprop. Gary read it late at night, and, then, in the morning...

Groth shared his grumbling with Spiegelman and Crumb, both of whom agreed that McCloud's predictions amounted to little more than half-baked evangelism masquerading as insight.

It doesn't say whether they'd read it or not, though. The implication from the article is that, over breakfast the next morning, Gary said "I read *Reinventing Comics* last night. This is dangerous agitprop," and Art Spiegelman said "Yeah?" and R. Crumb said "Is there any coffee over that end of the table?" and Gary said, "It's half-baked evangelism masquerading as insight, you know," and Messrs. Spiegelman and Crumb said "Sure sounds like it, Gary," and "Yup. Can you pass the toast?"

I've had my share of arguments with Scott about *Reinventing Comics* and his passion for the web

> ("...of course, the downside is I can't sell original art any more, as there isn't any."
>
> "Well, why can't you republish the online *Zot* on paper?"
>
> "Ah, Neil, not only can I not republish online *Zot* on paper, but the resolution was poor enough that it won't even go to a better monitor...")

and will undoubtedly have many more, but I can't imagine a world in which his ideas would actually be dangerous. (To whom? You try publishing comics on the web. Either you starve or you don't, or you do something else for money and you do the web comics for fun. You make good art or you make bad art. And your readership may well eventually wind up bigger than the paper equivalent. Inevitably, like a hundred million other people, you'll need to try and figure out whether and how to make money from the web, or whether what you do for money subsidises what you do on the web...But that's not dangerous. That's just life in 2001.)

And good evangelism—which means, of course, spreading the good news—should never be fully-baked, anyway, otherwise it gets stale quickly. It should be like those loaves of half-baked bread that you finish off in your oven at home. Half-baked evangelism is the best kind.

& so to bed.

posted by Neil Gaiman 2:53 AM

You know, I really do owe the world a wrap-up of the whole book tour thing. It would give us all closure and allow us all to feel that We'd Been Through Something Together.

But seeing that I've got to write a history of Harlequins and the *commedia del arte* today, here's a link to Zadie Smith's wrap up of her book tour instead. I enjoyed it a lot; it wasn't my book tour, but there are several moments I recognised. And anyway, it's funny.

posted by Neil Gaiman 1:59 PM

Monday, August 13, 2001

I asked Terry Gilliam how the *Good Omens* movie was going. His reply?

> I'll warn you in advance that we created a very different climax. And we dropped favorite characters. We added some scenes involving cattle drives in the Old West and song and dance sequences from our favorite Bollywood films. We also tried to make the Metatron more Jewish for the sake of the financiers. Woody Allen would be perfect…or maybe Mel Brooks. Then there is the snuff movie that Crowley is producing which we get to see in utterly graphic detail…we thought it would make him more active in be-lievable evil. And we eliminated most of the comedy. I felt it held the book back from being the "great and profound work" which we hope the film will be.

So I don't think we're going to have anything to worry about…

posted by Neil Gaiman 1:02 AM

There's an elegantly written, erudite and delightful *Guardian* article at http://books.guardian.co.uk/reviews/sciencefiction/0,6121,535420,00. html— it's about Douglas Adams, and his love and admiration for Lewis Carroll.

> Carroll, it tells us along with Wodehouse, was one of Adams's comic heroes, and his affection for him tinges his writing. Like Carroll's fabulous mock-epic poem, *The Hunting of the Snark* (1876), the *Hitchhiker* series is a brilliant skit on quests for ultimate meaning of any kind. Carroll's crew fruitlessly pursues the Snark, while Adams portrays the Earth as a miscued mega-computer vainly dedicated to calculating the answer to *Life, the Universe and Everything*. That it eventually spits out "42" is a nod to Carroll, who was obsessed with the number.
>
> Adams also shared with Carroll a love of pataphysical nonsense, as in the Vogon Captain's lovelorn ode, which

causes Arthur Dent such unimaginable suffering early in *Hitchhiker:* 'Oh freddled gruntbuggly!/ Thy micturations are to me/ As plurdled gabbleblotchits in a lurgid bee/ Groop I implore thee my foonting turlingdomes/ And hopptiously drangle me with crinkly bindlewerdles'. This is, in its deranged and glorious musicality, a clear homage to Carroll's 'Jabberwocky' poem—"Twas brillig, and the slithy toves/ Did gyre and gimble in the wabe".

Where Lewis Carroll, an academic mathematician, insinuated Victorian abstract algebraic thought into the Alice books, so Adams, a techno-zealot, quickly incorporated late twentieth-century science into his writing.

and so on.

There's only one thing wrong with it.

Douglas Adams hadn't read any Carroll. He didn't like Carroll. When I was writing *Don't Panic!* I asked Douglas about *Alice's Adventures in Wonderland* (and the Rule 42 line) and he said he'd started to read it as a kid and hated it, and stopped, and he'd started to reread it as an adult, and hated it in the same way, and had stopped.

But it's not the kind of thing a fact checker is ever going to check, is it? It's too big and too basic.

Worried e-mails have started trickling in about yesterday's post. Should I point out that this is from Terry Gilliam again?

posted by Neil Gaiman 11:55 PM

Thursday, August 16, 2001

Who was it who said that a lie can be half way around the world while the truth is still blinking up at the bedroom ceiling blearily wondering whether to clean its teeth before or after having an early morning cup of tea and then starting to think very seriously about rolling over in bed and trying to get just another ten minutes of sleep before starting the day?

Anyway, whoever said it, I hear from the Well that the Terry Gilliam quote I posted the other day has now started showing up on the *Inside Movie News* kind of sites as the inside skinny on *Good Omens*—the film.

So...

It was a joke. Terry Gilliam was joking. It was funny. I posted it because it made me laugh out loud, and I thought it might make some of you laugh too. I figured the stuff about the cattle drives might have been a dead giveaway if the bit about the Bollywood song and dance numbers wasn't, and that, if anyone was still in any doubt, the final line about taking out all the jokes would have set their mind at rest. We won't even go into the bit about Mel Brooks or Woody Allen playing the Metatron.

So. I've now read a draft of the script for *Good Omens,* by Terry Gilliam and Tony Grisoni, and yes, it's very funny. It's a Terry Gilliam film, and it's closer to the book that Terry Pratchett and I wrote than I would have thought possible given the different shapes and dynamics of books and films. Yes, some beloved bits are gone. An astonishing number of beloved bits and characters are still there.

The baby is there, and so is 90% of the bathwater. So please stop worrying.

Now we just have to hope that Mel and Woody will read this and stop calling Terry Gilliam. (Note for Internet movie rumour places: The last line was simply not true. Mel Brooks and Woody Allen have not been calling Terry Gilliam as far as I know, except possibly to complain about the noise.)

posted by Neil Gaiman 7:29 PM

Friday, August 17, 2001

Sooner or later I'll figure out who to talk to to get things happening on this website, and we'll get some of the cool weird stuff up that I keep promising, like the bibliography, and all the scans of all the foreign book covers that we did several months ago, and all the places that say "Coming Soon" will actually come soon…

In the meantime, here's something cute, from Bryan Talbot's lovely website: http://www.bryan-talbot.com/gallery11/imagine.html

Which is of significance only insofar as it contains my first published piece of fiction that anyone paid me for. It's a story named "Featherquest". A sort of Arabian Nights sort of thing. If memory serves I had to cut about 2000 words from it to get them to fit the space they had. I didn't think it was ever good enough to bother restoring the missing words and putting into a collection. *Imagine* published my next short story as well, about six months' later—"How to Sell the Ponti Bridge". It had a good bit or two in it, but it, too, is happier uncollected. (There's also a story from *Knave* from that period, "Mss. Found in a Milkbottle", which also remains uncollected. The last time Mike Ashley asked me for a story for his Comic Fantasy books I pulled that last one out, and reread it, and winced a lot and put it away again.)

Everything else has been published, or will be, in the next collection…

posted by Neil Gaiman 9:34 PM

Saturday, August 18, 2001

"A miracle, even if it is a lousy miracle, is still a miracle." And if *American Gods* was about anything, it was about that, I think.

It's a quote from Teller. Teller is very wise. http://www.deceptions unlimited. com/v2i2p2.html is an interview with Teller.

I love looking at stage magic, reading about it, thinking about it, mostly because all the things I think about magic and magicians are applicable to writing, to genre, to comics, to prose and to film. It's about thinking outside the box, and about craft, and about skill, and about the willingness to surprise yourself and, maybe, sometimes, to make miracles. Because even lousy miracles are still miracles.

posted by Neil Gaiman 12:18 AM

Wednesday, August 22, 2001

Hullo. Bet you thought I was dead.

Nope. Recovering from an intense bout of food poisoning (during the course of which I got to learn firsthand just how much vomit can come out of an adult male author. Try and guess. Nope, more than that…nope, much more than that. Honest. It surprised me, too.) Several hundred e-mails behind, not to mention days and days of blogger entries, but starting to catch up again.

So, today I watched my son head off across the country for his first semester at college, both of us suddenly feeling odder and older as we hugged goodbye. (And, as if to balance that, I took a small daughter to school to meet her second grade teacher, only to be taken by surprise when her principal told me how much she liked this website.)

Currently Jennifer Hershey from HarperCollins and I are starting to figure out things to fix or redo with this website. We're writing notes back and forth about the various COMING SOON bits and what we're doing with them. I want the AUDIO section to be the next thing up—somewhere you can listen to some of George Guidal's wonderful reading of *American Gods,* and listen to some of my readings on *Warning: Contains Language,* and where there are links to some of the scifi.com audio productions.

And I have to write a *Coraline* page, while I think of it…

If any of you have suggestions for things you'd particularly like to see on the site, or really want to see changed, send then off as an FAQ.

Lucy Anne and Puck are posting lots of (mostly *American Gods*) interviews and reviews over at the Dreaming website (it's http:// www.holycow.com/dreaming) and you may want to go and look at them. Lots of fun ones, of which my favourite is http://www.nationalpost.com/ search/story.html?f=/stories/20010804/637258.html&qs=Gaiman— something I barely remember writing as an e-mail from a hotel room when on the road.

(There have been several interviews I've read in the last few weeks, done with me on tour, that I have no memory of saying the stuff I'm quoted as saying at all. I read them and go "well, it certainly sounds like me, and nobody else would have said that, so I suppose I must have done...")

My before-bed reading recently has been Kelly Link's *Stranger Things Happen*. I'd read many of the stories in earlier incarnations, and read the book as a proof, so now am reading half a short story a night purely as a treat for me. Kelly Link is absolutely brilliant. She writes the kind of short stories that make you want to marry the author. (Oddly enough Gavin Grant must have thought the exact same thing, because he is marrying her in a week or so, and this journal would like to extend all felicities in their general direction.)

posted by Neil Gaiman 8:24 PM

Thursday, August 23, 2001

And of course one of the things that we need to overhaul on the site is the links area. There are more fan sites than the Dreaming of course. There's one called the Gaiman Archive over at http://home.bip.net/rivieran.

Meanwhile, I'm not quite sure what's happening with the official UK site at http://authorpages.hoddersystems.com/NeilGaiman/ it seems to run through an opening screen sequence and then give me an error message.

And I hear that *Rambles*.net is going to be reviewing the Flash Girls CD any day now. (Just what I need, thinks author wryly—an assistant on tenterhooks.)

And I was fascinated to see that Lord Lloyd Webber has started reviewing books...wonder how long it will be before Amazon.com take it down.

posted by Neil Gaiman 1:06 PM

There really are links on this journal, you know. You can see them if you put your cursor on the text. It's one of the things we'll get fixed here one of these days.

In the meantime, a review of *American Gods* by Charles de Lint at http://www.sfsite.com/fsf/depts/cdl0109.htm—and Charles neglects to mention, as he points out that other people have written stuff using similar themes to *American Gods,* that one of those people is Charles de Lint. But I can. He's a wonderful writer. Go and read him.

The review is from the September issue of *F&SF*. (You'll find a story by me in the Oct/Nov issue of *F&SF,* which should be on sale any week now—the "all-star 52nd anniversary issue" it says on the cover. It's a short-short story I wrote on a plane at the beginning of the year, just to get it out of my head, and I nearly threw it away, as I was sure that Fredric Brown had probably written it first, but after having shown it to a few people who said that he hadn't, I sent it to Gordon Van Gelder at *Fantasy & Science Fiction*. It's called "Other People", which is Gordon's title for it and a much better title than "The Skinning Knife, the Choke-Pears and the Screw", which is what I would have called it.)

And there is a review of the Flash Girls album up at http://www.greenmanreview.com/wildqueen.html.

posted by Neil Gaiman 7:52 PM

Friday, August 24, 2001

Sixteen years ago I made much of my living reviewing books. Haven't done it in a long time (although I've recently seen a few quotes from seventeen-year-old reviews surfacing with my byline, as if they're current blurbs, proving, I suppose, that they are not entirely forgotten), but was recently asked to review a book for a major newspaper, and agreed. I suppose I thought that book reviewing was like riding a bicycle or kissing—something you never forget how to do, no matter how long you don't. In reality, I'm finding, it's more like speaking a foreign language or playing a musical instrument: if you don't do it for a long time, you lose it. Not completely, and it comes back to you after a bit. But that easy, unthinking facility is gone.

So now I just have to turn a bunch of sentences into an article.

In the meantime, hurrah for Chris Ware, nominated for the *Guardian* First Book award. Read http://books.guardian.co.uk/firstbook2001/story/ 0,10486,541770,00.html

posted by Neil Gaiman 8:24 AM

Saturday, August 25, 2001

Not only has the Andrew Lloyd-Webber Amazon page vanished, but they've removed all the reviews from the system.

Poor old Amazon. I miss the days when you could write something in the "I am the author and I want to talk about my book" section. I was told that it had vanished following complaints from A Fantasy Author after someone impersonated him.

Now, I sent them a grumpy e-mail after an "I am the author" thing cropped up on the *Good Omens* site which said something along the lines of

> I wrote this book with Terry Pratchett it was very funny
> we laughed a lot I hope it will be a film soon well thank
> you fans I will write another book one day Neil Gaimen

asking them to take it down, which they did. But I didn't demand they scrap the whole thing because it was open to abuse, because it was too

cool and sensible and useful a tool for that. Unfortunately one day someone with no sense of proportion did.

I'd love to put up an "I am the author" note for Amazon.com's entry
for a book by me they list as coming out next year called *Cordelia* which
explains that I've never heard of this book before, and are they sure they
don't mean *Coraline?*

The suggestions for things to do with the site are being sent over to
HarperCollins... thanks everyone for your patience and your ideas.

posted by Neil Gaiman 9:10 AM

Sunday, August 26, 2001

http://www.rambles.net/flash_playeach.html is the latest Flash Girls
review for *Play Each Morning*. I have no idea why you can't seem to get
the CD through Amazon etc. yet, but DreamHaven always have things
like this for sale.

Today I started signing my way through a large box of cards, which
Yoshitaka Amano has already signed. Most of them have a signature in
English, but there are occasional cards which he's also written messages
on in Japanese. Knowing Mr Amano they probably just say his name in
kanji and do not spell out some rude message about signing things. But I
can't help wondering.

And I am currently reading—again, doling out a story a night before
sleep—*McAuslan Entire*. You can find the publisher's blurb on it here. It's
by George MacDonald Fraser, and is a delightful, sensible, world-affirming,
beautifully crafted bunch of stories. (And it's the sort of thing you need to
read after working your way through another chunk of the two volume
Collected Strange Stories of Robert Aickman.)

As a young man I preferred Fraser's *Flashman* stories to his *McAuslan/
Dand MacNeill* stories; now I'm not so sure. (Possibly because I'm still
out of sorts with a story in the last Flashman collection. Dammit, Flashman
can't meet Sherlock Holmes. There was a compact with the reader about
Flashman, and that breaks it—it says, unequivocally, that Flashman is a
fictional character, not a historical one, whereas up until that point the
only fictional characters were from *Tom Brown's Schooldays*. In *Royal Flash*
Flashman doesn't meet Rupert of Hentzau, he meets the inspiration for
Rupert of Hentzau, and so on.)

Sorry, I'm wittering.

And for those who do not need their lives—or anyone else's—affirmed
in any way, here's a page on the two volume Robert Aickman book I
mentioned above. I'm not honestly sure whether or not it's still in print

or back in print, but if you like to be unsettled by the best then try and find it. Yes, it's very expensive. Still, it's worth every penny and will save you several thousands on buying the original books that the stories appeared in, if you can find them all.

posted by Neil Gaiman 11:40 PM

Monday, August 27, 2001

Let's see…for any of you who use the message board, yup, I'm aware that it's broken, and now HarperCollins is too, and I expect that tomorrow Authors on the Web will be too.

And, yes, if they ever get the FAQ journal up and running, the questions will be answered. Probably not all of them (right now there's 693 of them) but that is still the plan…

posted by Neil Gaiman 9:55 PM

Wednesday, August 29, 2001

The relationship between authors and booksellers is a strange one. Especially from an author's point of view. (From a bookseller's point of view I am sure that mostly authors are just another kind of book buyer, only one more prone to find their books Spine Out and put them Face Out than the other kinds.) For an author, of course, it's a much more complicated relationship. It's more like a marriage. Although the booksellers never mind if the authors forget their birthdays. And they never grumble at you for leaving the toothpaste top off, or get you out of trouble by sliding over just as you're trying to remember whether the person at the funeral you're talking to is your wife's cousin or her dentist by saying "I'm pleased to see you've already run into Harry-who-runs-that-restaurant-you-like" so you can wrench the conversation off of the relative advantages of bridgework versus titanium tooth implants (which neither of you were doing very well at anyway) and head for the relative safety of aubergines. Which Americans call eggplants.

Come to think of it, it's not much like a marriage at all.

Which is a train of thought I wandered onto after getting two phone calls in close succession, one from a family member who went out to buy a copy of *American Gods* from their local bookshop, and who was told that They'd Sold Out Of All Their Copies Surprisingly Fast, so they Didn't Have Any. And on enquiring when they'd be getting more copies in, was told, disapprovingly, that It Was A Hardback. So they had No Plans to Order Any More, but the paperback would be Out Next Year.

And the other telling me that Booksense, which is an association of Independent Booksellers, has a list called the *Booksense 76*—books chosen by Independent Booksellers as books they like handselling, and feel need more attention—go to booksense.com for more information—and that *American Gods* is on the next *Booksense 76* list, at #2.

posted by Neil Gaiman 7:17 AM

Friday, August 31, 2001

Personally, I think the German *Smoke & Mirrors* cover (the book is now called *The Queen of Knives*, I think, after the poem)—visible at http://images-eu.amazon.com/images/P/3453177983.03.LZZZZZZZ.jpg is really fun. I suspect it'll disappoint a lot of German readers looking for something, um, spicy, though. (The Hungarian cover of *Smoke & Mirrors* made the content look pretty risqué too.)

Had fun tonight doing an hour of live radio on Wisconsin's *Spectrum West*, talking mostly about writing, with the redoubtable Jack Beaver. ("This is my fifth career," he said. "And I only got into it because I wrote a poem." But then volunteers Jessica and Katie needed to be taught how to answer the studio phones, and so I never found out just how the poem figured in Jack's career structure.) My favourite call-in question was from a lady who had just got out of prison and thought the prison stuff in *American Gods* rang truer to life than any movie she'd seen, and wanted to know about research.

Made a giant list of everything I was committed to doing over the next six months. Then made a list of all the books I want to write, trying to leave nothing out. I think *Neverwhere 2* (It's a novel called *The Seven Sisters*) may have to wait a while before being written, as I realised I only knew a little bit of the story, which means that the novel after *Coraline* will probably be either *Wall* (The Jenny Kertin novel) or *Anansi Boys*.

posted by Neil Gaiman 1:02 AM

Sunday, September 02, 2001

I think I said already somewhere that this was a particularly strange year for gardening. The sunflowers turned into 25-foot-high triffids, while the plum trees produced a grand total of three (3) plums, and the pumpkins are just weird. I brought back several packets of unusual pumpkin seeds from Amsterdam Airport when I went to Ireland in January, and now am trying to figure out what the odder ones are. If I was a *real* gardener I'd be able to remember where I put the empty seed packets to find out. But then I wouldn't have the fun of going "What *are* these things?" Particularly about the flattish ones that look like enormous vivid orange toadstools. I go out there in the morning and look at them nervously, like a character in an early Ray Bradbury short story.

A gift arrived from HarperCollins a few days ago. It's a black-leather-bound, gold-edged, handmade, one-of-a-kind edition of *American Gods*—a thing of unbelievable beauty. It makes me happy just to look at it. It's the kind of thing that makes me wish I had a display case for wonderful things, awards, gifts and whatnot, rather than just finding room for them on mantlepieces and in corners and things. But I don't. They just have to find their places.

In the old days when people used to ask me in interviews what I missed most about the UK I'd tell them the radio. Now I'm getting gradually spoiled, thanks to streaming audio broadcasts: as I type this, *The Archers* is burbling away in the background on Radio 4. *The Archers* is probably the longest-running radio soap opera in the world, perfect aural wallpaper, and I am ten years behind (which, oddly enough, doesn't matter, as, give or take the odd fire, rape, mad cow or bankruptcy, nothing ever actually happens on *The Archers*), and noticing that my-friend-the-lovely-Tamsin-Greig-from-the-BBC-*Neverwhere* is now in it.

Now I just have to persuade Jonathan Ross to move his Radio 2 show to my waking hours. Or find some brilliant technical way to listen to streaming UK radio on a six hour delay…

And while we're waiting for the FAQ etc thing to get up and running (ho! says older-but-wiser author in a hollow and sceptical voice) I thought I'd answer a few more questions. My favorite recent one was that someone wanted to know about me and Charles Fort, and whether I considered myself a Fortean. I suppose I do. I had to hunt down my Charles Fort books when I was a young teenager, after reading some article in an old SF magazine trashing him (from memory, the article was called something like "Lo! The Bold Forteans" and was by someone like Willy Ley, and I realised that this was the same Fort that Eric Frank Russell and R. A. Lafferty talked about), and I went down to my bookshop and ordered a copy of the Dover books *Complete Charles Fort*. And was struck by the poetry, and the delight in ideas. The pickle people. The jelly in the sky (which is why stars twinkle, of course.) Maybe we're property. How to measure a circle. Raining Fish (which one day I was to have a lot of fun with in *Good Omens* although I'm pretty sure it was Terry who first popped Fort into Adam's hands in the book—I remember the sheer joy of writing the Fortean version of Radio 4's perennial Gardener's Question Time…) I read him with the same delight, and with the same part of my head, and at the same time as I read e.e. cummings' prose essays.

There's a story about Charles Fort and Karl Marx that sits in my head in the attic of unwritten stories, on the same shelf in my mind as the one about Kenneth Williams and Kenneth Halliwell. One day…

Hmm. I wonder if those strange flat pumpkin things are really Fortean Phenomena. I should write in to Gardener's Question Time (and *Good Omens* readers who want background on that bit of the book can go and listen to it here).

posted by Neil Gaiman 11:49 AM

Tuesday, September 04, 2001

Fay Weldon has just set the literary world on its ear by doing product placement in her new novel, *The Bulgari* something or other. Bulgari sells expensive jewellery, and commissioned the book. Lots of people are gasping that this is the first time anything like this has happened and that it's the thin end of the wedge and that literature is now doomed. (http://books.guardian.co.uk/departments/generalfiction/story/0,6000,546800,00.html)

Actually, of course, the rot set in last year when my old friend Bill Fitzhugh started plugging single malts. (Read all about it here at http://www.kgbmedia.com/text/novel.html). Although I think that all Bill got out of it was bottles of fine single malt, while Fay Weldon probably got proper folding stuff with which to buy jewellery (or single malt scotch, I suppose, if that was the way her fancy led her).

Personally, I think it's a triffic idea, and would like to announce that any manufacturers of fine fountain pens who want to get plugged in the text of the next novel should just drop me a line. And a sample fountain pen or two. Also people selling small South Sea islands—I will happily plug your South Sea island sales company in my next novel in exchange for a small island of my own.

Just in case you were wondering.

posted by Neil Gaiman 7:38 PM

Wednesday, September 05, 2001

Yesterday's journal entry (the one about product placement) brought the following e-mail from my friend John M. Ford (talking about his first contact novel *The Final Reflection*):

> Promise I am not making this up. I can show you the book, if you think your nerves can stand it.

> Toward the end of the German edition of *Reflection*, just before Dr. Tagore says goodbye to Krenn for the last time, there's about a half-page of "blacked-out" lines, and then the text starts talking about how tiring it is for

old guys like Emanuel to beam up and down, but a hot Maggi bouillon cube will fix everything up just ducky. This goes on for a page or so, and then there are some more blacked lines, and the book resumes. Now, so far as I know, I didn't get a Deutschmark for this, or even a case of Maggi soup (which I wouldn't have minded having, especially the potato-leek) but it sure enough was a weird thing to see. Still is.

And, of course, I do believe him—I remember Terry Pratchett telling me about his incredulity at discovering a soup advert in the text of I think it was *Sourcery*, again the same sort of thing—"By now you might think our heroes would be pretty exhausted from all this running around. I bet they wished they had a nice cup of Maggi Soup..." If memory serves (and my apologies if it doesn't), Mr Heyne of Heyne publishing had done the deal with the soup company himself, and was only dissuaded from this course after a number of foreign authors (and probably some German ones as well) threatened to take their books away from Heyne.

There's a rather wonderful review of *American Gods* at http://www. compulsivereader.com/article1044.html...

A look at the *Locus* Bestseller roundup shows that *American Gods* remains up there on the *San Francisco Chronicle* bestseller list (up 6 places to number 4), after 10 weeks. Which makes me happy.

And things really and truly honestly and actually seem to be happening now with the website—journals will be changing, FAQ things will start to occur, content will begin to appear, or so I am assured. So if there's any problems with pages you've bookmarked (like this one), head back for the neilgaiman.com home page and come forward from there...

Which means that I get to see whether or not DirecPC will actually ever put in the two way internet satellite thingie I signed up for back in May. (A Kafkaesque story I shall tell when I get around to it.)

posted by Neil Gaiman 8:33 PM

Sunday, September 09, 2001

Yesterday was a strange day of oddnesses and coincidence and one disaster.

Of course, I'd have missed most of it if I'd known that Maddy had two violins.

So...

The Flash Girls, who have been mentioned more than once in this journal, are The Fabulous Lorraine and Emma Bull. They've been described as gothic folk, and they've been described as lots of other things too, all of them complimentary. The ladies formed the band at my first ever Guy

Fawkes Night after moving to the US (which would be somewhere around November 5th, 1992). Later, Lorraine came to work as my assistant (actually she came to help me organise the bookshelves and never went away). Still later, after a couple of Flash Girls albums, Emma Bull and her husband and partner in crime, Will Shetterly, moved to LA. This made life for a Minneapolis-based two-girl band much more problematic.

Still, last year they got back together and made a third album called *Play Each Morning, Wild Queen.* (The other albums are *The Return of Pansy Smith and Violet Jones,* in the liner notes of which I wrote a very odd short story, and *Maurice and I.* Maurice is a dried alligator head.) The official launch party for *Wild Queen* was last night, at DreamHaven Books. Emma flew in from LA for it last week, and she and Lorraine vanished off to the top of the house together every day; strange music echoed down from the attic.

Yesterday Emma and Lorraine, and several of their friends from distant parts, like Halifax and Kentucky, went off to the Minnesota Renaissance Festival. Emma and Lorraine were going to do a few Flash Girls gigs there, along with all the other things Lorraine does (like fiddle for a belly dance group and be the female side of a mead-swigging band named Bedlam). Then they were going to the DreamHaven party in the evening.

I was meant to spending yesterday writing, but when I got up I noticed that Maddy's violin was still here, and I felt bad for her. Maddy is seven, and had been planning to play with Emma and Lorraine at some point. She's had her heart set on it. So I sighed and put the violin in the back of the car, and off I drove.

I was just getting to the festival when I noticed that the pass that would have got me in was missing. I made a couple of phone calls to locate it, got the news, and so kept driving, past the festival and on to the local hospital.

Emma had slipped on a patch of water on a slick wooden floor, at the festival. She'd broken her right arm—smashed up her elbow quite badly. And the day turned into a hospital sort of day, waiting in waiting rooms for word on what was happening down the do-not-enter corridors.

The third time Lorraine came out she explained that Emma was going to have to go back to their hotel and sleep, and that she wasn't going to be able to play, and the launch party would have to be cancelled.

I said that wasn't a good idea, and went off to the car park to make a few phone calls. Life for everyone was made much easier as I'd shown up, mostly because I had a car.

We went over to Emma and Lorraine's hotel. I saw my wife, and Maddy. "It was so lucky that you came out," said my wife. "I thought you were going to stay home and write."

"I was," I said. "But when I saw you'd forgotten Maddy's violin…"

"I didn't," said Mary. "The one you brought is the one that's too big for her, so we rented another. Didn't you know she had two violins?"

I didn't, of course. But it had made life a lot easier for a lot of people that I hadn't known.

The DreamHaven launch party went ahead. Several hundred people showed up. Lorraine was there, although she didn't play—I made a short speech and told people what was happening, Lorraine produced a green mobile phone. People shouted "hello" to Emma over the phone. The entertainment was provided by a combination of Boiled in Lead and the long-defunct Cats Laughing, including Robin Anders, Adam Stemple and Lojo Russo. Lorraine signed a lot of CDs. A get well card was signed.

Keep your fingers crossed for Emma. (It's not a good thing for a writer/musician to lose the use of her right arm.)

And I'll be without an assistant for a few days.

(Useful links: http://www.amazon.com/exec/obidos/ASIN/B00003ZAN1 is the amazon link for *Maurice and I*; http://www.player.org/pub/flash/flash.html is the Flash Girls home page; http://www.fabulousrecords.com/ is Fabulous Records, the record company; and http://www.dreamhavenbooks.com/ is DreamHaven Books.)

posted by Neil Gaiman 11:48 AM

Will Shetterly just sent this out, and I'm posting it with his permission…

Excuse the mass mailing, but it seems the easiest way to deal with this:

Emma is in excellent spirits, so don't worry too much about her—just a little bit. Here's the story as I know it:
She went up to Minneapolis to play in a CD-release party for the Flash Girls' new album on Saturday night. She and Lorraine planned to spend that day playing at the Renaissance Festival. But at a lunch show, as Emma was heading in with a number of other performers, she slipped on a wet spot on the stage.

Being a pro, she got up and dashed offstage to keep from alarming the audience. That's where she realized things Were Not Good.

The Ren Fest has cabriolet guys–essentially their version of rickshaw drivers–who took her to Medical Services crying, "Make way for the new owner of the Renaissance Festival!" which made her laugh despite her pain. She got hustled off to the local ER, where she got the diagnosis:

The good news is that the break is clean. The bad news is that it is in her right elbow, where it will require surgery–otherwise, the tendon will pull at the bone and keep it from closing properly. She's going to get it taken care of up there; they're using insurance info from the Ren Fest and it looks like they'll cover the expenses, and, frankly, I feel better about her being taken care of in Minnesota's health care system than California's. (Those of you who know me well: insert a rant here about how much more sensible the health care systems of Canada, Japan, and most of western Europe are when compared with the US's.)

She's an outpatient and getting excellent care from her many friends; if this had to happen someplace away from home, I'm glad it happened near Minneapolis. She says the drugs have been swell. She sounds great on the phone. Lorraine, amazing personal assistant that she is, has been neglecting her boss for Emma's sake, and Betsy, nurse and force of nature that she is, has put Emma up at her house and is now hustling her through hospital and insurance regulations.

The CD release party went on, not quite as scheduled. Emma stayed in bed, but many fine folk showed up, so the audience had a good time: Neil Gaiman introduced Lorraine, who told the crowd what they had planned to do. I'm not sure whether Lorraine played anything. It sounds like most of the music for the evening came from Lojo Russo, Adam Stemple, Robin Adnan Anders, and Scott Keever, a swell bunch of musicians. I think the thing that makes Em and me sorriest about the whole thing is that she didn't get to play AND we both missed what sounds like a great show.

DreamHaven, the folks putting on the party, said they sold heaps of stuff, so they were as happy as they could be under the circumstances. Emma promised to sign things lefthanded with an "X"; there are apparently stacks awaiting her when she gets into the store.

The surgery is scheduled for Monday; they'll be putting in a plate. We're not sure how soon she'll be able to fly back, but I'm hoping to have her home before the end of the week.

UPDATE: I just got a call; she may also have fractures in her left elbow and in one hand. She's going through yet another set of X-rays to give them more information. Her left arm is swollen, but it has most of its range of movement–except for a worrisome little bit that hurts, which is the reason for the next set of X-rays.

Emma hasn't checked her email since she left for Minnesota, and now it'll probably be a while before she can. I'm not sure how big her email storage is, so I suggest holding off on sending her electronic get wells.

Hoping no one has stories to top Emma's—

Will

—Emma Bull and Will Shetterly's site: http://homepage.mac.com/emmawill/

posted by Neil Gaiman 6:03 PM

Monday, September 10, 2001

And again, from Will Shetterly, on Emma Bull's condition, as of Monday evening:

Today's surgery seems to have gone well. The situation with her right arm was a little worse than expected; they had to do a bone graft and put in a larger plate than they had planned on. Emma'll have to do some physical therapy; I've got a recommendation from one of LA's best doctors (science fiction fans crop up in the darndest places) for an elbow specialist whose offices are fairly close to us. She'll also probably have a removable cast for her left hand, and she'll have to keep that arm immobile.

We're assured that she'll be typing and playing the guitar soon—but soon is a relative term. The Fabulous Lorraine and I have already been talking back-up plans for the concert they planned to give at MadCon at the end of October; Emma should be able to sing, but there'll probably be a guest Flash Girl or two.

I continue to hope to have her home toward the end of the week. Lorraine and Betsy and Neil and and many fine people in Minneapolis are giving her the very best of care, so things really are as well as they possibly could be under the circumstances.

Will

And as for me, I'm writing away as best I can. (Currently rewriting one movie, making extensive notes for a second, and beginning the first of the stories for the ENDLESS book.)

It turns out that they did actually set the FAQ reply blogger thing up, a while ago. They just got my ID wrong when they did it…

So as soon as they sort that out I'll get some FAQ answers rolling. Most of the Questions coming in aren't FAQs and they are the most fun, so I suspect that that's what we'll transmute this journal into.

Forgot to mention that I'd seen the *Sandman Sandglobe* the other day. And, as I was told a long time ago by a cartoon rabbit, if you can't say something nice about someone, don't say anything.

posted by Neil Gaiman 7:37 PM

Tuesday, September 11, 2001

And a web site user writes:

> Hmm, so, you're disappointed with the *Sandglobe*. But have you seen the reprint of the Vertigo Tarot deck? The card stock is flimsy, it feels really fragile, I'm afraid to shuffle with it. Again, not the greatest quality product from Vertigo… I'm considering seeing how practical laminating the cards would be, as a not cheap, but effective way to keep the deck intact and still use it. Thanks for listening,
>
> Gareth Edwards

I've been chatting to Karen Berger, editor in chief of Vertigo, about the flimsiness of the cards, and she's investigating, as she had chosen a heavier card stock (which for reasons no-one understands doesn't seem to have been used). If the Tarot gets to a second printing—which it may well, given the demand,—then I am assured that the cards will certainly be on a heavier stock.

posted by Neil Gaiman 9:05 AM

The phone lines to New York aren't doing anything, and the cell phone numbers I've been dialing are dead. I'm scared for my friends. Watching CNN, worrying.

posted by Neil Gaiman 9:12 AM

Now got BBC America on. Many e-mails from friends to say they are alive… Many more I'm waiting to hear from.

Was meant to be going to the UK in a couple of days for Douglas Adams' memorial service, and then to Trieste in Italy for a festival. Right now we'll see whether or not planes are going to be flying...

posted by Neil Gaiman 10:24 AM

Thursday, September 13, 2001

This is what I did today.

I picked up lots of fallen sunflowers and propped them against the side of the house for no real reason other than they looked nice like that. I did some baking. I wrote some of a movie. I phoned friends I hadn't talked to in a while, just to say hello. I failed completely to get hold of anyone in New York by phone. I answered the phone a lot, because there were people calling in from New York. I decided not to fly to London on Saturday. I watched the documentary on *The Wicker Man* on the DVD (puzzled that the version I taped from the TV years ago is longer than the theatrical version, and shorter than the 99 minute "extended" one). I read a book about the Lazzi (or comedy routines and business) of the *commedia dell'arte,* with a weird sort of theory that they might make a metaphor. Cleaned the catboxes. Worried about the last couple of friends of mine in New York I've not heard from yet. Read Maddy tonight's chapter of *Howl's Moving Castle*. Made a Red Cross donation at Amazon.com. Taught Maddy several card tricks.

Trying to assert normality.

There are worse ways to spend a day.

posted by Neil Gaiman 1:16 AM

The strangest recent FAQ submission let me know that it had been "proved on usenet" that Caitlín Kiernan had ghost-written *Stardust* for me, and did I have any comments? Denying it, I was told, would only demonstrate that I was intent on covering it up. Could I prove they were wrong?

A puzzler, that, like being asked to prove that you are not an identical clonal double impersonating yourself. So yes, I suppose I could (I wrote the book in longhand, after all).

But I'd rather admit that Cait wrote *Stardust* while I was busy fighting crime off-planet. When you're battling Denebian slime-worms, who has time to write? Thank heavens for the Legion of Substitute Neils. Gene Wolfe wrote *Neverwhere* for me, while the late Ian Fleming wrote *American Gods* via planchette.

posted by Neil Gaiman 9:42 AM

Friday, September 14, 2001

Long chatty post replying to questions eaten by blogger last night, which then crashed, I assume from strain on the servers. No time this morning to rewrite it all, so I shall simply send all of you my best wishes.

posted by Neil Gaiman 9:30 AM

An e-mail arrived in the FAQ thing explaining, very reasonably, that *American Gods* made the World Trade Centre Disaster happen. It began by quoting Jerry Falwell's recent comments,

> The abortionists have got to bear some burden for this because God will not be mocked. And when we destroy 40 million little innocent babies, we make God mad. I really believe that the pagans, and the abortionists, and the feminists, and the gays and the lesbians who are actively trying to make that an alternative lifestyle, the ACLU, People for the American Way—all of them who have tried to secularize America—I point the finger in their face and say, 'You helped this happen.'

And then explained that the reader had read much of *American Gods* before realising that even reading it was an act of idolatrous demon-worship, and had burned his copy. (Or her copy, I suppose.) It wanted to know if I was happy now?

The implication, I guess, was that God was just about tolerating the pagans, Lesbians, ACLU etc., but then *American Gods* was published, and it tipped Him over the edge.

Insert picture of author here, sighing, shaking his head, getting back to work.

posted by Neil Gaiman 2:14 PM

Lots of nice letters from religious people of all stripes and sects who like reading books, disavowing both Mr Falwell and the previous correspondent. S'okay. While I didn't take it any more seriously than the American Family Association "boycott" of *Sandman* (like Donald Wildmon and his people were buying *Sandman* to begin with) I did take it as a cautionary tale, and a reminder: as long as you know who God wants you to hate and to hurt then anything you do to them is justified.

Abbot Arnold's line in the Albigensian Crusades (around 1210 from memory) still turns up on Tee shirts. The Albigensian Crusade was an internal French Crusade to root out heresy. When Arnold was asked how the troops would know how to tell the heretics from the believers in the city of Beziers, he replied simply, "Kill them all. God will know his own."

posted by Neil Gaiman 9:23 PM

Saturday, September 15, 2001

Go and read http://www.guardian.co.uk/wtccrash/story/0,1300, 552408,00.html if you haven't already. It's an article by Ian McEwan.

posted by Neil Gaiman 8:11 AM

My *Washington Post* review is up at http://www.washingtonpost.com/ wp-dyn/style/books/A28549-2001Sep14.html—it's of the King/Straub collaboration *Black House*. (The *Post* people have done a solid edit—the only line I really miss is the quickie description of Lord Malshun, "Sauron as used-car salesman".)

posted by Neil Gaiman 1:33 PM

Monday, September 17, 2001

So. I'm going to Trieste, for the Fantasy Festival (you'll find something about it here at http://www.corriere.fantascienza.com/ and the official site here at http://www.sfx.it/).

I'm leaving this coming Wednesday.

Pretty much everyone I talk to seems to think this is a very bad idea, and I think I've rather managed to upset several people I care about by deciding to go.

I'm going because I got up this morning, fully prepared to cancel—I'd already cancelled the flight to the UK last Saturday, to go to Douglas Adams's memorial today—and then I thought, "You know, if I don't go, if I just sit here for the next week, I'll feel like those twerps have won. And to the extent that people stop travelling and stop doing things, to the extent that we withdraw from the world, then that's the extent that whoever did these appalling things wins and the rest of us lose."

Which may not be particularly profound, but I phoned the travel agent and established that, yes, I could fly out on Wednesday, and I established that, yes, the festival did still want me. And so I'm going.

I'm not sure that it's particularly brave of me—in all honesty I doubt that I'm likely to incur much personal risk (it's probably safer to fly right now, when security is at its tightest, than it will be in a couple of years, when everyone's relaxed). I don't think that Trieste or Venice (where I fly into) are likely to be major terrorist targets. If things internationally go severely wobbly while I'm away, I might be stuck on the other side of the Atlantic for a while. I don't actually expect it will come to that. If it does, I'll go to England and hole up in Dave Mckean's spare room, or see if I can ride home on the QE2 or something like that. (I could hitch a ride on a tramp steamer, like people do in books, if I knew how to recognise a tramp steamer.) I'll take the Libretto. I'll post from the road. I'll be fine.

posted by Neil Gaiman 11:00 PM

Y'know, I've not said how pleased I was to learn from *Publisher's Weekly* (via Lucy Anne) that Darryll and the rest of the staff of the Borders Books in the World Trade Center were okay. (I started the *American Gods* signing tour there, on June 19th, and they took great care of me.)

posted by Neil Gaiman 11:30 PM

Tuesday, September 18, 2001

And an e-mail comes in on FAQ with a heartfelt request:

> Will you try to use your status as a celebrity to protect against the violence done to Muslim Americans? I'm sure and other famous people speaking out against these acts would be great...

Well, sure, for whatever good it will do. The people who would do violence to Muslims, or to Americans of Arab descent, are probably not reading this blogger. (And considering the first death in "retaliation" of an American was some people in Arizona shooting a Sikh [from the Punjab, and, as a Sikh, obviously not a follower of Islam], I don't even think that, for example, explaining that the Taliban no more represents Islam than Torquemada and his thugs represented Christianity or the Nazi Party represented neo-paganism would do much good. The Arizonans who killed the Sikh spotted the guy with the beard in the turban and figured that the gentleman had committed the crime of being brown-skinned and foreign, and that was enough for them.)

(And me, I wish people would reread *Sandman* # 50, "Ramadan", and the ifrit chapter in *American Gods*.)

posted by Neil Gaiman 12:33 AM

Yup. Something's wrong, and we don't know what it is. Close the window that opens. Do not try to run the exe file.

My immediate paranoid reaction was to assume that it was a gift from the Falwell-influenced "*American Gods* made the Bad Thing Happen" person or people, but it looks like it's on every Authors On The Web site.

Subject: Important from AuthorsOnTheWeb.com

All-Important note: Please do not try to access any Authors On The Web websites at this time. A file is coming up that is alien to these websites. We have a technical crew looking into this, but it will take time to ascertain the problem and get it corrected. To complicate things, our websites are hosted at Globix, which is south of Canal Street and thus running at less than 100% operation due to last week's disaster.

As we are not sure what the issue is at this time, it would be best if you were not accessing these websites until we have a handle on what is going on. We are going to try to take the server offline.

posted by Neil Gaiman 11:38 AM

So, this is the website with the information on the worm—http://vil.mcafee.com/dispVirus.asp?virus_k=99209?characteristics which contains the relevant patch and the information about what's going on. And if you're running Windows and Internet Explorer you should definitely download the patch in question.

posted by Neil Gaiman 5:10 PM

This is the user patch http://www.microsoft.com/technet/treeview/default.asp?url=/technet/security/bulletin/MS01-020.asp

posted by Neil Gaiman 5:27 PM

Friday, September 21, 2001

In Venice. The One in Italy. Honest. A man tried to sell me a paper Mickey Mouse that danced on the air today. He said, showing me a paper-doll, that it worked by magnets and was activated by music. I said I thought it worked by hanging the mouse on a piece of monofilament that went from his bag, with a little motor in it that jiggled the string, to the boombox. He showed me that he had a knife, so I went away, feeling I had won the argument but lost the war. Nobody likes a smartass.

So, now it's god-knows-when in the morning and I can't sleep. I'm a poor sort of insomniac, usually, sleeping easily and deeply, but I don't think my body believes it's really the middle of the night. I think it believes it's early evening back in Middle America and I'm trying to pull a fast one.

All authors should find themselves with nothing to do for a whole day in Venice, now and again. It's good for the imagination and the head.

This is what I did in reality: I went shopping for presents for other people. Also I ate lunch and dinner. Being a rotten shopper, I came away from a day's shopping with several notebooks of different designs, and a book on literary Venice. None of these are the kinds of things you can give other people. (I'll buy them presents in Trieste. They'll never know the difference.) Also two ancient postcards.

This is what I did on the inside: I made stuff up. I sketched out some stories, and began writing one of them. I wrote a poem for a benefit book.

Over dinner, the couple at the next table (he was Italian, she was English) spoke in Italian, but moved into English when they didn't want to be overheard; bad sex-comedy dialogue. I wrote the worst lines down in my new notebook, feeling deliciously guilty.

I suspect that Venice is full of ghosts. Not of Venetians, but of all the visitors who came, and fell in love with the place, and promised themselves they'd be back, dead or alive.

For any of you who are still reeling from the NIMDA virus (or who think you might be) check out http://www.symantec.com/avcenter/venc/ data/w32.nimda.a@mm.html. And my apologies if you got it from neilgaiman.com (if it's any consolation, so did I).

And those of you who logged on to the journal and were met with the entry from June the 18th about me signing at the Borders on the World Trade Center tomorrow, apologies again. Nobody seems to know how it happened or why. Probably the virus, unless it was something else.

posted by Neil Gaiman 7:18 PM

Sunday, September 23, 2001

Now In Trieste. Also In Italy But Only Just. "Trieste," says Lorenzo, who got me here for the festival, "is where dreams come to die." I'm not sure if he's quoting someone or not, but it seems about right for this strange crossroads town, once the southernmost bit of the Austrian Empire. We saw the home of Maximilian, briefly Emperor of Mexico, this morning. Seeing the journal's been off-line I've been filling up a Moleskine notebook with jottings, and I may put a few of them onto the computer tomorrow. Trieste seems like the intersection of so many places, so many stories…

It rained all day today—grey, and misty. Yesterday, also in the rain, we walked across the Square of Unity, and found ourselves watching jugglers and suchlike, in unconvincing costumes, and a parade of re-enactors from nearby towns, wearing things people didn't wear, carrying weapons they didn't have. It's all going Ren Fest, I think. The whole bloody world. Not that I minded; there's nothing to cheer you up like other people wearing wet chainmail.

En route today to the home of Maximilian, the rain forced us into a dry space which happened to be holding an exhibition of Robert Capa photographs: astonishing stuff, of the Spanish Civil War, of the Second World War, of the Japanese-Chinese War of 1938, and I found myself looking at the photos of combat, of wounded civilians, of people whose worlds had crumbled and fallen, without any sense of irony. These people were us. Whatever side they were on. They were us, and the images had a truth and an immediacy I couldn't have imagined until recently.

Spent several hours this evening doing a round table discussion at the Festival, talking about comics, myths, magic, language.

The Moleskine notebook (I bought it in Venice) is one of my favourite possessions already (although they sell it now as "Bruce Chatwin's Notebook!" which seems, I dunno, in faintly bad taste, although I'd be hard put to tell you exactly why I think so). Just the right size. Just the right weight. An elastic band to hold it closed, a pocket to put invoices and so on. You can see a bit about it at http://www.modoemodo.com/carta.htm—now I have to find somewhere to buy them in the US.

Home tomorrow...It seems odd to be going home the day that Jet Lag catches up with me.

posted by Neil Gaiman 3:00 PM

Monday, September 24, 2001

Home safe, thank you. Tired, but home. More tomorrow.

posted by Neil Gaiman 9:28 PM

Oops. Forgot to mention that Harlan Ellison, Peter David and yours truly (me, Neil Gaiman, that is, please try to keep up) will be talking at MIT in Boston on October 6th.

Details are not really to be found at http://lsc.mit.edu/current_term/lectures.html which was all a hasty Google search gave me.

I'll try and get more info up in the next day or so.

posted by Neil Gaiman 9:41 PM

Tuesday, September 25, 2001

I'll be doing an on-line chat tonight, Tuesday the 25th, at Scifi.com at 9:00pm US Eastern Time. So if there are questions I've not yet answered, you could certainly try asking them there.

Last night was first frost, and a pretty serious frost it was. Now I have to start harvesting the pumpkins (if I hadn't been travelling back from

Italy I might have covered the plants in black plastic, and staved off the inevitable for a little).

Lots of questions waiting—a few people want to know whether *American Gods* was inspired by Diana Wynne Jones's novel *Eight Days of Luke*. Not exactly, although they bear an odd relationship, like second cousins once removed or something. About six or seven years ago, I had an idea for a structure for a story, all about the gods and the days of the week. I chewed it and played with it and was terribly happy with it. And then the penny dropped, and I realised, gloomily, that I'd managed, working back from first principles, to come up with a wonderful structure for a story—but one that Diana had already used, in her brilliant *Eight Days of Luke*. So I put it down as one of those places where our heads went to the same sort of place (it happened with the nursery rhyme "How Many Miles To Babylon," and in several other times and places) and, with regret, I abandoned it. Or almost. I kept Mr Wednesday, and the day of his meeting, in the back of my head, and when I came to put *American Gods* together, he was there, ready and waiting.

The first review of *Coraline* came in today, from *The Bookseller* (which is the UK *Publisher's Weekly*). It finishes, "With absurd humour reminiscent of Lewis Carroll, and a sense of comic spookiness to rival Edward Gorey, this is a delicious literary treat with strong appeal for both boys and girls across a broad age range." Which is very nice indeed.

I'll try and get an updated list of appearances up ASAP, but in brief, to the end of the year, it's

BOSTON (MIT) With Harlan Ellison, Peter David, Oct 6th

MAD MEDIA Convention in Madison, WI, Harlan Ellison et al, Oct 26-28th

CHICAGO HUMANITIES FESTIVAL Nov 9-11 - check their website for details. I get to give a talk, interview Will Eisner, and be on a round table panel chaired by Michael Chabon. Buy your tickets early— BUT if they're sold out and you're there, it's worth coming anyway and getting a ticket at the door: the festival sets aside tickets for students, who then too often don't use them. (My talk last year was sold out, but the room was only 3/4 full.)

EXOTICON New Orleans where I am going chiefly to confer, consort and otherwise hobnob with the other G of H, Steve Brust, who I never see now he's moved to Las Vegas. Nov 16-19.

posted by Neil Gaiman 11:21 AM

And the info on the MIT event is at http://web.mit.edu/lsc/www/fiction/ (Thanks to Bill Gauthier for the link.)

posted by Neil Gaiman 1:52 PM

Wednesday, September 26, 2001

I ought to post something tonight, but jetlag has caught up with me, like an elephant sitting down on a grapefruit. With me being the grapefruit, I suppose, because I don't feel very elephantine. Wrote stuff today, did phone calls, and picked and ate Haralson apples from a tree in the garden I planted a few years ago. Also got the latest pages of the story from Gene Wolfe that we're writing together (basically we're doing about a thousand words each, back and forth) and I read it chuckling and delighted. It will be published for the World Horror Convention next year. It's a guide book, of a kind.

Good night.

posted by Neil Gaiman 9:19 PM

Thursday, September 27, 2001

Hah, I fixed the FAQ thing. Do not ask how. But I am VERY pleased with myself.

posted by Neil Gaiman 9:11 AM

FICTION

The "Hallowe'en" piece is the final part of a round robin Hallowe'en ghost story in London's *Time Out* magazine. We were given only the previous section, nothing else, and had to take it from there. My friend Kathy Acker wrote the segment before mine, and words and lines from my chapter echo and quote from bits of hers. When I read the published story (Peter Straub wrote a section, I think; so did Christopher Fowler) I was astonished at how much sense it all made, more or less.

(Roger Zelazny, as is recorded elsewhere in this book, told Steve Brust and me that most of his better short stories were the final chapters of novels he had not written. Hallowe'en is the final page of a short story I had not read.)

December 7th, 1995 was written for my friend Tori Amos, after she sent me a CD of the album that would become *Boys For Pele*. When I played it, I imagined the songs as people, and their stories, and I wrote it down for her, and sent it as a thank you.

The piece on writers and their faces was done for Patti Perret's *Faces of Fantasy*, a book of photographs of authors.

The Flints of Memory Lane was written for a book of true ghost stories, and is as true as recollection allows. *Good Boys Deserve Favours,* on the other hand, walks that twilight place where fiction and memory collapse gently into each other, and demonstrates that while things need not have happened to be true, by the same token just because something really happened, it is still not to be relied upon.

HALLOWE'EN

As abruptly as they had started, the visions were over.

She was alone in the room, and the man was still staked to the floor. He was a woman-murdering man: someone had told her that in her dream. It was part of the knowledge she had brought back with her. She had left her name behind; she must have known it once, but now it was gone, exchanged for a vision of her dead mother. She left the man on the floor, walked through the flat hoping for a clue to her own identity, for some kind of key to unlock this bizarre Hallowe'en.

Under his bed she found a box of photographs. The top snapshot showed her and the man on a seafront somewhere, both waving happily at the camera. The man had his hand on her shoulder. They seemed happy and close.

The other photographs were of teenaged girls. In some the girls were tied to iron rings set into concrete, in others they were lashed to a metal bed. One of the girls was only a child. Things were being done to them with a variety of objects, some hard, some sharp, by a man in a black leather mask. Beneath the photographs was a black leather face-mask, crusted with sweat.

She went into the kitchen. The fridge contained no food, only condiments—sauces, and seasonings, and a half-finished bottle of cheap cooking wine. The chest-freezer was another matter: the girls' heads were the saddest things, each frosted up in its own vapour-clouded clear plastic bag, eyes staring out into frozen nothing.

She took the largest of the butcher's knives from the wooden block on the sideboard, and the bottle of wine from the fridge, and she went back to the lounge. She swigged back a mouthful of cold wine, vinegary and vile, and poured the remains of the bottle over his face. He sputtered, and shook, and his eyes opened.

"You killed all those girls," she told him.

He shook his head.

"Hallowe'en," she recited, taking the words from her vision, "belongs to females. They pass through time-space in order to give gifts to their living blood."

272

He said nothing.

"They did this to you," she told him. "They found you, and they staked you out, and they brought me here. They gave you to me, as a present. Now, I'm giving you back to them."

She ran the butcher's knife over his body, gently at first, and then with increasing roughness, until he had become nothing but red meat and offal and bones and, above and beneath everything, blood.

Then she walked to the kitchen window, and watched the sun rise somewhere beyond Canary Wharf. Tendrils of mist kissed the pavement, and there was a frost on the windows of the nearest house. She wondered if, behind those closed curtains, other women had received their gift from the ones who walked before them, had given them blood in return. She thought she could hear tiny parrots and rats, squeaking and chirruping in the room she had left. When she returned, the room was empty, but the blood had gone from the floor.

She left the flat, then, and walked down the stairs. The noises were all around her, the high, twittering voices of the hungry dead. She turned, to see them on the half-light of the steps: her mother, and, behind her, half a dozen young girls. They were bubbles of blood, thinner than paper, made of nothing but the crimson oil-rainbow of surface tension, and of breath. Soon enough they would need meat, and bones, and hair, and eyes; but for now, the blood was sufficient.

They walked out into the London street together, a cold procession in the chilly November dawn.

December 7, 1995

It began in darkness; the little girl hesitantly touching the piano-key. She made up a song to sing to the darkness. She sang about the big girls, the pretty ones. She sang all her fear of growing up, all her fear of what she knew she would never be.

When the song was done she lay down, beneath the piano, in the dark.

The piano sang her a lullaby. The black keys and the white keys began to grow, and twine, and blossom, and she was dreaming: and they came into the bare room, all the dream people, crowding and strutting and scuttling and dancing.

There was a woman with a rose in her dark hair, a rose the colour of blood. She had a bruise on her cheek, and her eye make-up was smudged and streaked. She stared at the other people as if she was scared of them; as if any one of them might hurt her again.

There was a hairy-legged man with horns and a tail; he looked like a devil, but when the little girl asked he told her he had been around before ever the devils walked, and he smelled of rain and the forest. The Prophet, his beard dusty with the desert sand, fixed his lipstick, and whispered, "Hey, is that a thunderbolt in your toga, or are you just pleased to see me?" but nobody heard. Wild horses thundered past, their hooves drowning out the noise of the lost lovers, damaged children, wakened babies...

And by then the party was underway, and all the boys were partying, even the boys who were girls, and the World War One flier and the secret genetic agent, all of them grabbing the party food and spilling their drinks and laughing nervously and too loudly. Each of the people had a shadow, and the little sleeping girl found herself staring not at the people but at their shadows, as they danced their flickering shadow party on the floor and on the walls and ceiling, as they caressed and fought and fucked and died in their silent shadow carnival.

A beautiful woman—much too beautiful ever to be a beauty queen, with a tongue split, like a snake's—was carrying a window underneath her arm. Through the window the little girl could see a mirror, and reflected in the mirror was the dark smoke from the mountain. The man with the black-and-white-striped eyes shivered, and began hunting for a door, but none of the guests had remembered to bring a door with them. The virgin began to cry, as her friends strapped her to a chair. They took her gun away from her before they threw the switch, dropped the pill into the water-glass, got her in their sights: four live bullets, one blank; that's the tradition. The American way.

The houngan was feeling up the junkie widow. "I shouldn't be here," she said. "I really shouldn't be here. Maybe I'm not." She pissed herself, then, a thin trickle of vivid yellow urine which ran over his hand and down her stained legs and collected in a pool at her feet.

The floor juddered and trembled. The moon shone through the window, past the volcano, through every mirror in the world.

One by one all the dream people climbed into their shadows. One by one the shadows crawled beneath the piano, nestled under the little girl. The shadows slept inside her dream.

And when she woke, there was nothing there to show that anything had ever happened at all, only a distant star that twinkled in the window that someone had left propped up against the wall.

She played a song to the star on the piano, one note at a time, while the shadows billowed and swelled and filled the room with darkness, extinguishing the lamps, swallowing the candle-flames one by one, until there was nothing left at all.

Only the dark; and in the darkness, just a twinkle.

GOOD BOYS DESERVE FAVOURS

My own children delight in hearing true tales from my childhood: The Time My Father Threatened to Arrest the Traffic Cop, and How I Broke My Sister's Front Teeth Twice, When I Pretended to Be Twins, and even The Day I Accidentally Killed the Gerbil.

I have never told them this story. I would be hard put to tell you quite why not.

When I was nine the school told us that we could pick any musical instrument we wanted. Some boys chose the violin, the clarinet, the oboe. Some chose the timpani, the pianoforte, the viola.

I was not big for my age, and I, alone in the Junior School, elected to play the double-bass, chiefly because I loved the incongruity of the idea. I loved the idea of being a small boy, playing, delighting in, carrying around an instrument much taller than I was.

The double-bass belonged to the school, and I was deeply impressed by it. I learned to bow, although I had little interest in bowing technique, preferring to pluck the huge metal strings by hand. My right index finger was permanently puffed with white blisters until the blisters eventually became callouses.

I delighted in discovering the history of the double-bass: that it was no part of the sharp, scraping family of the violin, the viola, the 'cello; its curves were gentler, softer, more sloping; it was, in fact, the final survivor of an extinct family of instruments, the viol family, and was, more correctly, the bass viol.

I learned this from the double-bass teacher, an elderly musician imported by the school to teach me, and also to teach a couple of senior boys, for a few hours each week. He was a clean-shaven man, balding and intense, with long, calloused fingers. I would do all I could to make him tell me about the bass, tell me of his experiences as a session musician, of his life cycling around the country. He had a contraption attached to the back of his bicycle, on which his bass rested, and he pedaled sedately through the countryside with the bass behind him.

He had never married. Good double-bass players, he told me, were men who made poor husbands. He had many such observations. There were no great male cellists—that's one I remember. And his opinion of viola players, of either sex, was scarcely repeatable.

He called the school double-bass *she*. "She could do with a good coat of varnish," he'd say. And "You take care of her, she'll take care of you."

I was not a particularly good double-bass player. There was little enough that I could do with the instrument on my own, and all I remember of my enforced membership in the school orchestra was getting lost in the score, and sneaking glances at the cellos beside me, waiting for them to turn the page, so I could start playing once more, punctuating the orchestral schoolboy cacophony with low, uncomplicated bass notes.

It has been too many years, and I have almost forgotten how to read music; but when I dream of reading music, I still dream in the bass clef. *All Cows Eat Grass. Good Boys Deserve Favours Always.*

After lunch each day, the boys who played instruments walked down to the music school, and had music practice, while the boys who didn't lay on their beds and read their books and their comics.

I rarely practiced. Instead I would take a book down to the music school, and read it, surreptitiously, perched on my high stool, holding onto the smooth brown wood of the bass, the bow in one hand, the better to fool the casual observer. I was lazy, and uninspired. My bowing scrubbed and scratched where it should have glided and boomed, my fingering was hesitant and clumsy. Other boys worked at their instruments. I did not. As long as I was sitting at the bass for half an hour each day, no one cared. I had the nicest, largest room to practice in, too, as the double-bass was kept in a cupboard in the master music room.

Our school, I should tell you, had only one Famous Old Boy. It was part of school legend—how the Famous Old Boy had been expelled from the school after driving a sports car across the cricket pitch, while drunk, how he had gone on to fame and fortune—first as a minor actor in Ealing Comedies, then as the token English cad in any number of Hollywood pictures. He was never a true star, but, during the Sunday afternoon film screening, we would cheer if ever he appeared.

When the door-handle to the practice room clicked and turned I put my book down on the piano, and leaned forward, turning the page of the dog-eared *52 Musical Exercises for the Double-Bass,* and I heard the Headmaster say "...the music school was purpose-built of course. This is the master practice-room..." and they came in.

They were the Headmaster, and the Head of the Music Department (a faded, bespectacled man whom I rather liked), and the Deputy Head of the Music Department (who conducted the school orchestra, and disliked me cordially), and, there could be no mistaking it, the Famous Old Boy himself, in company with a fragrant fair woman who held his arm and looked as if she might also be a movie star.

I stopped pretending to play, and slipped off my high stool and stood up respectfully, holding the bass by the neck.

The Headmaster told them about the soundproofing, and the carpets, and the fund-raising drive to raise the money to build the music school, and he stressed that the next stage of rebuilding would need significant further donations, and he was just beginning to expound upon the cost of double-glazing when the fragrant woman said, "Just look at him. Is that cute or what?" and they all looked at me.

"That's a big violin—be hard to get it under your chin," said the Famous Old Boy, and everyone chortled dutifully.

"It's so big," said the woman. "And he's so small. Hey, but we're stopping you practicing. You carry on. Play us something."

The Headmaster and the Head of the Music Department beamed at me, expectantly. The Deputy Head of the Music Department, who was under no illusions as to my musical skills, started to explain that the First Violin was practicing next door and would be delighted to play for them and—

"I want to hear *him*," she said. "How old are you, kid?"

"Eleven, Miss," I said.

She nudged the Famous Old Boy in the ribs. "He called me Miss," she said. This amused her. "Go on. Play us something." The Famous Old Boy nodded, and they stood there and they looked at me.

The double-bass is not a solo instrument, really, not even for the competent, and I was far from competent. But I slid my bottom up onto the stool again, and crooked my fingers around the neck, and picked up my bow, heart pounding like a timpani in my chest, and prepared to embarrass myself.

Even twenty years later, I remember.

I did not even look at *52 Musical Exercises for the Double-Bass*. I played…*something*. It arched and boomed and sang and reverberated. The bow glided over strange and confident arpeggios, and then I put down the bow and plucked a complex and intricate pizzicato melody out of the bass. I did things with the bass that an experienced jazz bass player with hands as big as my head could not have done. I played, and I played, and I played, tumbling down into the four taut metal strings, clutching the instrument as I had never clutched a human being. And, in the end, breathless and elated, I stopped.

The blonde woman led the applause, but they all clapped, even, with a strange expression on his face, the Deputy Head of Music.

"I didn't know it was such a versatile instrument," said the Headmaster. "Very lovely piece. Modern, yet classical. Very fine. Bravo." And then he shepherded the four of them from the room, and I sat there, utterly drained, the fingers of my left hand stroking the neck of the bass, the fingers of my right caressing her strings.

Like any true story, the end of the affair is messy and unsatisfactory: the following day, carrying the huge instrument across the courtyard to the school chapel, for orchestra practice, in a light rain, I slipped on the wet bricks, and fell forward. The wooden bridge of the bass was smashed, and the front was cracked.

It was sent away to be repaired, but when it returned it was not the same. The strings were higher, harder to pluck, the new bridge seemed to have been installed at the wrong angle. There was, even to my untutored ear, a change in the timbre. I had not taken care of her; she would no longer take care of me.

When, the following year, I changed schools, I did not continue with the double-bass. The thought of changing to a new instrument seemed vaguely disloyal, while the dusty black bass that sat in a cupboard in my new school's music rooms seemed to have taken a dislike to me. I was marked another's. And I was tall enough now that there would be nothing incongruous about my standing behind the double-bass.

And, soon enough, I knew, there would be girls.

The Flints of Memory Lane

I like things to be story-shaped.

Reality, however, is not story-shaped, and the eruptions of the odd into our lives are not story-shaped either. They do not end in entirely satisfactory ways. Recounting the strange is like telling one's dreams: one can communicate the events of a dream, but not the emotional content, the way that a dream can colour one's entire day.

This is my ghost story, and an unsatisfactory thing it is too.

I was fifteen.

We lived in a big house, built in the garden of our old house. I still missed the old house: it had been a big old manor-house. We had lived in half of it. The people who lived in the other half had sold it to property developers, so my father sold our half-a-house to them as well.

This was in Sussex, in a town that was crossed by the zero meridian: I lived in the Eastern Hemisphere, and went to school in the Western Hemisphere.

The old house had been a treasure-trove of strange things: lumps of glittering marble and glass bulbs filled with liquid mercury, doors that opened onto brick walls; forgotten toys; things old and things forgotten.

My own house—a Victorian brick edifice, in the middle of America—is, I am told, haunted. There are few people who will spend the night here alone any more—my assistant tells of her nights on her own here: of the porcelain jester music box which spontaneously began to play in the night, of her utter conviction that someone was watching her. Other people have complained of similar things, following nights alone.

I have never had any unsettling experiences here, but then, I have never spent a night here alone. And I am not entirely sure that I would wish to.

"There is no ghost when I am here," I said once, when asked if my house was haunted. "Perhaps it is you that haunt it, then," someone suggested, but truly I doubt it. If we have a ghost here, it is a fearful creature, more afraid of us than we are of it.

But I was telling of our old house, which was sold and knocked down (and I could not bear to see it empty, could not stand to see it being torn apart and bulldozed: my heart was in that house, and even now, at night, before I sleep, I hear the wind sighing through the rowan tree outside my bedroom window, twenty-five years ago). So we moved into a new house, built, as I said, in the garden of the old one, and some years went by. Then, the house was halfway down a winding flint road, surrounded by fields and trees, in the middle of nowhere. Now, I am certain, were I to go back, I would find the flint road paved, the fields an endless housing estate. But I do not go back.

I was fifteen, skinny and gawky and wanting desperately to be cool. It was night, in autumn.

Outside our house was a lamp-post, installed when the house was built, as out-of-place in the lampless countryside as the lamp-post in the Narnia stories. It was a sodium light, which burned yellow, and washed out all other colours, turning everything yellow and black.

She was not my girlfriend (my girlfriend lived in Croydon, where I went to school, a grey-eyed blonde of unimaginable beauty who was, as she often complained to me, puzzled, never able to figure out why she was going out with me), but she was a friend, and she lived about a ten-minute walk away from me, beyond the fields, in the older part of the town.

I was going to walk over to her house, to play records, and sit, and talk.

I walked out of our house, ran down the grass slope to the drive, and stopped, dead, in front of a woman, standing beneath the street-lamp, staring up at the house.

She was dressed like a gypsy queen in a stage play, or a Moorish princess. She was handsome, not beautiful. She has no colours, in my memory, save only shades of yellow and black.

And, startled to find myself standing opposite someone where I had expected no one, I said, "Hello."

The woman said nothing. She looked at me.

"Are you looking for anyone?" I said, or something of the sort, and again she said nothing.

And still she looked at me, this unlikely woman, in the middle of nowhere, dressed like something from a dream, and still she said nothing at all. She began to smile, though, and it was not a nice smile.

And suddenly I found myself scared: utterly, profoundly scared, like a character in a dream, and I walked away, down the drive, heart beating in my chest, and around the corner.

I stood there, out of sight of the house, for a moment, and then I looked back, and there was no one standing in the lamp-light.

I was fifty paces from the house, but I could not, would not, turn around and go back. I was too scared. Instead I ran up the dark, tree-lined flint lane and into the old town, and up another road and down the road to my friend's house, and got there speechless, breathless, jabbering and scared, as if all the hounds of hell had chased me there.

I told her my story, and we phoned my parents, who told me there was no one standing under the streetlight, and agreed, a little reluctantly, to come and drive me home, as I would not walk home that night.

And that is all there is to my story. I wish there was more: I wish I could tell you about the gypsy encampment that was burned down on that site two hundred years earlier—or anything that would give some sense of closure to the story, anything that would make it story-shaped—but there was no such encampment.

So, like all eruptions of the odd and strange into my world, the event sits there, unexplained. It is not story-shaped.

And, in memory, all I have is the yellow-black of her smile, and a shadow of the fear that followed.

Essay for Patti

These are not our faces.

This is not what we look like.

You think Gene Wolfe looks like his photograph in this book? Or Jane Yolen? Or Peter Straub? Or Diana Wynne Jones? Nonsense. They are wearing play-faces to fool you. But the play-faces come off when the writing begins.

Frozen in black and silver for you now, these are masks. We who lie for a living are wearing our liar-faces, false-faces made to deceive the unwary. For if you believe these faces, we look just like everyone else.

Protective colouration, that's all it is. Read the books, though: sometimes you can catch sight of us in there. We look like gods and fools and bards and queens, singing whole worlds into existence, conjuring something from nothing, juggling words into all the patterns of night...

Read the books. That's when you see us properly: naked priests and priestesses of forgotten cults, our skins glistening with scented oils, scarlet blood dripping down from our hands, bright birds flying up out from our mouths. Perfect, we are, and beautiful in the fire's orange light...

You think we sit with our old faces on, making up stories, writing them down?

There was a story I was told as a child, about a little girl who peeked in through a writer's window one night, and saw him writing. He had taken his false-people-face off to write and had hung it behind the door, for he wrote with his real face on. And she saw him; and he saw her. And, from that day to this, nobody has ever heard of the little girl again.

Since then, writers have looked like other people even when they write (though sometimes their lips move, and sometimes they stare into space longer and harder than anything that isn't a cat); but their words describe the real faces; the ones they wear underneath.

This is why people who encounter writers of fantasy are rarely satisfied by the wholly inferior persons that they meet.

"I thought you'd be taller, or older, or younger, or prettier, or wiser," they tell us, in words or wordlessly.

"This is not what I look like," I tell them. "This is not my face."

ON GAIMAN

(Here are what other people—and possibly Neil Gaiman himself?—had to say about Neil Gaiman...)

Neil Gaiman used to have more Eisner Awards than anyone else, but he suspects that Alan Moore, Kurt Busiek or James Robinson must have caught up by now. His most recent works are *Stardust,* a four-part short novel illustrated by Charles Vess; *Neverwhere,* a longer novel illustrated only by the power of the imagination; and *Beowulf,* a re-telling of the original saga which he wrote with film-maker Roger Avary, and which goes into production in 1998. Unless it doesn't, this being Hollywood, after all.
(Introduction to *Astro City: Confession)*

Neil Gaiman is mentioned only once in the Lovecraft Canon: the mysterious Dr Charriere, in the posthumous Lovecraft-Derleth collaboration "The Survivor," we are told, has a portrait of Gaiman on his wall, along with certain cabalistic charts, and pictures of large reptiles. Gaiman won the 1995 International Horror Critics' Guild Award for best collection for his book *Angels and Visitations,* and has won pretty much every award, American and International, that it's possible to get for writing comics, and one award, the aforementioned World Fantasy Award, for Best Short Story (for *Sandman #19),* that it's impossible to get for writing comics any more.
(Concerning Dreams and Nightmares: H. P. Lovecraft)

Neil Gaiman is best known for writing the series of graphic novels that comprised *The Sandman*, published in ten volumes by DC Comics. It is the recipient of more awards internationally than any other work written for the comics medium, including the World Fantasy Award, making it the only comic to have received an award intended for prose fiction. Having recently written the saga of Beowulf as a Hollywood movie, he is currently working on a short story collection and a new, prose novel.
(Introduction to *The Einstein Intersection*)

Neil Gaiman is the author of *Sandman: Season of Mists,* a baroque theological fantasy, and co-author, with Terry Pratchett of *Good Omens,* a very funny novel about the end of the world according to the *Book of Revelations.* It was nominated for a British award for religious fiction, which came as a real surprise to Neil and Terry, who were rather expecting bricks through their windows.
(Introduction to *The Screwtape Letters*))

THE NEW ENGLAND
SCIENCE FICTION ASSOCIATION (NESFA)
AND NESFA PRESS

Recent books from NESFA Press:

- *Entities* by Eric Frank Russell $29
- *Quartet* by George R.R. Martin* $15
- *Strange Days: Fabulous Journeys with Gardner Dozois* $30
- *From These Ashes* by Frederic Brown $29
- *Frankensteins and Foreign Devils* by Walter Jon Williams* $14
- *First Contacts: The Essential Murray Leinster* $27
- *An Ornament to His Profession* by Charles L. Harness $25
- *Shards of Honor* by Lois McMaster Bujold $22

The Complete SF of William Tenn
- *Immodest Proposals* (Vol. 1) $29
- *Here Comes Civilization* (Vol. 2) $29

The Essential Hal Clement:
- *Trio for Slide Rule & Typewriter* (Vol. 1) $25
- *Music of Many Spheres* (Vol. 2) $25
- *Variations on a Theme by Sir Isaac Newton* (Vol. 3) $25

*Indicates trade paperback.

Details and many more books available online at: www.nesfa.org/press

Books may be ordered by writing to:
NESFA Press
PO Box 809
Framingham, MA 01701

We accept checks, Visa, or MasterCard. Please add $3 postage and handling per order.

The New England Science Fiction Association:

NESFA is an all-volunteer, non-profit organization of science fiction and fantasy fans. Besides publishing, our activities include running Boskone (New England's oldest SF convention) in February each year, producing a semi-monthly newsletter, holding discussion groups relating to the field, and hosting a variety of social events. If you are interested in learning more about us, we'd like to hear from you. Write to our address above!

ACKNOWLEDGMENTS

These are the people who helped us make this book happen:

George Flynn (gold star)
Mark L. Olson
Alice N. S. Lewis
Davey Snyder
Lorraine Garland
John M. Ford

Special thanks for the efforts of Erik Olson.

— Tony Lewis and Priscilla Olson
(December, 2001)

For the trade paperback edition, we particulary want to thank Davey
Snyder and Chip Hitchcock for their fine work.

(July, 2002)